THE KEYNESIAN REVOLUTION

THE KEYNESIAN REVOLUTION

SECOND EDITION

BY

LAWRENCE R. KLEIN

WHARTON SCHOOL OF FINANCE AND COMMERCE
UNIVERSITY OF PENNSYLVANIA

MACMILLAN

London · Melbourne

1968

First published in the United States of America 1966
by the Macmillan Company of New York

Published by
MACMILLAN AND CO LTD
Little Essex Street London W C 2
and also at Bombay Madras Melbourne Calcutta
Macmillan South Africa (Publishers) Pty Ltd Johannesburg
The Macmillan Company of Australia Pty Ltd Melbourne

Printed in Great Britain by
Lowe and Brydone (Printers) Ltd London

To My Parents

PREFACE TO THE SECOND EDITION

On the occasion of a visit to Japan during the autumn of 1963, I found myself putting together new thoughts about *The Keynesian Revolution*. This book has enjoyed some success in postwar Japan, and my reconsiderations of the Keynesian contribution formed the subject of addresses given to Japanese university students. The written content of these lectures was published in *Economic Studies Quarterly* in November 1964, and M. Shinohara suggested that the material might usefully be included in a new Japanese translation. This suggestion inspired the new English language edition. It is essentially the old *Keynesian Revolution* with two added chapters, one being the paper from *Economic Studies Quarterly* and the other being a more careful econometric statement of the Keynesian system.

The revisitation published in *Economic Studies Quarterly* is not likely to come to the attention of most Western economists. This accounts for the new Chapter VIII. After more than 20 years of intensive econometric research inspired by the Keynesian Revolution (and Tinbergen's League of Nations study), I felt that it was time for a pause to relate an up-to-date version of my econometric researches to my original doctoral work. When I first visited Cambridge, England, after having worked in relative isolation in Cambridge, Massachusetts (under the guiding light, of course, of my supervisor, Paul Samuelson), I found great interest among some of Keynes' colleagues in my econometric attempts to build statistical models of their system. This interest inspired me to continue working along these lines, but as systems and areas of application grew the results seemed to become more remote from the *General Theory* as such; therefore the time is now appropriate to return to my starting place.

The *esprit* that gripped me in 1944 while I was writing *The Keynesian Revolution* as a dissertation will never be recaptured. Therefore, I did not want to make changes in the original chapters and appendix except to point out amendments of errors, misstatements, or

vii

viewpoints. Economic life naturally looks more complicated to me at 45 than it did at 23. I have retained the book's youthful vigor by not tampering with it in the main, except to right some wrongs, and have added the less racy materials in two new chapters, VIII and IX. Chapter VIII, as I pointed out above, is a reconsideration of the Keynesian analysis and theoretical system. In Chapter IX, I lay out an empirical model and other econometric materials to show how far we have gone in the measurement of the Keynesian system, a second-order stage of intellectual development.

I would like to thank Mr. Harry Eisenpress of the IBM Corporation for his considerable assistance in the programming and carrying out of the computations for the estimation of the model in Chapter IX. Modern econometric research has become more and more a team effort. I would also like to thank those associates, colleagues, and research assistants who have toiled with me over the years in econometric studies. The material presented here is based on cumulated effort and would not have its present form or power were it not for the arduous years of build-up of econometric research and knowledge.

L. R. K.

PREFACE TO THE FIRST EDITION

What is essential and what is unessential in the economic theories of the late Lord Keynes? What are the minimum assumptions that must be made in order to obtain the theoretical results usually claimed by the adherents of Keynesian economics? How did the revolutionary book *The General Theory of Employment, Interest, and Money* develop out of Keynes' earlier writings? To what extent is the Keynesian theory indebted to those of older writers, and how does it compare with the theory of classical economics? What is the relationship between the economic theories and the economic policies of Keynes and his followers? Do the policy measures advocated by the Keynesians lead to socialism, or do they endeavor to preserve capitalism? These are the leading questions which this book attempts to answer.

The Keynesian theory is viewed in the following pages as a revolutionary doctrine in the sense that it produces theoretical results entirely different from the body of economic thought existing at the time of its development. The "Revolution" discussed here is a revolution in thought, not in the economic policies of governments. The first six chapters deal with the development of the theory and an analysis of the implications of the theory. The final chapter evaluates the influence of the theories of Lord Keynes upon the forces of economic and social reform.

The Keynesian Revolution is addressed to a mixed group of readers. For the non-professional economist Chapters I (exclusive of parts of the last section), II, and V deal with the historical development of economic theories, Chapter III with the structure of the Keynesian system, Chapters III and VI with the use of Keynesian theories to analyze the economic problems of deflation and inflation, and finally Chapter VII with the practical consequences of this theory for economic policy. All these ideas are presented in non-technical terms. For the professional economists, in addition to those parts which are of interest to the layman, a section in Chapter I gives a technical analysis of the theory of *A Treatise on Money;* a section in Chapter III compares Keynes with the classical writers; Chapter IV attempts to clear up controversies on the interest rate, the savings-investment equation, and the effect of wage cuts on unemployment; finally an appendix develops mathematical models of Keynesian economics. The lay reader will probably do well to skip over some of these technical discussions, but the remainder of the book is quite understandable to those without any formal training in economic theory. This book is so designed that most of the major problems are treated in simple terms that laymen can follow with an application of careful thought. It is, however, frankly not intended to be "Keynes for the Layman." That is another subject which deserves to be treated separately.

Much of this material was originally contained in a doctoral thesis written in 1944 at the Massachusetts Institute of Technology, during the author's tenure as May Fellow at that institution. However, in the two years elapsing since the original writing the manuscript has been considerably revised with the end in view of making the material more understandable to the general reader, although, it is hoped, without an undue sacrifice of standards of scholarship. In addition, the final chapter contains material which was not presented in the original version. This chapter on economic policy was written primarily for the general reader in order to relate the abstract arguments to the concrete problems that now confront us.

There are many persons associated with the author's intellectual development whose teachings led to the ideas set forth in this book. It was the late Struan T. Robertson who first interested the author in the writings of Keynes, and Professors William Fellner and Norman S. Buchanan who convinced him of the usefulness of studying economic problems. But no single person is more responsible for *The Keynesian Revolution* than Paul A. Samuelson. It was the lectures of Professor Samuelson that first pointed out to this author the truly essential points of Keynesian economics. If any of the ideas of this book are accepted as contributions to economic thought, Paul Samuelson should receive credit. The author, of course, assumes full responsibility for any errors.

Numerous friends and colleagues have read the manuscript and have made important suggestions and criticisms. They are R. Bishop, D. V. Brown, O. Lange, J. Letiche, J. Lintner, G. Malanos F. T. Malm, J. Marschak, C. Myers, D. Patinkin, and S. Pu. Miss Beatrice Rogers of the Industrial Relations Section of the Massachusetts Institute of Technology was very helpful in editing the original thesis.

The author gratefully acknowledges receipt from the following of permission to quote from their publications: Bankers Publishing Company; Free-Economy Publishing Company; Harcourt, Brace and Company; London School of Economics and Political Science; The Macmillan Company; the Ronald Press; the *American Economic Review;* the *Economist;* the *New Republic;* the *Quarterly Journal of Economics*, and the *Review of Economic Statistics*.

L. R. K.

CONTENTS

xiii

THE KEYNESIAN REVOLUTION

CHAPTER I

KEYNES AS A CLASSICAL ECONOMIST

One thing that must be kept in mind throughout the reading of these pages is that Keynes was always a classical economist. Much space will be devoted below to the manner in which he made a significant break with classical doctrine; but as all economists know, it is almost impossible to get rid of early impressions, especially after they have stuck for two decades or more. It was not until Keynes had lived through a few years of the world's greatest economic catastrophe that he was able to divorce himself from some of the standard doctrines. In this chapter we shall look carefully at the body of economic theory and policy (always so important with Keynes), which was being espoused by Keynes, in order that we may get a clear picture of the development which must have been going on in his own mind up to the early part of the thirties.

KEYNES OF THE PREWAR WORLD

It was not until the Treaty of Versailles that Keynes achieved his great fame and began to make public the theoretical system on which he based his original contributions to economic policy. But he had, himself, pointed out in 1911 in a review of Professor Irving Fisher's *The Purchasing Power of Money*[1] that English monetary theory was then principally a matter of oral tradition — the Cambridge oral tradition — and that the theory supported by the British economists had not been widely set down in publications. However, he did at that time remark upon what he considered to be the best work in monetary theory since Ricardo, namely, Marshall's testimony (1887) before the Gold and Silver Commission and before the Indian Currency Committee. These comments by Keynes mark him definitely as one steeped in classical tradition. Many years

[1] See *Economic Journal*, Vol. XXI, 1911, p. 393.

elapsed before he began to question these first theoretical impressions.

Keynes began his professional career with a solid, substantial book, *Indian Currency and Finance*,[2] which was favorably accepted by his professional colleagues, but which was by no means an indication of his later brilliance and cleverness. Some economists today would like to make much of the fact that Keynes, from the outset, departed from orthodoxy, since here he had made a plea for a managed currency. Actually, his policy recommendation that India have a gold exchange standard was reached on the basis of straightforward, classical analysis, not seriously challenged by his contemporary, orthodox colleagues. Briefly, this book asked for a central bank to be set up in India which would centralize the gold reserves so that extraordinary monetary drains could be met in times of crisis. He thought that this plan would lend greater stability to the Indian currency system than could be obtained through the use of a strict gold standard. It was a commonplace at that time that the Western countries had made India the sink for the world's excess gold supply, giving those nations a very good cushion against inflationary price movements. This led directly to price fluctuations and undesirable currency speculation in India. Such conclusions as the above are certainly evident to the classically trained economist working along the lines of the quantity theory of money. Primarily, Keynes was interested in achieving price stability for India, and he supported his program for stability by quite orthodox analysis. Whether the policy recommendation was the most orthodox plan or not, it cannot be doubted that Keynes' economic analysis was derived entirely from classical theory.

Surprisingly enough, our prolific hero was very quiet during the war years. At the outset of the war, Keynes went to the British Treasury as an economist and worked on problems of French finance, especially in relation to the reparations question. His publications during this period were of a very conservative nature and were marked by a complete absence of innovation. He reviewed some German publications on that country's war economy and

[2] *Indian Currency and Finance*, Macmillan, London, 1913.

wrote some articles on the behavior of the money markets and banking system during that critical period, but there seems to be no indication of any important contribution on his part to the discussions of inflation, or of the real costs of the war, that were so prominent then.

THE TREATY

But in 1919, from a freely flowing pen, economists and the public in general were entertained with a best-selling analysis of the Treaty of Versailles.[3] As was to be increasingly the case, Keynes was dealing in a spectacular way with important issues of the day, and in this instance the questions were: Are the provisions of the treaty economically justified; and more specifically, What is the extent of Germany's ability to pay? With most of that book and its sequel we should not be primarily interested, because they give us little evidence of the author's theoretical system — the point at issue in this chapter. However, in *The Economic Consequences of the Peace*, Keynes did devote a chapter to a discussion of the economic process as it led up to the World War. In this chapter, Keynes looked with pangs of nostalgia at the prewar economic system in which there were no barriers to trade, unlimited investment opportunity, capital accumulation, and growing population. This period, to any classical economist, was a time of capitalism at its best, and the growing possibilities of postwar restrictions and monopolistic practices did not present a happy outlook. A few quotations will show the perspective into which the prewar period was put.

What an extraordinary episode in the economic progress of man that age was which came to an end in August 1914![4]

Europe was so organized socially and economically as to secure the maximum accumulation of capital.[5]

The interference of frontiers and tariffs was reduced to a minimum.[6]

The analysis of this economic millennium is quite interesting, especially when compared with the later views of *The General Theory of Employment, Interest, and Money*. Keynes saw the high

[3] J. M. Keynes, *The Economic Consequences of the Peace*, Macmillan, London, 1919.
[4] *The Economic Consequences of the Peace*, p. 11.
[5] *Ibid.*, p. 18.   [6] *Ibid.*, p. 15.

level of investment and consequent growth of capital stock made possible through the inequalities inherent in the capitalistic income distribution. In fact this inequality was Keynes' justification of the capitalist system. The rich had excess income which they had saved and were able to invest profitably. It was only because the rich were wise enough to abstain from consumption that capital accumulation was able to achieve its great size. But the important part of this analysis is that Keynes saw only two possible obstacles to this progressive economic growth: (1) population might grow too rapidly and outrun accumulation, and (2) war might consume the stock of capital. He was never worried at this time about a lack of profitable investment opportunities which could offset the savings generated out of the capitalistic income distribution and thus lead to a possible high level of unemployment. Although Keynes is famous for many predictions, he was not able to predict the economic stagnation of England during the twenties — because he was too classical in his analysis.

POSTWAR MALADJUSTMENTS

The postwar economic ills provided the stimulus to much of Keynes' writings for several years. The issues which he was trying to clear up were (1) inflation vs. deflation; (2) the gold standard vs. a managed currency (sometimes phrased as stability of exchange vs. stability of prices). The first problem is very important to us, for the following reasons: Although Keynes was consistently in favor of price stability,[7] if economic maladjustments had to be corrected by price manipulation, he was invariably on the side of inflation as opposed to deflation. This preference for inflation is quite important in understanding much of the argument of the *General Theory*. His statement on this issue is

. . . it is worse, in an impoverished world, to provoke unemployment than to disappoint the *rentier*.[8]

This notion was a part of his more important conception that a high level of investment activity is necessary for economic progress

---

[7] This favoritism goes back at least as far as his *Indian Currency and Finance*.

[8] *Monetary Reform*, Harcourt Brace, New York, 1924, pp. 44–45.

under capitalism. Though investors would prefer the certainty of price stability, rising prices were considered to be a stimulus to business activity, while deflation was looked upon as an obstacle to investment and enterprise Rising prices brought windfall profits to business and in this way enhanced the expectations of potential investors, a necessary stimulus for the promotion of a high level of income and employment. But it must be admitted that the level of investment depends upon much more than price expectations, and in this respect the early Keynesian analysis was weak. It was not until investment opportunities had sunk to a level much lower than that reached during the decade of the twenties that Keynes recognized their complicated character and the necessity for vigorous measures in order to send the economic system into a revival. However, we must keep in mind the fact that Keynes was always for a little inflation, and his reasons were not unrelated to the promotion of investment. Another reason why Keynes always favored inflation as opposed to deflation was that inflation is carried on at the expense of the *rentier* class, an inactive class in the economy which Keynes had always wanted to eliminate. He regarded deflation as a transference of wealth from the active to the inactive (*i.e. rentier*) class. This attitude accounts for his interest and activity in the problem of determining the level of the franc. In an "Open Letter to the French Minister of Finance,"[9] Keynes argued that the level of the franc would be determined by the proportion of income which the taxpayers would allow to be transferred to the *rentiers*. He argued that it would be more desirable to diminish the claims of the *rentier* rather than to increase the tax burden. Of three alternatives open to the Minister of Finance — capital levy, reduced interest rates, or price rises — Keynes recommended the inflationary method of price rises as the most expedient method of solving France's monetary problem.

The desire for price stability is quite in line with Marshall's teachings. Marshall, too, desired stability because he saw the possible evils of price fluctuations upon the various classes of society. He pointed out the effects of rising and falling prices on

---

[9] *Essays in Persuasion*, Harcourt Brace, New York, 1932, p. 105.

producers' expectations and hence on the level of output. Marshall very specifically noted the fact that wages were sticky as compared with prices, so that workers lost where employers gained. His observations on the movements of wages' relative to prices have some bearing on the more recent Keynesian writings. On the whole, Marshall feared the results of extreme and frequent fluctuations and consistently favored moderation in price movements.

The question of devaluation vs. deflation of the monetary unit was a considerable part of the above matter of inflation vs. deflation, and was being considered in the light of the gold standard issue. The matter can be phrased thus: Should England fix the value of its currency, no matter on what standard, at the existing, postwar exchange rates, or should she return to the prewar value of the pound by a process of deflation. Secondly, should the monetary system be constituted so as to achieve a stable internal price level or a stable foreign exchange rate? Once the second question had been answered, it would have been possible to decide whether or not to return to the strict gold standard, and the answer to the first question would have indicated the exchange rate to be chosen, no matter what standard was used. Keynes was certainly unequivocal in his preference for domestic price stability over exchange rate stability so that the monetary authorities could maintain control over the domestic economy. Whether Keynes' specific proposal was what we call a gold standard or not is unimportant; the point to be made is that he definitely did not want to return to the old-fashioned gold standard system that existed before the war, and that he did not want to restore the pound to its prewar parity under any system. His specific proposal was for the Bank of England to quote a weekly buying and selling price for gold (spot and future) not at the level of prewar prices. Some economists may assert that a gold standard is in existence when there is a fixed buying and selling price for gold, and it can be seen that Keynes' scheme did not even fall under this liberal definition of a gold standard, for he was very much against a pegged price for gold. The bank's weekly price for gold was not to remain fixed, but was to fluctuate as conditions warranted. Of course, Keynes felt that stability of exchanges, as long as it was not incompatible with stability of prices, was a desirable thing, and that, if possible, the Bank of England should keep the buying and selling prices of gold stable.

As in the previous problem of the Indian monetary situation, in order to recommend a policy of price stability it was necessary to base the recommendation on a theory of the determination of the price level. An economist cannot recommend a policy for the stabilization of prices unless he knows clearly how prices are determined. And so in both cases we see that the theoretical apparatus employed by Keynes was the quantity theory of money, along the most orthodox lines. For the entire period of the twenties we find this incessant insistence upon price stability, with the policy measures formulated on the basis of an orthodox quantity theory of money, or something closely related to it. One almost gets the impression that Keynes was viewing the business cycle as the "dance of the dollar" and that price stability, in itself, would cure our economic ills. It was not until the true nature of the saving-investment process became evident to Keynes that he was able to get rid of some of his classical and neo-classical ideas in order to develop a more satisfactory theory of economic behavior.

Returning once more to the theory of the determination of the price level, let us consider the quantity theory as held by Keynes in *A Tract on Monetary Reform*. There he worked with the well known equation:

$$n = p(k + rk')$$

where n is the cash in circulation, p is the price level, k is the number of consumption units which the public decides to hold in cash, r is the banks' ratio for checking accounts, and k' is the number of consumption units which the public decides to hold in checking accounts. Keynes regarded n and r as institutionally given, *i.e.* determined by the personal decisions of the heads of the banking system. He considered k and k' to fluctuate over the course of the cycle but also to be institutionally given by the public's psychological spending habits at any point of time. Hence the only variable in the equation is p, which can always be determined in terms of institutionally given parameters. The proper manipulation of n and r by the banking system was suggested in order to counteract the fluctuations over time of k and k', thus giving the desired price stability. This theory of the determination of p was admittedly based on the theory of Marshall's *Money, Credit and Commerce*, except for the fact that Marshall did not distinguish between the decision to hold consumption units in the form of checking accounts and in the form of circulating currency.

As we shall see further on, the main difference between Keynes of the *Tract* and Keynes of *A Treatise on Money* is concerned with the treatment of the quantity theory of money. For in the *Tract*, the motives of the public for holding money were inadequately analyzed. Money was regarded as having only one function — as a medium of exchange — and its function as a store of value was not considered. This is evident since k and k' were both defined as the equivalents of the number of consumption units which the public elects to hold in the form of cash or deposits. In other words, he assumed that people have only one motive for holding money, the transactions motive. Keynes actually did go on to qualify this slightly and to introduce the precautionary motive, but the important thing that he omitted was the speculative motive which is linked to the function of money as a store of wealth, an idea entirely absent from the *Tract*. However, we shall see later that the major theoretical innovation of the *Treatise* was an analysis of the functions of money and the motives which lead people to hold cash balances.

Again the Marshall influence is evident. We find in Chapter I of Marshall's *Money, Credit and Commerce*, a discussion of the function of money in which Marshall mentioned it only as a medium of exchange and as a standard of deferred payments. He and his pupil Keynes both overlooked the influence of money as a store of value.

The modern reader will undoubtedly raise high hopes in anticipation of something quite revealing in the economic process after a reading of the preface of *A Tract on Monetary Reform*. There the first words read:

We leave Saving to the private investor, and we encourage him to place his savings mainly in titles to money. We leave the responsibility for setting Production in motion to the business man, who is mainly influenced by the profits which he expects to accrue to himself in terms of money.[10]

[10] *Monetary Reform*, p. v.

In vain does one look in the body of the book for some early insight into the saving-investment problem and its influence on the level of output and employment. This passage, however, is one of the first indications that Keynes recognized the problem of offsets to savings and the nature of the decision to save, as opposed to the decision to invest. Herein lies the great Keynesian contribution, but we are to hear little more of it in the *Tract*, except for the discussion of inflation and deflation, which examined the effect of price fluctuations on investment and business decisions.

In the transition period between the appearances of the *Tract* and that of the *Treatise* there was one problem which troubled England greatly and which Keynes was constantly attempting to solve. This was the problem of prolonged unemployment and depressed economic conditions in general. Up to 1929 there was a steady rate of unemployment of about one million or more persons (a large figure for Britain), and depressed conditions existed in many industries. All this was going on while other countries were fairly prosperous, a point which led Keynes to attribute the faults entirely to policies of the British government rather than to world conditions in general. The unemployment was largely concentrated in basic industries such as iron and steel, shipbuilding, and coal, while light industries fared much better. The unemployment was not great in such industries as electrical engineering, printing, distributive trades, or banking. This concentration of unemployment at that time in heavy industries is quite important in understanding some of the remedies later to be proposed by Keynes.

The main characteristic of the Keynesian policies for the improvement of the level of employment is that they almost all involved some sort of monetary control and manipulation. Unemployment was looked upon as one of the most serious of our economic problems, yet Keynes confidently believed that it could be fully solved within the framework of the capitalist system by employing the proper monetary policy. While most of the policy measures proposed were justified by strict classical analysis, it should be noted that there was one fundamental point of view which was quite unorthodox, namely, the contention that the system was not perfectly self-adjusting and that *laissez faire* policies were not the ones to bring about recovery. However, this departure from classical reasoning might be more apparent than real, if one recognizes that many of Keynes' reasons for the lack of self-adjustment related to frictions, maladjustments, and political conditions of the day, which could not have been foreseen by the founders of classical doctrine. In fact, he characterized this state of prolonged depression during the twenties as one of pseudo-equilibrium [11] and not a smooth-working economic adjustment. Also, in answering Beveridge's thesis that overpopulation has little effect upon the level of employment, Keynes stated what he believed to be the real cause of unemployment — a phenomenon of maladjustment. The maladjustments, he remarked, may have arisen from such causes as transitions from lower to higher price levels, a change-over from supplying one type of external market to supplying another, attempts of organized labor to obtain higher real wages than the existing economic conditions would permit. This latter maladjustment was considered closely related to overpopulation, and he concluded that perhaps Malthus was correct about a terrible devil.[12]

The classical influence is no more strongly represented anywhere in Keynes' writings than in his earlier views on free trade.[13] He stated that the case for free trade was based on two propositions which he accepted with certain obvious exceptions: (1) It is better for each country to produce those goods in which it has the comparative advantage and trade for those in which it has comparative disadvantages. (2) There can be no disadvantage in importing useful goods. The exceptions had to do with trade restrictions for such purposes as influencing the trade in goods which are particularly desirable or undesirable for non-economic reasons, building up industries for national defense, supporting infant industries, and dealing with dumping. He argued that protection would lead either to interference with commodity exports or to an increase in capital exports. The latter event he wanted to avoid because he was using the old argument of unlimited investment opportunities [14] —

[11] *Essays in Persuasion*, p. 241.
[12] "Is Britain Overpopulated?" *New Republic*, Vol. XXXVI, 1923, p. 247.
[13] "Free Trade for England," *New Republic*, Vol. XXXVII, 1923, p. 86.
[14] This is the argument of Say's law.

exported capital merely diverts capital from use at home; *i.e.*, capital will always be employed, either at home or abroad. In Keynes' own words we have the following statements:

> For if there is one thing that protection *cannot* do, it is to cure unemployment.[15]

> But the claim to cure unemployment involves the Protectionist fallacy in its grossest and also in its crudest form.[16]

We shall see later how much these views were modified.

Britain's return to gold in 1925 at the prewar parity brought forth a huge stream of critical articles by Keynes, for this was a deflationary measure which he had opposed since the close of the war. Moreover, this step was opposed not only on grounds of his preference for inflation over deflation, but also because it represented an attempt to restore an automatic mechanism of currency adjustments, directly in opposition with Keynes' views on monetary management. In *The Economic Consequences of Mr. Churchill*,[17] he argued that the whole source of difficulty in the British economic scene could be traced to the fact that relative prices at home and abroad were completely out of line, to the disadvantage of England. The prices of British export goods abroad were considered to be too high, thus working a hardship on the export trade in maintaining a balance of payments. But it is significant that Keynes agreed at this stage to change one of his views regarding the cause of unemployment and excessively high export prices. An orthodox conclusion to be drawn might have been that the workers were being remunerated too handsomely for what they produced. Keynes objected to this view and said that the real cause of troubles in the export industries was that sterling was overvalued; the return to gold at the prewar parity raised the value of sterling by 12 per cent abroad, thus making British goods more expensive in foreign markets. If the average money wages prevailing at that time in the various countries be converted into a common monetary unit at the then going exchange rates, one would find the British wages far above those of the rest of the world, but this seeming competitive

---

[15] *Ibid.*, p. 87.   [16] *Ibid.*, p. 87.
[17] *The Economic Consequences of Mr. Churchill*, L. and V. Woolf, London, 1925.

advantage for British workers was a purely monetary phenomenon. The real wages of British workers were much nearer the level of those in other countries than was true of the gold wages. Keynes thus argued that the difficulty could not have been due to high real wages in the export industries. The possible lines of action that were open to Britain, according to Keynes, were to let the sterling exchange depreciate abroad with constant prices at home, or to force home prices and wages down into adjustment with the sterling exchange. Of course, he ruled out the latter alternative because of his constant fear of deflationary complications. He also recognized the institutional rigidities which would stand in the way of wage cuts because he foresaw the possibility of strike action on the part of the workers in order to prevent wage reductions. Another element in the return to gold which drew criticism from his sharp pen was the fact that the Bank of England was forced to raise its discount rate and restrict credit, precisely at a time when the level of investment activity was low.

A long controversy between Keynes and Ohlin took place in the latter part of the 1920's on the transfer problem; however, since the issues involved here have been so extensively reviewed in books on international trade and since the questions involved do not illustrate much about Keynes' monetary theories which we cannot find elsewhere, there is little point in discussing the matter further. But in passing, we should note that this argument on the transfer problem is quite in line with classical thought, the theme of this chapter.

It is with the election of 1929 that interesting points arise again, for here is the first inkling of the later and more famous Keynesian doctrines which will be examined at some length below. The occasion of the new Keynesian policy was a political pledge by Lloyd George to reduce the volume of unemployment through spending on public works. Keynes in collaboration with H. D. Henderson [18] examined the commonsense reasoning behind this pledge and argued that it followed from economic analysis. Keynes had by no means deviated as yet from classical thought, and for this reason the argument is weak at certain crucial points. But the most significant

[18] *Can Lloyd George Do It? An Examination of the Liberal Pledge*, Nation and Athenaeum, London, 1929.

enlightenment to draw from this piece of writing is that we can see clearly the sense in which the Keynesian doctrines represent a true innovation. In later chapters we shall show clearly that all the important parts of the *General Theory* can be found in the works of various predecessors, but in spite of this fact no one was thinking seriously along these lines at the time of the Great Depression. *The Keynesian theory was essentially new as compared with the existing body of doctrine held in the late 1920's and the 1930's.* The arguments against Lloyd George's Liberal Pledge clearly show the status of some of the non-Keynesian thought.

As always, Keynes was very optimistic about the success of his policy recommendations — this time a public works program — in bringing about full employment, especially since he predicted, in addition to the direct stimulus to the construction industry, induced effects whereby other industries would indirectly be influenced as a result of the increased purchasing power of the workers employed on the government projects. In fact, he even suggested that Lloyd George wanted to spend too much and that the plan could be successful even if based on smaller outlays. He was rather naïve in accounting for the frictions, leakages, and other obstacles, about which we learned so much in our depression experience.

The fact that men (economically productive factors) were idle and being supported by costly unemployment benefits when they could have been set to work on useful tasks which would have increased the stock of wealth was, for Keynes, an outright contradiction. The contradiction was especially flagrant since this state of unemployment had been going on for eight years (excepting 1924) with at least one million persons constantly out of work. He considered, and rightly so, the cost of the Lloyd George program to be trivial as compared with the wastes of unemployment.

Keynes' recognition of the great possibilities of induced effects over and above the initial government outlays presents the germ of his later developments, for his opponents always considered the costs of the plan in relation only to the volume of primary, direct employment that would result from public works projects. But one must not get the idea that Keynes had yet come to the strategic doctrine now called the "multiplier," which shows the accumulation of all induced effects; *i.e.*, the total increment to national production, accumulated over all future periods, which results from a given public outlay. It is an exceedingly big step for a formal economic theory [19] to go from the vague concept of repeated expenditures by successive income recipients to the theory of the multiplier without getting lost in explaining the successive rounds of spending by each income recipient. Keynes always got lost in successive spendings after the first two or three rounds. But he did point out very clearly that there would be cumulative effects of induced purchasing power, although he remarked that it would not be possible to measure the accumulation with any precision.[20] Also he emphasized very much the spread of employment from the immediate site of the public works to the indirect employment in complementary industries — the notion of investment induced by a given autonomous impulse. However, since he had not examined thoroughly a formal multiplier theory, he did appear to be falling into one pitfall. He imagined that by this spending the government would be able to lift itself by its own bootstraps. He concluded that there would be such an increase in income as a result of the spending that with fixed tax rates the government would get large increases in its tax revenue in order to offset the budget deficit. Other sources of relief to the budget, he stated, would be reduced armament expenditures and reduced unemployment benefit payments, but, in fact, the reduction of spending on these latter two items by the government would merely mean that spending would be transferred out of these lines into public works if full employment were to be achieved. There would be no net relief to the budget.

There are also indications in this article that the stagnant economic position of Britain had at last impressed upon Keynes' mind the problem of offsets to savings. His opponents contended that employment on public works schemes would merely divert employment from jobs in private industry. They were clearly operating with the classical assumption of full employment — sending workers into one job merely takes workers away from another job. It is

[19] Though not for economic policy.
[20] Compare this with the optimistic attitude about the precision of the measurements in *The Means to Prosperity*, Harcourt Brace, New York, 1933.

amazing, in the light of British experience, that people could argue this way. That Keynes saw the problem is evident, but he was far from having developed a satisfactory theory. He claimed that the savings which would flow into the investment undertaken by the Lloyd George scheme would not come from funds that would otherwise be used to finance other capital equipment; instead that the resources would be furnished from savings which were then disbursed to the unemployed, from savings which would run to waste through lack of credit, or from reduced foreign lending. The recommendation that the government offset otherwise redundant savings brings us to the core of the later Keynesian policy.

A THEORETICAL MODEL

A period of swift intellectual growth was concluded with the appearance in 1930 of the famous *Treatise on Money*.[21] Economists eagerly awaited this long publicized work, which Keynes had been writing over many years. We are told in the preface that many of the author's ideas underwent great change during the process of writing this *Treatise;* and one reviewer has characterized the book as a transitory phase of rapid development. The most striking characteristic of the *Treatise* is its loosely knit theory with many lines of thought incomplete. But we can accept this book as the summation of all the lines of thought covered in the several debates of the 1920's, as discussed above, with the possible exception of the question of public works schemes brought up in the elections of 1929. We shall take the *Treatise* and some of the review articles built upon it as the status of Keynesian theory at the start of the Great Depression. In the next chapter, we can then go on to consider the extremely important transition from the *Treatise* to the *General Theory*, with the important steps exposed.

We can describe the *Treatise* as a book in classical economics based on two important and well known theories. These two theories are the business-cycle theory which makes investment fluctuations the prime mover of the capitalistic system as supported by Tougan Baranovski, Spiethoff, Schumpeter, Robertson and the

[21] *A Treatise on Money*, Harcourt Brace, New York, 1930, 2 vols.

theory that the rate of interest is determined in equilibrium by the equality of savings and investment.[22] With these two theories superimposed upon a classical model, it is possible to develop the important arguments of the *Treatise*, with the exception of one significant new contribution to economic theory, the foundations of Keynes' later liquidity-preference theory of interest. It may seem odd that the liquidity-preference doctrines should come out of a work based on the interest theory of the *Treatise;* however, this only illustrates the confused state of Keynes' ideas at the time. The seeming contradiction is easily resolved, since the liquidity-preference theory of interest grew from the seeds of the bearishness theory of the determination of the price level of investment goods (or non-liquid assets), as it was presented in the *Treatise*, rather than from the determination of the rate of interest.

Briefly, the argument of the *Treatise* ran as follows: The business cycle is caused by fluctuations in the rate of investment relative to the rate of savings. This notion is based on the theories of Tougan Baranovski, Spiethoff, Schumpeter, and Robertson. In fact, Schumpeter's theory of innovations was unreservedly accepted by Keynes as the moving force of the capitalist fluctuations.[23] According, however, to the interest theory, fluctuations in the market rate of interest about the natural rate (the rate which would equate savings and investment) are uniquely related to fluctuations in the discrepancy between savings and investment which in turn are related to fluctuations in the price level. Then Keynes argued that investment is the really dynamic factor which fluctuates when the market and natural rates of interest diverge, and that the fluctuations in prices are a result of the discrepancies generated between savings and investment. The whole aim of the *Treatise* was to tell us how to keep prices stable; or, what is the same, to keep savings and investment equal; or, what is the same, to keep the market rate of interest equal to the natural rate. Thus Keynes' concrete

---

[22] The interest theory as presented in the *Treatise* was somewhat Wicksellian, although Keynes intimated that he personally considered his interest theory to be different from that of Wicksell.

[23] Although Professor Schumpeter would have us believe that his views are 100 percent non (anti (?))-Keynesian, he must admit that there are great similarities between their cycle theories.

proposals were schemes of monetary control; the banks by manipulation of the rate of interest would influence the level of investment until equilibrium could be achieved with the more stable rate of savings. This would give the desired end of price stability. If interest rate manipulations proved unsuccessful, then open-market operations were suggested as the control measure. In many respects this part of the *Treatise* does not differ much from the *Tract on Monetary Reform*. In that latter book he also wanted price stability in order to stimulate a satisfactory level of investment activity. But the *Treatise* was certainly a step forward in that the investment-savings process was much better analyzed and the influence of the rate of interest, although perhaps exaggerated, was incorporated into the economic model. The analysis of the factors that determine the level of investment in fixed, working, and liquid capital and the distinctions between the process of saving and the process of investment were great contributions of the *Treatise*, in spite of the fact that these notions were not wholly original with Keynes but were drawn from other theories.

Keynes apparently thought that he was bringing out the heart of his theory in the exposition of his pretentious "fundamental equations," but the "fundamental equations" were not the essential contribution of the book, and it is quite unfortunate that the reviews and discussions of the book always centered on these equations, instead of on more useful material. Of course, Keynes' attitude and his label of "fundamental equations" did not help to promote the discussion of the *Treatise* to a higher level of scientific achievement. The "fundamental equations" were merely definitions which did not rest upon refutable hypotheses — hypotheses which could be verified or refuted by available data. They were on a level with other famous equations in economics such as $MV = PT$, which do not tell us anything about fundamental economic behavior.

Essentially, the fundamental equations represented an attempt to improve upon the classical quantity equations and link the interest rate, as well as the stock of cash balances, to the determination of the various price levels, particularly the price level of output as a whole and the price level of consumption goods. Keynes wanted to show with these equations how variations in the market rate of interest relative to the natural rate would cause discrepancies between the level of savings and investment, which in turn would cause the price level to oscillate. It must be pointed out that Keynes did not regard his equations as formally incompatible with the quantity theory; rather he thought that they brought to light certain processes obscured by the traditional doctrine.

This exposition may seem to be nothing more than a statement of the Wicksell theory, from which the terminology was certainly borrowed. But Wicksell was not ready to substitute an alternative for the quantity theory. His theory held that equality between the two rates of interest implies stability of the price level as well as equality between the levels of savings and investment, but he did not look upon these conclusions as flagrant contradictions of the quantity theory and took the attitude in his *Interest and Prices* that the quantity theory, although not a perfect explanation of price movements, was the best theory to use until a better formulation could be provided. Wicksell openly admitted that his ideas about interest rates and the price level were so imperfectly thought out in his own mind that he did not dare formalize them in mathematical equations. Keynes thought that Wicksell's theory and that of the *Treatise* might come to the same thing, but he was never quite certain of what Wicksell wanted to say.

At this time Keynes' bone of contention with the classical writers was that the price level is affected by variations in magnitudes other than the stock of money or velocities of circulation, namely, by variations in the interest rate. According to the classicists, though, interest fluctuations could influence the price level only through induced fluctuations in the stock of cash balances. That is to say, they thought that changes in the market rate of interest make bank credit easier or more restricted according as the interest rate is lowered or raised. The net change in bank deposits when added to the existing cash was their mainspring behind price movements.

Let us consider now the "fundamental equation" for the determination of the price level of output as a whole in relation to the quantity equation, to see what were the points at issue.

Keynes defined what we now call net national income produced, Y, as the sum of income paid out to the factors of production plus windfall profits. The income paid out, E, was defined as salaries and wages, unemployment benefits, interest on capital, regular monopoly gains, rents, and the normal remuneration of entrepreneurs. Normal remuneration of entrepreneurs was defined as that rate which would leave entrepreneurs under no motive to alter the scale of their operations if they were free to make new bargains with the factors of production at the going rates of return. Thus, net returns, over and above the normal rate, became windfall profits. Windfalls were also defined as the difference between the market value of new investment and savings. The second definition came to the same thing as the first, since "savings" was defined as the difference between income paid out (net of windfalls) and consumption.[24] while the market value of investment was defined as total income produced (inclusive of windfalls) minus consumption.

If we denote output as O, the price level as Π, and windfalls as Q, then we get:

$$Y = \Pi O = E + Q$$

Keynes wrote the right-hand equation as:

$$\Pi = \frac{E}{O} + \frac{Q}{O} = \frac{E}{O} + \frac{I - S}{O}$$

Here I and S represent investment and savings respectively.

Perhaps it was unfair to say above that this equation was a definition and not based on any refutable hypothesis. The mere formal existence of the equation, Keynes thought, depended on the truism that income could be conveniently broken up into two parts: (1) Income paid out, E; (2) windfall profits, Q. In so far as this was his theory, it was not based on any refutable hypothesis. But he implicitly attached certain hypotheses to some of these variables in order to study the mechanism of price change. As is true of all these definitional equations, variations in one variable may always counteract variations in another, so that conclusions with regard to the movements of yet other variables may be obscure. In the quantity equations, $MV = py$, if movements of the velocity of cir-

---

[24] This is a satisfactory definition of saving in agreement with common usage only if people spend on consumption goods exclusively from income paid out and spend on capital goods from windfall profits and incomes paid out.

culation (V) and/or of the physical volume of output (y) counteract movements of the stock of money (M), then we cannot be certain about movements of the price level (p). The classical theorists solved this problem by taking the velocity as an institutionally given constant, and output as given at the full employment level. They justified the first assumption by claiming that velocity or, if you like, its inverse, the Marshall "k," depends upon consumer spending habits, practices with regard to the frequency of income disbursements, banking practices, and the general psychology.[25] Thus at any point of time the general social and economic setting would give them the hypothesis of an institutionally determined parameter, $k = \bar{k}$. The other assumption of full employment output followed from their theory of the structure of the real sphere of the economy. They thought that the marginal productivity theory of wages defines a demand curve for labor in terms of real wages. This demand curve, according to them, interacts with a supply curve of labor (also in terms of real wages) to determine the level of employment and the level of real wages. They also envisaged a technological relation between output, employment, and the stock of capital. Taking the stock of capital as fixed, in the short run, a relation exists between the level of output and employment such that they could determine the former from their knowledge of the latter. Keynes, being a good classical economist, implicitly accepted the above theory of the level of output. Hence, in his fundamental equation we can assume that output is given, $O = \bar{O}$. That this is a correct interpretation is substantiated by a statement in the preface of the *General Theory* which said, "My so-called 'fundamental equations' were an instantaneous picture taken on the assumption of a given output."[26]

The variable E which represents income paid out to the factors of production was never adequately accounted for by Keynes, this being the principal fault of the *Treatise*. This variable represents effective demand, and the lack of any theory of effective demand

[25] This is the same sense in which Keynes of the *Tract* assumed that the number of consumption units held in the form of cash is an institutional constant. See p. 7 above.

[26] *The General Theory of Employment, Interest, and Money*, Harcourt Brace, New York, 1936, p. vii.

was precisely the fault which prevented Keynes from producing a satisfactory result at this time. He dodged the issue of the determination of effective demand by assuming the ratio $\frac{E}{O}$, which he called the rate of efficiency earnings of the productive factors, as a stable term which changed only gradually with a trend path. Thus the only other determinant of the price level in the "fundamental equation" which remains unaccounted for is the strategic variable Q or $(I - S)$. The behavior of this variable was formulated from the main hypothesis of the book. Keynes posited that Q depends upon the difference between the market and natural rates of interest, such that Q is greater than zero when the latter rate exceeds the former, equal to zero when the two rates are equal, and less than zero when the former rate exceeds the latter.

From these hypotheses, Keynes derived the result that the price level fluctuates about a rather stable equilibrium value, $\frac{E}{O}$, according as the market rate fluctuates about the natural rate and induces fluctuations in the profit variable, Q. The theory of price fluctuations could, of course, be stated in terms of the relative behavior of savings and investment flows since Q was defined as $(I - S)$. The explanation in these terms is perhaps more illuminating, since it tells more about the economic mechanism. For example, if there is an increase in the quantity of money, in the first instance there should be an upward pressure on the price level via the term $\frac{E}{O}$ of the equation. More money will be spent in the payments to the factors of production which accounts for the increased ratio $\frac{E}{O}$. But in the next step, we find that the increased cash will tend to increase the reserve position of banks and make them willing to lend on easier credit conditions; i.e., the bank rate will be lowered. The change in the rate of interest will, according to this theory, stimulate investment and discourage savings so that there is a discrepancy generated between these two flows. This discrepancy, which was called Q, will further increase the price level; hence there is a stimulus to prices in addition to that caused by increased income payments. The process does not end here, because the increased demand for investment reacts upon the demand for workers to produce investment goods and thus exerts a further upward pressure on prices.

In so far as the quantity equation is written in the Cambridge form

$$\overline{M} = \bar{k}p\bar{y}$$

in which the stock of money, $\overline{M}$, the fractions of income which people choose to hold in the form of cash, $\bar{k}$, and full employment output, $\bar{y}$, are all given, the classical theory does not agree with the theory of the *Treatise*. Keynes agreed with the assumption that $\overline{M}$ and $\bar{y}$ are given, but objected to the assumption $\bar{k} = k$ which he had previously accepted in *A Tract on Monetary Reform*. Keynes was really trying to say that k is influenced by the rate of interest. This can be shown in the following way: One of the great innovations of the *Treatise* was to analyze the motives for which people hold cash balances. Total cash balances were split into income deposits, savings deposits, and business deposits which can be linked very easily to his later well known classification of funds held for the transactions, business, precautionary and speculative motives. He said that the incomes paid out are equal to the income deposits multiplied by their velocity of circulation, or $E = M_1V_1$. Hence the "fundamental equation" can be written:

$$\Pi O = M_1V_1 + Q$$

Just as the classical writers assumed k given, so did Keynes assume V_1 given. He wrote, "Generally speaking, one would expect the average value of k_1 [the inverse of V_1] in a given economic society to be a fairly stable quantity from year to year."[27] He accounted for the stability of k_1 by pointing out the same habits, customs, and business practices to which earlier economists had referred. In this relation, he thought that interest fluctuations would cause movements in Q, independently of M_1 and V_1, which would, in turn, cause the price level to oscillate. *We may conclude that the classical theory took a fraction of $E + Q = Y$ as a stable given*

[27] *A Treatise on Money*, Vol. I., p. 44.

value, while Keynes took a fraction of merely E as a stable given value.
The monetary flow directed at that part of the value of output
denoted by Q was really taken to depend upon the rate of interest
and was not given institutionally. The quantity equation can be
written:

$$(M_1 + M_2)V = E + Q = Y$$

Here M_2 is the stock of business deposits. Keynes asserted that
the sum of income deposits plus business deposits constituted cash
deposits and represented the total sum available for spending. The
other element of the money supply, savings deposits, was assigned
a zero velocity of circulation and treated only as a store of value.
The equation with $M_1 + M_2$ as the stock of money agrees also
with the classical treatment of money exclusively as a medium of
exchange. Furthermore, since Keynes wrote $M_1V_1 = E$, we can
legitimately write $M_2V_2 = Q$, where V_2 is the velocity of circulation
of business deposits, defined as the ratio of Q to M_2. If Q is a function
of the interest rate, then V_2 is also defined as a function of the
interest rate.[28] Now the "fundamental equation" can be written:

$$\Pi = \frac{(M_1 + M_2)V}{O} = \frac{M_1\overline{V_1}}{O} + \frac{M_2V_2}{O}$$

The classical V is merely a weighted sum:

$$V = \left(\frac{M_1}{M_1 + M_2}\right)\overline{V}_1 + \left(\frac{M_2}{M_1 + M_2}\right)V_2$$

It must also depend upon the rate of interest because it is made up
of an autonomous element $(\overline{V}_1)$ and a function of the rate of interest (V_2).

It is very important to see here that Keynes' divergence from
the quantity theory was not related to his treatment of money as a
store of value because he excluded the influence of savings deposits
from his "fundamental equation." His later position based on the
liquidity-preference theory, however, was to include in his money
equation the sum of money used for transactions and for idle

[28] Except for the exceptional case in which M_2 is a particular function of the interest rate such that the rate cancels out of the numerator and denominator of $\frac{Q}{M_2}$.

hoards. His divergence from the quantity equation was, in the *General Theory*, due directly to the treatment of money as a store of value. In the *Treatise*, savings deposits, as we shall see below, were treated in a relation entirely separate from the "fundamental equations."

The theory behind the determination of the price level of consumption goods was quite similar to that of the case of the general price level. To determine P, the price of current consumption goods, Keynes developed another "fundamental equation." He first wrote:

$$P = \frac{E}{O} + \frac{I' - S}{R}$$

Here I' is the cost of production of new investment, and R is the physical volume of consumption. It was soon pointed out by Professor Hansen that this equation involved an unwarranted assumption about the relative rates of change of the costs of investment goods and consumption goods. But it is shown in the appendix to this volume that this invalid equation did not affect the determinacy of prices in the system — and Keynes' main goal was to explain the theory of price determination.

The theory of the determination of the other price level, P', for investment goods introduced a far more interesting theory. D. H. Robertson in commenting on the *Treatise* [29] remarked that Keynes' exposition was not complete because he never stated explicitly how P' is determined. Keynes replied [30] that in his discussion of bearishness and bullishness, he had implicitly given enough factors to determine this price level. His theory was that the price level of non-liquid assets is determined by the equation of the quantity of hoards which people want to hold with the quantity of savings deposits which the banks are willing to create. The variable P' was conceived as the allocating mechanism between the holding of idle balances on the part of the public and the creation of idle balances on the part of the banks.[31] Formally, he looked upon the determina-

---

[29] "Mr. Keynes' Theory of Money," *Economic Journal*, Vol. XLI, 1931, p. 395.

[30] "A Rejoinder," *Economic Journal*, Vol. XLI, 1931, p. 412.

[31] For a brilliant anticipation of the theory of liquidity preference based upon this argument of the *Treatise*, see J. R. Hicks, "A Suggestion for Simplifying the Theory of Money," *Economica*, N.S., Vol. 2, 1935, p. 1.

tion of P' as the result of the intersection of two economic schedules. On the demand side he drew up a schedule relation between the demand for savings deposits and the price of non-liquid assets. This schedule is the bearishness function.

For each price level of non-liquid assets, people may choose whether they want to hold their wealth in the form of savings deposits or non-liquid assets. The price level of non-liquid assets is the discounted value of the expected future income stream to be derived from the holding of a unit of these assets. If expectations are known as a psychological datum, then there is a simple relationship between the price of non-liquid assets and the discount rate. The discount rate shows how profitable it is to hold non-liquid assets and enables one to choose the form in which he wants to hold wealth — in savings deposits or in non-liquid assets. The discount rate enables one to make this decision because when compared with the interest rate paid on savings deposits, it shows the relative advantage or disadvantage of holding wealth in the form of non-liquid assets as opposed to savings deposits. Consequently, Keynes stated that there is a demand schedule relating the demand for savings deposits to the price of investment goods.

On the supply side, Keynes believed that the banking system had control over the volume of savings deposits. He said, "We have claimed, further, that the banking system can control the supply of savings deposits. . . ." [32] This assumption certainly makes P' determinate, for if the supply curve is controlled by the banks, and the bearishness function is known, we can find the equilibrium between the demand and supply of savings deposits. Ordinarily there will be a unique price (P') which will be consistent with this equilibrium. The assumption that the banks can control the supply of savings deposits seems somewhat tenuous. At best, we now assume that they control the supply of the total stock of money and not the various kinds of deposits separately.

Keynes was assuming that a particular discount policy determines the size of the various types of cash balances. It should be parenthetically remarked that the control of the banks over the discount

---

[32] *A Treatise on Money*, Vol. II, p. 346.

rate is not independent of their control over the stock of cash balances. If the two are not independent, perhaps the classical economists were not so wrong in tracing fluctuations in the interest rate to fluctuations in the stock of money and to fluctuations in the price level. At any rate, it must be admitted that the control over· the bank rate of interest is highly interrelated with the control over the stock of money.

Now that we have analyzed Keynes' theories of the determination of prices, we can see immediately how his policy-control scheme fits into the theoretical framework. He tried desperately to answer the question: Does the central bank have enough power to control the price level? Granted that this control is possible, he believed that cyclical fluctuations would be eliminated. The central bank would have to exercise control over the volume of savings deposits and the market rate of interest so that P', P, and Π would be kept stable. By means of the bearishness function, control over savings deposits would result in control over P', and by means of the "fundamental equations," control over the market rate would result in control over P and Π. He did not claim that the monetary authorities could always produce these results simultaneously; or that non-monetary disturbances might not arise unforeseen; or that it would be possible to avoid relative price movements; or that a country could carry out domestic monetary policy regardless of international considerations. In general, however, he had a very optimistic outlook as to the possibility of regulating a capitalist economy, and thought that interest rate and credit manipulations carry great weight in economic decisions.

The principal defect of the theoretical side of the *Treatise* was, as has been shown, the failure to explain how the level of effective demand gets determined. Keynes wanted to explain an equilibrium situation in which prices would be stable. The main criterion of this equilibrium situation was pictured by him as the equality of the flows of savings and investment. Herein lay a great mistake, for savings and investment can be in equilibrium at various levels of employment. For Keynes, an equilibrium between savings and investment at low levels had exactly the same influence on price stability in the "fundamental equation" as an equilibrium at high levels. It is only when the levels of savings and investment are related to the level of employment that we get significant results. The theory of the *Treatise* is entirely independent, in equilibrium, of the size of offsets to savings. Keynes, however, was not the only one to fail to associate his equilibria with the volume of employment. Wicksell's theory had the same defect. He was interested only in the equality of the market rate and the natural rate of interest, or in other words, in the equality between savings and investment.

This defect of the theory could become quite serious. Since Keynes believed that many of the troubles of the early 1930's were due to a failure of savings to get invested, on the basis of his theoretical model he could have proposed two essentially different types of remedies. He could have proposed, as he did, measures which he thought would stimulate investment to such an extent that it would offset, at a high figure, the savings that people wanted to make. But his goal of price stability would have supposedly followed equally well if he had instead proposed measures to bring savings to an amount small enough to provide only the meager investment outlets available. One solution would represent a high level of capital accumulation and one a low level. Obviously, our prosperity would differ in the two cases, but the effects on the Keynesian criteria would not be apparent. That is not to say that the effects would not exist. There would be different reactions in each case on the term E in the equations, but these reactions would not follow from Keynes' theoretical point of view.

Not only was the theoretical model exposed to much criticism, but the applied theory of money also underwent many attacks. Keynes undoubtedly overestimated the number of significant economic variables which the banks could control as well as the results of such control. The principal lever in the whole scheme was the rate of interest. He recognized that the important rate for his theory was the long-term rate, for this is the rate which would influence the fluctuations in fixed capital. But since he knew that the banking system had no direct control over the long-term rate, he had to appeal to the statistical facts to show that there was a close correlation between the long and short rates so that control of the latter by the banks would lead to effective influence over the former. Later, when all the relevant data were brought up to date, it was found that this close correlation did not always persist, and Keynes was forced to back down on his statement about influencing investment through control over the bank rate.[33] In the event of the banks' failure to gain effective control over the market rate of interest, Keynes was forced to resort to proposals for the stimulation of investment by more direct methods.

A criticism of the *Treatise* which has also been levied against the *General Theory* is that the model was entirely static. This criticism is all the more serious since Keynes claimed dynamical virtues for his innovations. In a formal sense, the "fundamental equations," written as they were appear to be entirely static. To represent a determinate, dynamic system, a model must be able to indicate the behavior of each determined variable throughout time; *i.e.*, it must be able to show the value of each variable at any instant of its time path. The solutions of the equations must all be functions of time or constant over time. It certainly seems that we cannot get such formal dynamic solutions in the *Treatise*. But the case is not yet lost for Keynes. While he did not formalize a dynamic system, all of the reactions which he traced from the behavior of his statical variables were dynamic in character. In the "fundamental equation" for the general price level he did not say that a discrepancy between investment and savings changes the price level to a new figure. Instead he said that a discrepancy between investment and savings causes the price level to *oscillate* about its equilibrium level. It was only a formal aspect of his "fundamental equation" that was static. His analysis and conclusions were quite dynamical.

A point which should be mentioned is that in this entire discussion of the *Treatise*, we have been using the terms "savings" and "investment" exactly according to Keynes' definition of these terms. It is well agreed by now that arguments over definitions or terminology are fruitless; since, if definitions are precisely made and consistently followed, perfectly valid results can be obtained. While it is true that one will probably not make any great blunders

[33] See Edward C. Simons, "Mr. Keynes's Control Scheme," *American Economic Review*, Vol. XXIII, 1933. p. 264, and J. M. Keynes, "Mr. Keynes's Control Scheme," *American Economic Review*, Vol. XXIII, 1933, p. 675.

in formulating economic policy as a result of misconceptions concerning the savings-investment equation, the discussion of the equation is vital to the understanding of Keynesian economics. As a matter of fact, the discussion surrounding the *Treatise* shows clearly the inability of Keynes himself to understand the difference between definitions relating observable economic quantities and relationships between schedules of economic behavior.[34] Robertson[35] had suggested that Keynes might define income as earnings plus windfall profits, and savings as the difference between this income and consumption expenditure. Keynes rejected such a definition as absurd, because then savings would always equal investment. If Y is defined as income, then we have:

$$Y = E + Q$$
$$S = Y - PR = E + Q - PR$$
$$I = E + Q - PR$$
$$S = I$$

Keynes, like most of his contemporaries, was dealing with these flows as definitions of observable quantities and failed to treat them properly as schedules.

An aspect of the classical side of Keynes which has not yet been discussed in this text but which is very interesting is his final disposition of the quantity theory. In the most general case, with the market rate of interest moving in relation to the natural rate, the Keynesian theory differs from the quantity theory; but what happens in equilibrium? If the market rate equals the natural rate, then the windfall profits become zero and the "fundamental equation" becomes, according to Keynes:

$$\Pi O = M_1 V_1$$

This relation looks very much like the quantity theory, because we know from the above discussion that the restrictions, $O = \overline{O}$ and $V_1 = \overline{V}_1$, were imposed by Keynes. In the conditions of full

---

[34] This entire problem will be discussed at length in Chapters III and IV.
[35] "Mr. Keynes' Theory of Money," *Economic Journal*, Vol. XLI, 1931, p. 395.

equilibrium, the theory of the *Treatise* becomes strictly classical. As a matter of fact Keynes wrote:

> This means, indeed, that in equilibrium — *i.e.* when the factors of production are fully employed, when the public is neither bullish nor bearish of securities and is maintaining in the form of savings-deposits neither more nor less than the "normal" proportion of its total wealth, and when the volume of savings is equal both to the cost and to the value of new investments — there is a unique relationship between the quantity of money and the price levels of consumption-goods and of output as a whole, of such a character that if the quantity of money were double the price-levels would be double also.[36]

There can be no doubt that Keynes accepted the classical theory for the case of equilibrium.

[36]*A Treatise on Money*, Vol. I, p. 147.

CHAPTER II

THE BIRTH OF THE GENERAL THEORY

With the preceding chapter as background, we shall trace the very important steps that were taken prior to the great publication of 1936. The procedure is to be twofold: first tracing chronologically the developments in the Keynesian literature, and secondly comparing the Keynesian developments with the status of thought of the non-Keynesian writers. It is hoped that, by this method of tracing chronologically the Keynesian development, it will be possible to put a finger approximately on the date of the conception of the new theory. In the next chapter it will then be possible to make comparisons between the formal, theoretical models of the *General Theory* and the conventional theory held by economists outside the Keynesian camp.

THE KEYNESIAN DEVELOPMENT

Economists can sometimes go very far in the advocacy of proper, sound policy measures based on an inadequate formal theory. That such things are possible proves only that practical economics is simply common sense, while theoretical economics is "common sense made difficult." Keynes had a good idea as to what the troubles were in the economic system in the early years after the 1929 crash — in fact, even before the crash — and he supported policy similar to that built up around the *General Theory*, but he was not able to formalize his arguments into a satisfactory theoretical mold. His early analysis in the beginning of the depression was based entirely on the classical model of the *Treatise*. It was not his theory which led him to practical policies, but practical policies devised to cure honest-to-goodness economic ills which finally led him to his theory. Keynes was in much the same position as have been many of our colorful monetary cranks. These amateur economists have usually sensed what is wrong, and have often proposed workable corrective policies, but they have usually been

31

far wide of the mark in the formulation of their fantastic, theoretical systems. A consideration of Keynes' popular writings in the interim between the *Treatise* and the *General Theory* illustrates well this relation between policy and theory.

In the first months of the slump Keynes was telling us that the fundamental cause of the difficulty was a lack of new enterprise due to the poor outlook for capital investment. He advocated action to stimulate profit margins and hence to give rise to new investment. But he did not want to attempt to restore profits to a higher level through the cutting of costs, for he regarded such a move as deflationary. He argued that there were two ways of restoring profits; either by inducing the public to spend a larger fraction of their incomes or by inducing entrepreneurs to turn a larger fraction of their output into the form of investment. The argument was correct, but it was based on faulty reasoning. It was obvious to Keynes that increased consumer spending would be a net inflationary stimulus to the system, yet his advocacy of a higher rate of spending was based on the classical theory of the *Treatise* — saving would fall and would be in equilibrium with investment at the new low level, thus giving the desired end of price stability. He had not yet dropped the condition of a given output level so that he could imagine a case in which both consumption and investment could be raised simultaneously. He was still working under the assumption that increased consumption must be at the expense of investment and *vice versa*. A typical Keynesian characterization of the slump maladjustment was that producers were not dividing their output between consumption and investment in proportions which corresponded to the way in which consumers were dividing their income between savings and consumption. This argument was another way of saying that there were discrepancies between the terms I, S and I', S in the "fundamental equations" of the *Treatise*.

We must admit that Keynes advocated certain policies in the early thirties in spite of, rather than because of, his theoretical background. He made a radio address [1] in England in 1931 which

---

[1] Reprinted in *Essays in Persuasion*, p. 148.

was an excellent plea for increased spending to counteract the depression — intuition was far more powerful than a theory. In this address he attacked thrift, the classical virtue, because he saw the fallacy of providing large savings to be offset by investment when there were no available offsets in sight.[2] The housewife was urged to spend, and a plug was made for government public-works expenditures. These proposals sound very much like those of the modern Keynesians arguing on the basis of the *General Theory*.

In addition to the attack on thrift, Keynes soon changed some of his previous views on another classical doctrine. He suddenly decided that perhaps free trade does not pay in a period of serious unemployment, and made strong "buy British" arguments. He suggested that the Chancellor of the Exchequer choose a protective tariff for Great Britain in order simultaneously to relieve the budget and restore confidence. It hardly seems possible that the Keynes who in 1923 claimed that protection could never help increase employment could later advance such anti-classical policies. But a great change must have been developing in Keynes' thoughts because of the failure of his former theories to solve problems of underemployment situations.

In June, 1931, at the time when Keynes was advocating the various measures mentioned above in this section, there appeared the famous *Macmillan Report*.[3] Since the latter part of 1929 a committee of which Keynes was a member had been preparing this report. The most interesting conclusions from this book's point of view are those of Addendum I relating to domestic monetary policy. This addendum, which was unreservedly supported only by Keynes and three other committee members, stated that there were three alternatives in domestic monetary policy which could be used to meet the emergency: (1) a reduction of salaries and wages; (2) controls over imports and aids to exports; (3) state assistance to private enterprise and to investment.

---

[2] Recall the discussion of Chapter I on the *Economic Consequences of the Peace* concerning Keynes' appraisal of saving and the capitalist growth of the pre-World War I era.

[3] *Committee on Finance and Industry, Report*, Presented to Parliament by the Financial Secretary to the Treasury by Command of His Majesty, June, 1931.

C

True to the Keynesian traditions, the first alternative of wage cuts was rejected as deflationary. The *Report* argued that false analogies as to the advantages of wage cuts to the single employer were often drawn to apply to the economy as a whole. The committee members realized that output as a whole might suffer if purchasing power of wage earners should be reduced. This is precisely the argument which Keynes used in all his own writings. It is quite significant that the *Report* concluded that it would be better to leave money incomes fixed and change the monetary standard by lowering the gold parity of sterling in order to adjust the level of wages and salaries to a long-run equilibrium position. It is possible to see here the germ of the early arguments of the *General Theory* as regards real and money wage rates. Since it would have been very difficult to lower money wages all round, a better solution was thought to be the inflationary measure of causing prices to rise and real wages to fall.

The discussion of the second alternative made the point very emphatically that the free-trade arguments do not apply to a system in which there is unemployment, since tariffs could bring about a net increase instead of a mere diversion of resources. On similar grounds, aids to exports were recommended also.

In the case of the third alternative — schemes of capital development — the argument was on about the level of Keynes' discussion of Lloyd George's Liberal Pledge, considered in the previous chapter. Again the theory of the multiplier was implied roughly in the argument, but as in every other case the analysis never got beyond the first few rounds of expenditure. As opposed to what many other economists thought at the time, the writers of the *Report* were emphatic in pointing out that public spending on investment would not divert resources from private investment, since there was a high level of unemployment. From a practical point of view, one improvement was made over Keynes' previous analysis of public-works spending. This improvement was the recognition that such programs might have a harmful effect upon business confidence, another reason why protection was considered to be advantageous. However, the *Report* thought that on balance such spending schemes would be helpful and desirable.

When we compare the recommendations of the main body of the *Report* with those of Addendum I we see some striking contrasts. The former recommendations were much more conservative and orthodox. They comprised proposals for adherence to the gold standard at the existing parity, for a lower international value of gold in terms of wholesale goods, for price stability at higher levels, for bank regulation of interest and credit in order to stabilize the level of investment. When contrasted with the more radical proposals of the Keynesian Addendum I, we see that Keynes was forced to depart widely from the more conventional lines of thought of his colleagues. This point is to be brought out even more strongly later in this chapter when the testimony of Hawtrey and Pigou before the Macmillan Committee is considered.

From Keynes' lecture [4] delivered under the auspices of the Harris Memorial Foundation at Chicago in the summer of 1931, we see the continued influence of his old theoretical model. Though he made a good analysis of the current economic situation and suggested meaningful remedies, his theoretical views were basically unchanged and not entirely in accord with his commonsense judgments. One accurate prediction that he did make at this time was that the catastrophe in which the world then found itself would not be quickly overcome; instead he predicted that the slump might last much longer than people thought. He foresaw a long period of semi-slump conditions — an underemployment equilibrium, if you like. He continued at this time to emphasize the influence of the rate of investment on economic prosperity, and suggested remedies entirely in the light of attempting to stimulate investment. It seems that his principal tool for curing the depression was still the manipulation of the interest rate. He was very optimistic as to the influence of the rate of interest in investment decisions — a practical issue — and he was still working with the theory of the *Treatise* in which the interest rate was the main factor in bringing about an equilibrium between savings and investment — a theoretical issue. His goal at this time may be characterized as a situation in which investment would be driven up to equality

[4] *Unemployment as a World Problem*, Quincy Wright, Editor, University of Chicago, Chicago, 1931.

with savings at a level which would signify prosperity. **Savings was taken as the passive element, and investment as the volatile element of the economic process.** However, the Keynes of this period saw unlimited investment opportunities at sufficiently low interest rates, while the later Keynes saw limitations in investment opportunities due to a lack of effective demand. As a result of this theoretical system, Keynes proposed a program of reduction of the long-term interest rates and of restoration of confidence to borrowers and lenders. In spite of his restrictive theoretical system, Keynes also proposed a program of government construction.

An important scientific contribution was made, at this time, that was to develop a completely revolutionary mode of economic thought. Hayek, Robertson and others were discussing such questions as: Are Mr. Keynes' "fundamental equations" really different from the ordinary quantity equations? Is Mr. Keynes' E, the cost of production of current output, the same as his E, the factor earnings during the period in which the output comes on the market? And at the same time Mr. R. F. Kahn was formulating the theory of the multiplier,[5] the missing link between what Keynes was saying in policy and what he wanted to say in theory. The theory as Kahn formulated it was just the step needed to show that savings and investment determine in equilibrium the level of output as a whole and *not the rate of interest*. But let us not be misled and think that Kahn, Keynes, or anybody else could at this time see the issues involved and incorporate the contribution into a new theory of the determination of the level of employment. Kahn quite unambiguously stated that he had worked out his theory of the multiplier in an attempt to solve a practical problem of the day — to get a more precise evaluation of the beneficial repercussions of public-works projects. Furthermore Kahn has told us that he wrote this article with the theory of the *Treatise* before him. He obviously did not see the great theoretical implications of his work.

Kahn showed that an initial government outlay on public works will be distributed to workers in the form of wages. These workers will then spend a large fraction of this added income on consumer

---

[5] "The Relation of Home Investment to Unemployment," *Economic Journal*, Vol. LI, 1931, p. 173.

goods. The merchants, in turn, will spend a large fraction of this previous fraction and so on *ad infinitum*. Kahn's great contribution was to calculate the limiting value of the sum of these repeated expenditures.

Many other economists had thought about and written about the multiplicative effects of government deficit spendings due to successive rounds of consumer spending, but they were never able to formalize their thoughts into a theory of definite economic behavior. Why should we lay such great stress on the multiplier theory, as formulated by Kahn? The answer is that this formulation of aggregative consumer behavior changed entirely our views about the structure of a model economic system. As a result of his paper, we were able to see the important point that consumption depends, in a definite way, upon income and not upon the rate of interest. Such a functional relationship between consumption and income is necessary in order to generate the successive rounds of the multiplier sequences. Once we have recognized the relation between consumption and income, we can pass by means of a mathematical identity to the savings-income function,[6] and if income is taken to be the important variable in the consumption function, it must also be the important variable in the savings function. We should then be practically ready to discard the classical notion of a savings-investment · equilibrium via the rate of interest. All that was needed was a few more months of stubborn depression facts, and Keynes was able to see that investment opportunities are not unlimited at low interest rates. Rather, investment also depends upon the level of income and some non-economic (autonomous) variables. At any rate the standard functional relation between interest and investment did not fit the facts, and a theory of the determination of the level of income was needed to replace the theory of the determination of the rate of interest. Once this point was seen, a revolution occurred in economic theory. It was not a new theory of the rate of interest that was needed to replace the classical savings-investment theory, as some economists seem to think; instead it was a theory of output that was needed to replace the

---

[6] This is the case because savings are *defined* as income not spent on consumer goods.

old theory of the interest rate. When the latter step was carried out, a new interest theory followed as a residual which had to be accounted for.

We must repeat here that although Kahn furnished us with the necessary step in 1931, the Revolution did not occur then. Economists continued to think along the old lines while using this innovation in their formulation of policy. It required some two years before we can find evidence that Keynes made great use of the multiplier concept in his theoretical system. Although the egg was developing, the birth of the new theory did not occur until about 1933.

Keynes' own writings continued along the old lines for some time after Kahn's article was made available. In 1932, Keynes was worried about a financial crisis more than anything else. But he thought that the critical situation could be improved if only cheap money would become available. He seemed to feel that an abundance of credit would probably lead to a high level of investment and initiate a recovery, thus avoiding a financial crisis. He did qualify his cheap-money policy with a plea for more vigorous state intervention in the stimulation of investment in the event of a failure of a purely monetary policy. But a short article written in 1932 shows that he still had great faith in manipulation of the interest rate.[7] The conversion of the War Loan to an interest rate of $3\frac{1}{2}$ per cent was looked upon by Keynes as one of the most promising of all the anti-depression measures. He had always before regarded his program for the manipulation of the short-term bank rate as somewhat inadequate because such manipulation need not influence the more important long-term rate. But now he had an instance in which an important long-term interest rate was directly lowered, an event which he thought might hold great promise for the future. The continued insistence upon credit controls shows how little Kahn's arguments had yet convinced him.

Professor Samuelson has pointed out a very interesting development in the economic literature of 1933. We can never be quite sure what goes on behind the political scenes in Cantabrigian

---

[7] "A Note on the Long-term Rate of Interest in Relation to the Conversion Scheme," *Economic Journal*, Vol. XLII, 1932, p. 415.

economics, but we do know that there is a good deal of exchange of information among individuals within certain groups. If we take Joan Robinson as a reliable sounding board of opinion within the Keynesian group, we find a great change in ideas during 1933. In *Economica* of February, 1933, Mrs. Robinson wrote an article entitled "A Parable on Savings and Investment" in which she attempted to explain some of the more subtle difficulties of the *Treatise* to the simple-minded reader. It was an attempt to clear up the differences of opinion which existed between Keynes and his reviewer, Hayek. In this article we find a perfectly clear exposition of Keynes of the *Treatise*, which leads one to suspect that the ideas of the *Treatise* were still being talked about within the Keynesian group. However, in the autumn of that year, 1933, Mrs. Robinson felt called upon to write another article for Volume I, Number 1 of the *Review of Economic Studies*, called "The Theory of Money and the Analysis of Output." In this later article Mrs. Robinson again claimed to be giving an exposition of the *Treatise*, but such was not the case. Any reader of the *Treatise* or of the discussion presented in Chapter I of this book (if it has been accurate) knows that a theory which takes a given level of output is not a theory of the analysis of output. Mrs. Robinson was overgenerous to the master and was actually writing one of the first expositions, in which she is so lucid, of the really essential parts of the *General Theory of Employment, Interest, and Money*.

In the *Economica* article, Mrs. Robinson was attempting to demonstrate the working of the theories of the determination of the various price levels, P, Π, P', which had caused so much confusion because simple-minded people (in which category she placed herself) had to be shown clearly how a fall in P, for example, need not lead to a rise in P'. In other words, she was trying to explain the relations behind the two "fundamental equations" and the equation of bearishness. Her exposition followed that of the *Treatise* without a break. But when we come to the second article, which appeared in the *Review of Economic Studies*, we get material which is infinitely more interesting and powerful. She was a prophet in her own right when she said, ". . . the Theory of Money has recently undergone a violent revolution." The beautiful thing about this article is that the analysis of the *General Theory* was so clearly stated, and that such an important element as the savings-investment equation was presented in terms of the real issues involved instead of in terms of trivial, terminological controversy. The pre-*General Theory* Keynesians were much clearer than their successors! In this discussion Mrs. Robinson told explicitly how savings and investment can be equal at all points of time and yet not be identical schedules or curves. She first assumed a disequilibrium and then showed the conceptual process by which the level of real income would adjust to bring savings and investment into equality. She also demonstrated the working of another very important process in the maintenance of the savings-investment equation, namely the operation of "forced" investment. She assumed an increased rate of savings and a consequent fall in consumption so that the equation could not be maintained. Her explanation of the adjustment then was that inventories would pile up due to the decreased rate of consumption, thus forcing investment up to meet the increased level of savings. This is an argument commonly used by present-day Keynesians. The whole argument was summed up by the statement that there may be an equilibrium output at any number of different levels — levels of full or less than full employment. It is also interesting that she did not need, at this stage, to appeal to lower limits to the interest rate, or rigid money wages, or imperfections in competition to explain the phenomenon of unemployment.

The difference in theoretical structure between these two articles by Mrs. Robinson is quite amazing and should lead us to suspect the occurrence of the revolution in Cambridge during 1933.

One of the first articles by Keynes which shows the influence of Kahn was published in 1933.[8] In this work Keynes made a new argument for public-works expenditures which was in many respects similar to that made in 1929, except for the fact that this time he made very extensive use of a new tool, the multiplier theory. The arguments which were being put forth against government spending programs in the early thirties were very similar to

---

[8] *The Means to Prosperity*, Macmillan, London, 1933.

those used against the Lloyd George Pledge, but this time Keynes was able to counter with more explicit statements as to the ultimate level of employment created out of a given public expenditure and as to the net cost to the government budget. Recall that in 1929 Keynes had said that there would be induced and indirect effects which the opponents always neglected, but that these effects could not be measured with any precision. The important point for the reader to keep in mind is that in order to get precision, it is necessary to know a definite functional relationship between consumption and income, given certain other variables in the system as parameters; in other words, applications of the multiplier theory must be based on a theory of the consumption or savings function.

At this time Keynes estimated the multiplier to be about 2, but in order to be conservative calculated with a value of $1\frac{1}{2}$.[9] He used the same argument as before, concerning the strain upon the budget. He calculated the transfer saving on the dole and the increased taxes out of the increased income generated as covering half the costs involved. Thus he concluded that there was no dilemma between spending programs and the balancing of the budget. However, one is not quite sure whether or not he had fallen into the mistake of believing that the exchequer can lift itself by its own bootstraps.

There is no doubt that he then saw clearly the relationship between consumption and income, although this discussion was not intended to produce a theoretical system. He encouraged spending on the part of the population but realized that it would be impossible to spend much more out of an already reduced income. He also began to see more clearly the working of economic systems as wholes. Only a few years before *The Means to Prosperity*, he had announced a distinct favoritism for a protectionist policy in Great Britain. Now he was willing to give up this idea, since he realized that successful attempts by England to improve her foreign balance would only be at the expense of other countries. Furthermore he realized that competitive protection applied by

[9] In other words, every dollar spent on public-works projects creates $1.50 of national income.

all countries simultaneously would only be harmful to all. What he now proposed was world-wide inflationary loan expenditure to stimulate the world as a whole, especially in order to raise the world price level. He was now ready to advocate that all countries expand trade simultaneously through the abolition of exchange restrictions and tariffs. Keynes made a complete turn-about on the question of free trade.

As in the case of the *Treatise*, the appearance of the *General Theory* was well advertised in advance. We know that, for some time, Keynes was lecturing at Cambridge on the theory of employment and output according to the doctrine later written down in the *General Theory*.[10] Also some ten months prior to the signing of the *General Theory* preface, the *New Republic* carried an article by Keynes,[11] in which he brought out the main points of his new doctrines, which he compared with those of the heretics and cranks. Now he had come to believe that in the absence of frictions the system was not self-adjusting, as the classical economists had felt and as many economists feel today. If we can find a theory which describes a non-self-adjusting capitalistic, frictionless, perfectly competitive system, have we not found a revolutionary theory?

Keynes did not present at this time a complete outline of his theory, but he did say enough to indicate the core of the analysis. Some people have misinterpreted the essential innovations of the Keynesian Revolution, and there is a statement by Keynes in this article which may add to this misinterpretation. He claimed that the inability of the classical system to determine the level of effective demand and of employment was due to an unsatisfactory interest theory. Are we to take this to mean that the Keynesian Revolution lies in the new interest theory — liquidity preference?[12] We can admit that the theory of liquidity preference is an ingenious solution to the problem of the determination of the rate of interest, which is essentially different from the classical, neo-classical, or modern Swedish theories, but we need not regard the liquidity-

---

[10] A copy of some unpublished notes by R. B. Bryce, who was then at Cambridge, has been made available in mimeographed form.

[11] "A Self-Adjusting Economic System?" *New Republic*, Vol. LXXXII, 1935, p. 35.

[12] This theory will be explained in detail in Chapters III and IV.

preference theory as an essential element of the modern Keynesian system. It merely rounds out the theory and makes it complete. The way to interpret Keynes' above claim about the inadequacies of the classical interest theory is to point out that this theory used, as determinants of the rate of interest, flows which actually determine the rate of output; hence we were prevented from having a satisfactory theory of output as a whole because classically inclined economists were using the strategic determinants of output to determine something else. Keynes later remarked that, as it actually happened, he first conceived of the savings-investment equation as the determinant of the level of output. This left him without a theory of interest; so he then developed the liquidity-preference theory of interest. At this point we should like to anticipate an argument which may arise in the reader's mind; at least, it arose in the mind of D. H. Robertson. This argument would state that savings and investment should not be isolated as merely determinants of the level of output, for they can determine something else simultaneously, namely, the rate of interest. We admit that in a mutually interdependent system cause and effect cannot be isolated, but at this stage of the analysis we are working with building-blocks out of which a mutually determined system has been constructed. We are now solely interested in the strategic variables in each of the interrelated equations. However, this point is to be discussed more fully below.

SOME NON-KEYNESIAN THEORIES PRIOR TO 1936

If we are to see the full significance of the revolution, we must have a thorough idea of the theory against which Keynes revolted. It is true that Keynes directed his attack against what he called classical economics, with the implication that most economists of the day were thinking according to the classical system. This implication has caused some disagreement, with the result that many economists maintain that Keynes was knocking over straw men, since hardly anyone held these so-called classical notions, anyway. We can avoid this issue by simply going to the pre-*General Theory* writings and finding out just what other economists were thinking before the light was revealed to them. We shall attempt to present a cross-section of opinion in order to bring out the prevailing doctrines.

Just as Malthus engaged in a long controversy with the orthodox, classical school over the question of Say's Law (that supply creates its own demand), Keynes pictured himself as arguing the same issue with his orthodox contemporaries. While we shall probably never know how much stimulation Keynes received from many of his anticipators, we can be quite sure that he drew much from Malthus, whom he openly admired. The controversy between the Keynesians and the non-Keynesians in many respects was similar to the Ricardo-Say-Sismondi-Malthus controversies of the nineteenth century.

A very good exposition of Say's Law which brings out the major issues of the discussion of the 1930's can be found in a book from which many well known economists were undoubtedly taught, namely, Fred M. Taylor's *Principles of Economics*. This book was written in 1921 and was used as a textbook in American universities for several years. An examination of the arguments on Say's Law in this book, which is, on the whole, an excellent piece of work, is here in order. First, Taylor attempted to demonstrate the fallacy in the argument that disastrous acts of God can stimulate the level of economic activity. He took the example of a householder whose roof was blown off by a tornado. He observed that the spending by the householder in replacing the roof would react in successive rounds and increase the prosperity of the entire community. But, he asked, is this a net increase in demand? True to Say's Law and other classical traditions, he answered:

> The money which on account of the tornado our householder was compelled to spend putting on a new roof would ultimately have been spent anyhow, though in some other direction; and thus being spent, it would have created just the same demand for commodities or services.[13]

Here we have the strictest sort of classical argument; with the assumption of given output, expenditures on one sort of activity are merely diversion from spending elsewhere. Taylor could see that there was plainly no reason why funds spent on a roof would

---

[13] *Principles of Economics*, Ronald, New York, 1923, p. 197.

always otherwise be spent on consumption, especially if the house-holder should be sufficiently wealthy; so he assumed that the house-holder would otherwise have spent the money on investment activity, say the excavation of a cellar. This brings us to the crux of the matter. The exponents of Say's Law have always assumed unlimited investment opportunities. Householders could never have any savings which would not be invested somewhere in this perfect system.

Hence the tornado does not increase demand in the least, it merely *substi-tutes one chain of purchases for another.*[14]

The contribution made by any one person to the total demand for goods is, in the long run, bound to be just equal to his income, no more no less.[15]

In a sense, Taylor in 1921 was not quite as bad as were some other economists in the early thirties, for he recognized that in short-run depression periods when there is unemployment, Say's Law may not hold; *i.e.* government spending on public-works projects may not divert funds from the private investment market. But he was not one to say that this condition could persist for any length of time, for he stated unequivocally that Say's Law would hold in the long run. As a long-run optimist, he saw unlimited investment opportunities.

The principles underlying Say's Law also crept into the discus-sions of appropriate anti-depression economic policy. Hawtrey has expressed some ideas which are not unrelated to a discussion of this law and which can be conveniently considered at this point.[16]

Hawtrey was called upon to give testimony as an expert econo-mist before the Macmillan Committee, of which Keynes was a member.[17] The problem of the committee being to suggest policies which would bring England out of her stagnation, Hawtrey com-mented on possible methods of securing the desired ends. On the matter of government spending, Hawtrey stated that whether the spending came out of taxes or loans from savings, the increased

[14] *Ibid.*, p. 198.   [15] *Ibid.*, p. 198.
[16] See p. 53 below for brief comments on Hawtrey's monetary theory of the trad cycle.
[17] Reprinted in *The Art of Central Banking*, Longmans, Green, London, 1933.

governmental expenditures would merely replace private expenditures. He even considered the "radical" idea of government spending out of new bank credit, but predicted that the result of such a policy would be inflationary and a threat to the gold standard, thus forcing up the bank rate of interest and causing credit contraction. Such a plan, for him, would only defeat itself, since government expenditures out of bank credit would mean the end of cheap money for private enterprise. Arguments like these would be much more understandable coming from Taylor of 1921 than Hawtrey of, say, 1930. How could economists worry about the inflationary gap when there was such a high level of unemployment? The only answer we can give to this question is that they must have been working with assumptions of Say's Law and/or full employment. It was with similar arguments by British political lights that Keynes had to contend in his articles supporting public-works projects.

Whatever labor leaders or leftist economists have to say about Keynes' bourgeois emphasis, they must be brought to realize that he consistently worked against those theories which blamed the depression on labor. There was a large body of doctrine that traced the cause of the unemployment to rigidities which prevented the free working of the capitalist system, the major rigidity being obstructions to the downward movement of wages. How can people find employment if they ask a king's ransom for their work! Professor Pigou, like Hawtrey, was called upon to give testimony before the Macmillan Committee. He traced the current difficulties to two obstructions to the free working of economic forces, namely, the improper allocation of people among jobs, and the existence of wage rates above the level called for by the general demand conditions. Following these lines of argument, he supported a policy of wage cuts. Even today, Professor Pigou argues that unemployment is not possible if we admit flexible wages into our theoretical system. This issue is to be considered more fully in a later chapter.

Another exponent of wage cuts was Professor Cannan,[18] who wanted to explain general unemployment in exactly the same way

---

[18] See "The Demand for Labor," *Economic Journal*, Vol. XLII 1932. p. 357.

as one explains particular unemployment in an individual firm or an industry. He argued that in particular employment, more workers can be employed at lower wages if the demand for the product is elastic.[19] In total employment, demand for the product is indefinitely elastic; therefore any number of workers, up to full employment, can be hired if they do not ask for too high wages. Consequently he regarded general unemployment as the result of asking too much. He also included attempts at profit maintenance as part of the phenomenon of asking too much. If this point of view is representative of the theories of very many economists of this period, can there be any doubt that the Keynesian system is revolutionary?

In Professor Schumpeter we have an economist who is quite outspoken in his belief that there can be no persistent unemployment in a perfect, frictionless capitalist system. Aside from his theory of innovations which would explain relatively short-period movements, one would expect him to incorporate a theory of frictions and obstructions to explain unemployment. He provided such an explanation very early in the depression.[20] He claimed that the forces at work in the early period of depression were the agrarian crisis, protection, high taxes, high interest rates, high wages, and the lack of free price movements.

The examples of Pigou, Cannan, and Schumpeter are not atypical. Many economists felt that the capitalist system was self-adjusting in the absence of frictions and obstacles. They argued that the system had always recovered before from crises, and would again if only the imperfections could be removed from the system. As a matter of fact, Keynes thought along exactly these lines just after World War I, and his great change of view delineates the revolution perfectly.

But it is not necessary to consider exclusively the writings of economists who are known to follow closely the classical tradition in order to bring out, in a striking manner, the sense in which the

[19] Demand for a product is elastic if, roughly speaking, the demand is very sensitive to price changes.

[20] See "The Present World Depression: A Tentative Diagnosis," Supplement to the *American Economic Review*, Vol. XXI, 1931, p. 179.

Keynesian ideas represent a true discovery. An examination of the observations made during the formative period by some of Keynes' more recent followers shows this contention in a very clear light. Professor Hansen is an example of a Keynesian disciple who argued strongly, in the days of confusion, against the very things which he now so vigorously supports in the light of modern Keynesian economics. Hansen's remarks at this time appear to be almost unbelievable in the light of his policy recommendations of a few years later. For those who were not too stubborn and set in their ways of thinking the revolution meant a complete turn-about in both economic thought and economic policy. For example, Hansen in 1933 was very skeptical of the acceptance of Keynes' policy measures, especially those having to do with the stimulation of investment by governmental devices.[21] He feared "absurd" results as a consequence of the support of measures which try to increase investment and decrease the rate of saving by the use of such devices as governmental deficits, tariff policies, buy-now campaigns, unemployment doles, and public-works programs. Hansen worried very much about adverse effects of the Keynesian policies upon business confidence, and one gets the impression that he was using the classical argument, then so popular among economists, that a dollar spent by the state meant a dollar *not* spent by private enterprise. He agreed with Hayek that it was wrong to assume that the government could buy its way out of depression because of the burden which would be placed on the capital market. Hansen retained these conservative notions until the last minute; *i.e.* until the appearance of the *General Theory*. In 1936 [22] he was still in doubt about the usefulness of public-works programs in the stimulation of employment. He sided with those who looked upon public works as a mere stopgap, and, curiously enough, he was not impressed with the multiplier approach. Hansen's attitude shows how necessary it is to write down a complete, formal, elegant theory in order to convince professional economists of the validity of new

[21] A. H. Hansen and Herbert Tout, "Annual Survey of Business Cycle Theory: Investment and Saving in Business Cycle Theory," *Econometrica*, Vol. 1, 1933, p. 119.
[22] Alvin Hansen, Francis M. Boddy, John K. Langum, "Recent Trends in Business Cycle Literature," *Review of Economic Statistics*, Vol. XVIII, 1936, p. 53.

ideas. Apparently, all the Keynesian writings of the period 1930 to 1936 were not accepted until Keynes gave them his theoretical justification.

Among economists who have been far from the Keynesian doctrines there grew up a very popular business-cycle theory in the early thirties called the neo-Wicksellian theory. The basis for this theory rests on Wicksell's interest theory of the natural rate and the market rate. Swedish economists have been true to the "favorite son" and worked closely along Wicksellian lines, one of their best expositions being Myrdal's *Monetary Equilibrium*. But the Swedish economists were not the only ones who dressed up and elaborated upon Wicksell's theory; Mises and then Hayek developed a popular business-cycle theory, known also as the monetary overinvestment theory, which started its analysis from the relation between the market rate and the natural rate.

Although Keynes of the *Treatise* also made use of the Wicksellian interest theory (or something close to it), his analysis was quite different from that of Myrdal, Mises and Hayek. Myrdal has presented a very clear picture of the theory of the interest rate used by this school of writers. He considered the natural rate of interest to be given by any one of three relations: (1) the natural rate is that rate at which savings, in the schedule sense, is equal to investment, or what is the same, to free capital disposal, also in the schedule sense; (2) the natural rate of interest is that rate which is consistent with a stable price level; (3) the natural rate is the ratio between the *expected* net return on new investments and their costs of production. Myrdal does not make it quite clear, however, whether the natural rate, according to the third definition, should be the anticipated returns over cost on new investment or on total capital, but, at any rate, it shall be shown below how closely this concept is related to that of the marginal efficiency of capital in the Keynesian system of the *General Theory*. One question which comes up, with regard to these conditions, is that of their consistency. If expectations of future returns on investment are given and if the supply price level of investment goods is determined from other equations of a complete system, then is the natural rate obtained from these conditions the same as the natural rate obtained from the equation of savings and investment? The answer to this question depends upon the savings-investment theory used. The revolutionary development of Keynes was to formulate a savings-investment theory which made the answer to this question *no*, for the general case.

Other Swedish economists such as Lindahl, Hammarskjöld, Johansson, and Ohlin were very active during the early years of the depression. As in the case of Myrdal, they worked along lines that represented an extension of the Wicksellian analysis. At best, they had an elaborate theory of the price level and the rate of interest, but they did not have an explicit theory of effective demand or the determination of employment.[23] There were, however, some clever ideas among these economists which should be pointed out. Like Keynes of the *Treatise*, they had a clear conception of the difference between decisions to save and decisions to invest. This is a necessary though not sufficient condition for the development of a theory of effective demand. It is especially an inadequate condition if it is thought that sufficiently low interest rates can always bring decisions to save into equilibrium with decisions to invest. The Swedish interest theory does imply that interest-rate manipulation is an adequate measure to insure full employment.

A more significant development of the Swedish economists is their concentration on the role of expectations in economics. They pointed out the importance of entrepreneurial expectations in shaping the decisions to invest, but failed to integrate the theory of expectations with the current stage of world economic development. Had they been able to perform this integration, they would have obtained a different relation between interest rates and investment, and would have been forced to abandon their interest theory.

The monetary over-investment theorists (principally Hayek and Mises) argued from Wicksell's interest theory to a complete explanation of the cyclical process. They maintained that when the market rate of interest is pushed below the natural rate, a

---

[23] It is often contended today that the Swedish economists independently developed many of Keynes' ideas before 1936. It is important to remark that they never did develop a theory of the determination of the level of output, Keynes' major contribution.*

cumulative expansion process begins. Investment will be undertaken at this profitable relationship between the market and natural rates because the cost of borrowing is less than the rate of return on capital, and the structure of production will be elongated in the sense that industries producing non-consumer goods will be expended relative to industries producing consumer goods. The important part of their theory was however a statement of reasons why the expansionary process cannot continue indefinitely and must eventually come to an end. The explanation of the down-turn into the depression is quite different from the theory of the Keynesian system. The reason why the expansion has to end, *i.e.* why there has to be a shrinkage in the structure of production, was stated by Hayek to be that an insufficient supply of credit will always be forthcoming to fill the ever abundant investment outlets, or in their words, to complete the structure of production. Hayek claimed that the banking system will always fail to supply enough credit, and people will not be willing to forgo consumption in order to supply the necessary savings funds for the partially completed structure of production. According to this theory, if people will only save voluntarily, then the elongation of the production structure can remain intact, and depression will not occur. Hayek considered it impossible to complete the elongation of the production structure via forced savings. He also argued that excessive government expenditure and taxation or changes in the money supply will aggravate the shortening of the structure of production. Finally, he did not approve of the combating of depression through inflation of the money supply. In short, he was an ardent supporter of do-nothing economic policy. The business cycle is an immutable law of nature which cannot be defied, and the system, if left alone, will always recover to full employment.

The over-investment writers were clearly dealing with short-run cyclical phenomena and did not attempt to deal with the theory of prolonged depression. This follows from the notion that monetary factors can invariably be relied upon to bring about recovery from a depression. If only the market rate of interest can be pushed below the natural rate, the cumulative expansion process will begin. Obviously they overlooked some of the major points about the theory of the natural rate. If we accept the formulation of the natural rate as the ratio of the anticipated net returns on new investment to the cost of the investment, then we should naturally attempt to develop a theory of what determines the size of this rate. However, it never occurred to Hayek, Mises, or other writers of this school that the numerator of this ratio may get so low that no practicable fluctuations of the market rate of interest will stimulate investment. They believed that the natural rate is always so high that it will be possible to find market rates of interest low enough to stimulate investment.

It is very important to consider this theory of Hayek's in the light of the Keynesian Revolution, for the central notions of the Hayek school are directly opposite to those which have made the Keynesian theory so important. Recall that their central thesis of the collapse of prosperity is that there is a lack of savings available to finance ever present, unlimited investment opportunities. For Hayek, the boom never fails because of a lack of investment outlets, but its collapse is always due to a failure of abundant investment outlets to be financed by scarce savings. He insisted on working with a theory of an assumed output; hence one must spend either on consumption or on investment, and funds spent on consumption represent funds not available for investment. In fact, Hayek has claimed, in his review of the *Treatise*,[24] that the only point of view which could have led Keynes to a true explanation of the cycle is the view of the alternative character of increased output of consumption goods or of investment goods. How can this mean anything but an assumption of given employment? An important contribution of Keynes has been his stress on the limitation of finding increased investment outlets on the part of capitalistic, private enterprise. One cannot fail to see the differences which make the Keynesian theory entirely unlike Hayek's theory of abundant investment opportunities, given employment, alternative production of either consumption goods or investment goods, and a lack of voluntary savings. Hayek's description of the economic process just does not fit the facts.

[24] "Reflections on the Pure Theory of Money of Mr. J. M. Keynes," *Economica*, Vol. XI, 1931, p. 270, and Vol. XII, 1932, p. 22.

Finally, we can find in Haberler's famous book, *Prosperity and Depression*, a very good summary of the status of all the various business-cycle theories that were being espoused before economists started talking about the Keynesian ideas of consumption or savings functions, the multiplier, the marginal efficiency of capital, and liquidity preference.† It is in order at this point to examine each of the classes of theories presented there and to see how Keynes departed from their doctrines.

First, there is the purely monetary theory of Hawtrey which said that changes in "the flow of money," are the only causes of business fluctuations. The sensitivity of the merchant class to interest changes is the strategic element in this theory, for Hawtrey believed that an easy-money policy could stimulate any revival by inducing the merchants to invest in liquid and working capital, *e.g.*, inventories. With such a theory, economic stagnation is practically impossible. It is hard to see how an economist who lived in England through the 1920's could support such a theory.

In a sense, Hawtrey's theory has some likeness to that of the *Treatise* in terms of the influence of the interest rate upon investment. But while Keynes thought that low interest rates would stimulate investment, he did say that a cheap-money policy could only hope to have a great influence on fixed capital and not on working or liquid capital. Keynes thought that fluctuations in working and liquid capital are extremely important in the cyclical process, but he did not think that their fluctuations are sensitive to changes in interest rates. However, more relevant than a comparison of Hawtrey's theory with the theory of the *Treatise* is a comparison with the theory involved in the Keynesian Revolution. A major point of the new theory is that investment does not depend upon interest rates alone and that investment is not indefinitely expansible. It is impossible with any realistic formulation of the revolutionary Keynesian system to maintain that an easy-money policy will always stimulate revival. Hawtrey was supporting an extremely optimistic point of view which included little of the essential elements of the new Keynesian doctrines.

The theories with one of the largest followings are those which Haberler calls the over-investment theories. The monetary over-investment theories have been already considered, for this is just another name for the theory of Hayek. Other supporters of this theory were Machlup, Mises, Robbins, Röpke, Strigl. The differences between this and the Keynesian school are very great and have already been stated. But the non-monetary branch of over-investment theorists covers a slightly more interesting group of writers who are somewhat more closely related to Keynes, although they may not like to admit it. The truth of the matter is that Keynes has really drawn heavily upon some of their ideas. The authors in the non-monetary school include Spiethoff, Tougan-Baranovski, Cassel and possibly Schumpeter.

The sense in which the non-monetary over-investment theorists are similar to Keynes of the *General Theory* is the same sense in which they were previously similar to Keynes of the *Treatise*. In the latter work he admitted having favored their idea that the moving force behind the cyclical movements is the violent fluctuations in the level of investment. For Keynes, the mischief maker has for a long time been the ever changing rate of investment, a quasi-autonomous variable [25] which depends very much on probability judgments and expectations as to the future level of other variables. But we have followed the two theories as far as they go together. The non-monetary over-investment theorists do not explain satisfactorily the incidence of a crisis after a period of expansion. For them, a capital shortage brings about the catastrophe. They never consider the possibility that investment opportunities might be lacking. They fail to make use of their own theory of the uncertainty and expectational behavior behind the fluctuating level of investment. They would argue that prosperity could continue if people would only refrain from consuming too much — an activity which prevents investment goods from being available to complete the structure of production. On the other hand, Keynes has shown us that spending on consumption can be just as much a stimulus to the level of income and employment as can spending on investment. Theories which argue that the depression is caused by too much consumption are quite anti-Keynesian.

[25] An autonomous variable is one that cannot be explained by purely economic forces. It depends on political, sociological, technological and other forces. The term "exogenous" is also used synonymously in the literature.

Haberler characterizes the theories based on the acceleration principle, where investment is made to depend on the rate of change of consumption, as mere features of the more general over-investment theories. Similarly the acceleration principle can be quite easily incorporated into the Keynesian system; so it need not be considered further at this stage.

The other important group of theories considered by Haberler is the under-consumption school of business-cycle theories.[26] It is very interesting, indeed, to read that Haberler considers the scientific standard of these theories on a lower level than that of the over-investment or monetary theories. It is difficult to agree that this is an accurate statement, for many of these writers were nearer the truth than the so-called scientific theories. Fortunately orthodoxy is not the only criterion of scientific standardization. The writers of this school, Malthus, Sismondi, Hobson, Foster, and Catchings, include important anticipators of the *General Theory*.

There are two senses in which over-saving or under-consumption can be harmful. There may be over-saving relative to the level of investment opportunities; *i.e.*, there may be more savings than can be offset by investment outlets. Secondly, there may be over-saving in the sense that too much saving gets invested and hence more goods are produced than can be consumed. For the Keynesian theory, it has been saving which does not get offset which represents over-saving, but for many of the other under-consumptionists such as Hobson, Foster, and Catchings, it was often saving that does get offset, over and above a certain level, which constitutes over-saving. Thus the Keynesian theory is a distinct improvement over the under-consumption theories existing in the early depression period. But in spite of the fact that the under-consumptionists had a faulty theoretical structure, their policy measures are quite in accord with the arguments of Keynesian economics. Policies to stimulate the level of consumption, such as income redistribution, would in the Keynesian models help to raise the level of income. Many of the under-consumptionists, like other economists, thought that there were sufficient investment outlets for any level of savings, and this was their principal error.

[26] The under-consumptionists as anticipators of Keynes will be discussed much more fully below in Chapter V.

CHAPTER III

THE NEW AND THE OLD

What has been Keynes' revolutionary contribution? As shown in the preceding chapter, the revolution was solely the development of a theory of effective demand; *i.e.*, a theory of the determination of the level of output as a whole.

There are two major economic problems — the problem of achieving full employment, and the problem of allocating resources in a full-employment economy. Keynes has shown how the level of employment gets determined, and thus has provided a theory with which to attack the first problem. He did not presume to advance a solution of the second problem, except in so far as the first must necessarily be cleared away before thinking about the second can start.

The task of this chapter is to develop the Keynesian theory from the most fundamental and elementary economic considerations, to compare the theory with the facts of the world, and finally to compare the new theory with the classical model.

THE KEYNESIAN SYSTEM AND RATIONAL BEHAVIOR

The central problem of Keynesian economics is concerned with the operation of the system as a whole, while most economic theories have been concerned with the behavior of individual households and business firms. A problem which has never been adequately considered by Keynesians is the derivation of a theory in terms of communities of individuals and groups of commodities from a basic theory in terms of individuals and single commodities. In modern economic terminology this is the problem of passing from micro to macro economics, *i.e.*, aggregation.

The Keynesian theory has been severely attacked by some economists because it is couched in terms of aggregate concepts like total consumption, employment, income, etc. These aggregative concepts, it is argued, get away from the more fundamental economic concepts of the individual and are thus misleading. But the aggregative or macro approach is not only labeled as misleading; it is also labeled as incorrect. For example, economists ask how can there be a stable relationship between total community consumption and total community income unless the distribution of income within the community is taken into account?

It is a very technical mathematical solution to show how the difficulties of aggregation may be overcome. Only the general method and final results are to be stated here.[1]

The theories of individual behavior provide a complete set of inter-relationships within the economy; *e.g.*, they give us the demand-and-supply relationships of every commodity in the system. This is the famous Walrasian system of general equilibrium. A mathematical representation of this system would probably involve several million equations in several million unknowns, an incomprehensible maze. To make any useful economic judgments, one must simplify this system into a manageable number of relationships among aggregates of the fundamental prices and quantities.

If one defines a precise relation between each aggregative variable in which he is interested and all the individual components of that aggregate,[2] then a particular set of relationships between the aggregative variables may exist. It has been shown [1] that certain aggregation procedures lead to very simple formal analogies between the propositions of micro and macro economics. An example of this is the following: Under rational conditions of profit-maximization in a perfectly competitive economic system, the individual firms' demand for a particular type of labor will be such that the wage of that type of labor will be just equal to the value of the marginal product of that type of labor. A worker of the type under consideration will be added to the labor force as long as he contributes more to revenue than to cost. The analogous proposition in macro economics states that there will be a demand for more labor in the

[1] For a more rigorous solution see F. W. Dresch, "Index Numbers and the General Economic Equilibrium," *Bulletin of the American Mathematical Society*, Vol. XLIV, 1938, p. 134, and L. R. Klein, "Macroeconomics and the Theory of RationBehavior," *Econometrica*, Vol. XIV, 1946, p. 93.

[2] In other words, if an index number is defined.

system, as a whole, as long as the average wage rate is less than the value of the national product added by new laborers. In this book the volume of employment, the wage rate, the price level, and the volume of output are aggregates that are so measured in terms of the individual quantities that such analogues of the micro-economic relationships exist. It comes to the same thing as though the economic system were treated as made up of two goods (consumer and producer goods), two industries (consumer and producer-goods industries), and two productive factors (labor and capital). As mentioned above, however, this procedure is not unjustified.

The total production of goods and services in the national economy in a given period of time is commonly called national income. This income is made up of two parts, the production of consumer goods and the production of producer goods. Our first task is to determine what are the variables that influence the total demand for each of these two types of goods.

From the accepted theories of consumer behavior it is learned that if a household maximizes its satisfaction (or preferences) subject to the constraint that its budget does not exceed its income, then the demand for each type of good consumed by a particular household will depend upon the household income and the prices of all goods in the household budget. By appropriate aggregation methods, one can develop the analogue of these demand schedules which says that the demand of each household for real consumer goods depends on the general price level of consumer goods, the interest rate (which relates the price of future consumer goods to the prices of current consumer goods), and the household's money income. Matters can further be simplified by assuming that households would not alter their expenditures on consumer goods if all prices and incomes were to change by the same proportion. Then the relevant variable affecting consumption is real income, *i.e.*, income corrected for price changes, rather than money income and the price level separately. This simplification of the use of real income instead of money income and prices separately is not essential but is very convenient and will be incorporated into this discussion. The interest rate remains as before as one of the variables affecting consumption, because it is not related to the units of measurement of income and consumption. We have not yet derived the basic Keynesian relation that we set out to establish because we have one such consumption relation for each household. However, appeal to empirical family budget studies can be made in order to establish more specific characteristics of the consumption-income relationship. In the budget studies that have been made for the United States, the average consumer expenditures in each income class vary with the average income of each class along a positively sloped straight line over the income range which includes practically all the income.[3] This means that the change in consumption corresponding to a movement from one income class to another is constant for all income classes. Hence a redistribution of income will leave total consumption approximately unaffected. If $1 is taken away from someone in the $3,500 income class and given to someone in the $1,000 class, the drop in consumption of the former just equals the increase in consumption of the latter. Thus consumption is approximately invariant with respect to changes in the income distribution, and we can say:

Community consumption depends upon the rate of interest and the level of real community income

to a first approximation.

This fundamental Keynesian relationship has important characteristics. It is probably true that a change in the interest rate will have a negligible influence on the level of consumption. It cannot even be said in advance whether an increase in the interest rate will increase or decrease consumption. On the one hand, some people will become more thrifty and spend less on consumer goods, because they will get a higher premium for their unspent incomes. On the other hand, those people who are abstaining from present consumption in order to obtain a fixed annuity in the future will find that they have to abstain less in order to accumulate enough funds to realize their annuity. Consequently, they will spend more on consumer goods. It is impossible to say which influence will be greater. This is a problem which can only be solved empirically. We can test the available data on consumption, income and the

---

[3] For incomes as high as $5,000 per year.*

interest rate to see whether or not there is any influence of the latter variable. As far as statistical results are concerned, no econometrician has ever found a significant correlation between consumption and interest rates when the correlation between consumption and income is taken into account. It must be concluded that the consumption function is interest-inelastic; *i.e.*, consumption is not sensitive to changes in the rate of interest.†

The relation between consumption and income is obviously such that an increase in income leads to an increase in consumption. A further characterization of the consumption-income relationship which is not as obvious, though, is the proposition that a small increment in income will be accompanied by a smaller increment in consumption. In technical Keynesian terms this states that the marginal propensity to consume is less than unity. This idea is an important feature of the Keynesian system, because it is one of the stabilizing forces of the economy. If consumers customarily increased their spending by more than an increase in income, the dynamical course of the system throughout time would probably be explosive. Increasingly greater fluctuations would be experienced through history. The fact that the marginal propensity to consume is less than unity counteracts the disturbing forces which make for ever greater fluctuations, although it is not necessarily successful.

The data from family budget studies and from time series on consumption and income confirm the existence of the above-mentioned stability condition. The marginal propensity to consume calculated from both types of information is significantly less than unity (between 0.6 and 0.8 in most cases).

It has often been argued by economists that consumption expenditures should depend upon accumulated cash balances as well as upon income. It has been seen, above, that income entered the consumption function via its position as a budget constraint in the theory of consumer behavior. It is, of course, arbitrary to state that households plan their budgets so that consumption expenditures do not exceed their current incomes. They may very well spend more than their current incomes by drawing upon their accumulated liquid savings. A more general theory would say that a household's total expenditures are limited by its income and its liquid assets or by some increasing function of both. The question as to whether liquid assets as well as current income should be a strategic variable affecting the level of consumer expenditures is another issue that can be settled only by looking at the facts. Taking personal cash balances to be representative of liquid assets in the interwar period, we find that there is no significant correlation between consumer expenditures and cash balances if the consumption-income correlation is taken into account. It may be true in the postwar world that a large amount of liquid assets in the hands of individuals, *coupled with a dearth of durable consumer goods*, will have a great influence on the propensity to consume. But this is not to be expected as a normal peacetime relationship.

Whatever is said about consumption and its explanatory variables can be immediately translated into statements about savings, since there is, in the Keynesian system, a simple definitional relation between consumption and savings. "Savings" is defined as income not consumed. Whatever income is paid out to factors of production, plus undistributed profits that do not get spent on consumer goods, is exactly defined as savings. If consumption depends upon interest and income, then savings depend upon interest and income. If the marginal propensity to consume is positive and less than unity, then the marginal propensity to save is also positive and less than unity. The marginal propensity to consume plus the marginal propensity to save is, by definition, equal to unity.

The variation of savings in response to changes in the rate of interest will be opposite in direction to the variation of consumption, but equal in absolute value. Income less consumption is identically equal to savings for all levels of income, virtual and observed. Income minus the consumption schedule is identically the savings schedule. This is not to be confused with the statement that income minus observed consumption equals observed investment. This latter equality is not an identity which holds for virtual levels of income that are not observed; but more about this later.

The other type of good which is produced in our system is the producer good which is demanded by business firms rather than households.

The simplest type of economic theory describing the demand for producer goods is that which says that the economist can say nothing quantitative about it. This theory maintains that the demand for producer goods depends upon subjective anticipations regarding future markets, technological developments, population growth, and various other uncertain forces about which the economist has no adequate theory. These factors can be all lumped together as Professor Schumpeter's innovations. In fact we know that Keynes of the *Treatise* accepted unreservedly Schumpeter's theory of innovations as the moving force behind the cyclical process.

This view is undoubtedly extreme. While it is probably true that much investment activity is autonomous and depends on factors that are unrelated to the economic quantities that are to be studied here, it is still true that business firms in a capitalist economy are trying to make as much profit as possible and will adapt their demand for capital goods to the behavior of prices, sales, capital accumulation, etc.

The basic Keynesian theory of the demand for capital goods falls under the heading of marginal efficiency of capital. This theory is based on the most classically accepted doctrine of profit maximization. Again, it seems best to develop a treatment from the behavior of an individual unit following an optimal principle, and then to derive the aggregative relationship for the economy as a whole.

According to Keynes, the individual firm will purchase capital goods as long as the expected future earnings from this good, properly discounted, exceed the price of additional capital goods. The marginal efficiency of capital is defined as that discount rate which will just equate the discounted stream of anticipated earnings to the price of new capital goods. By following Keynes' procedure of profit maximization, it will be possible to develop a definite relationship between the demand for capital goods and certain strategic economic variables.

The individual firm tries to maximize its expected profits subject to the constraint that it operates within the framework of certain technological conditions. The profits depend upon prices, sales, the use of factors of production and the costs of these factors. Furthermore the technological constraint establishes a definite relation between the input of the factors of production and the output of the final product. The maximization of profit subject to the constraint leads immediately to Keynes' proposition that more capital goods will be demanded as long as their price is less than the discounted value of their expected future earnings.

The corresponding relation which holds for the economy as a whole, provided we have measured the aggregates properly, states that the community of entrepreneurs will demand more capital goods as long as their average price is less than the discounted value of their anticipated earning stream. There is a very elegant mathematical result, given below in the appendix, which shows that if the technological (input-output) relation for the economy as a whole follows certain very well established empirical forms then the equilibrium (profit-maximizing) demand for capital goods depends upon the ratio of the discounted future national income to the average price of capital goods and upon the accumulated stock of capital. If we make the further assumptions that the expected national income depends upon the most recently observed levels of national income (how else can expectations be formed?) and that there is only one price level in the system, then we have the following fundamental Keynesian relationship:

The demand for capital goods depends upon the real value of national income, the interest rate and the stock of accumulated capital.

The assumption that there is only one price level in the system is not important to the work that follows, but it is made here for simplification. Models can easily be constructed where this assumption is not made.[4]

The careful reader will note that in the case of the demand for capital goods we went immediately from the profit-maximizing condition for the individual firm to the profit-maximizing condition for the economy as a whole without any appeal to statistical facts. This was possible because the theory of the behavior of business firms deals only with objectively measurable quantities such as profit, output, employment, capital, etc., whereas the theory of

[4] See G. C. Evans, "Maximum Production Studied in a Simplified Economic System," *Econometrica*, Vol. II, Jan. 1934, p. 37.

the household is based on subjective quantities such as satisfactions or preferences which are not measurable or comparable for different individuals. It is relatively easy to combine the individual profits, outputs and inputs of the separate business firms into aggregates, but it is not possible to combine the non-measurable individual satisfactions; hence it was necessary first to develop the individual demand relations for consumer goods and then to aggregate them over the entire economy. In the present case it is possible to start immediately, with the aggregate production and aggregate profits, to derive the aggregate demand for capital goods.[5]

Consider the relative importance of the several variables influencing investment as they operate in the real world of economic activity. Just as it was concluded above that consumer expenditures are insensitive to changes in the rate of interest, it should also be concluded that producer expenditures for capital equipment are insensitive to changes in the rate of interest. The rate of interest enters the demand relation for producer goods or investment through its influence on the discount rate applied to expected future earnings. In a perfectly behaved world where individuals possess much foresight, the discount rate would be precisely equal to the interest rate. However, in the interesting case of the real world, great risks and uncertainties accompany investment opportunities in a capitalist universe. The appropriate discount rate must account for these risks and uncertainties and hence must be greater than the interest rate. The appropriate discount rate is made up of an interest component and a subjective-risk component. The latter element belongs as much to the study of psychology as to economics. The non-interest components of the discount variable may far outweigh the interest component, making any fluctuations in the interest rate of little importance.

Because of the great risks involved in the present-day world of affairs, business men have been led to act very "bearishly" in their investment decisions. They require that a capital asset must pay for itself in one to five years, although they know that the useful life of the asset is likely to be much longer than five years. This fact

⁵ See F. W. Dresch *loc. cit.* and L. R. Klein *loc. cit.*

has been established by actual questions put to business men.[6] If investment decisions are guided by discounting future returns over a very short horizon of less than five years, then interest calculations are not given a chance to be important. A discount factor computed at present interest rates cannot possibly grow to significant proportions unless the horizon of business men is considerably longer than five years. The engineering and other costs of investment will heavily outweigh any costs which arise from discounting an income stream at current interest rates over a five-year horizon. It may be true that in certain sectors of the economy where the horizon is long, interest charges are more important. Public utilities and transportation are examples of industries with horizons longer than the average. But in the system as a whole it does not seem that investment should be sensitive to changes in the rate of interest.

Another reason, in addition to that of the short horizon, which causes entrepreneurs to disregard interest fluctuations when making investment decisions is linked to the new phenomenon of internal financing. Business men appear to have psychological preferences for financing their investment operations from surplus funds which have been accumulated through undistributed profits, depreciation, and other reserves. Theoretically, the rational entrepreneur should charge himself imputed interest costs when he uses his internal funds for investment, but he does not behave that way, as a matter of fact. The use of internal funds for financing will lead investors to ignore fluctuations in the market rate of interest.

It is not true that every small firm which buys capital equipment is able to do so from internally accumulated funds. but large corporations which carry out a significant part of our investment decisions have huge sums of working capital upon which they can draw for expenditures on new plant and equipment.

These remarks about the interest inelasticity of investment have been well substantiated by different types of empirical investigations. Two studies made on the basis of questionnaires submitted to a large sample of business men show conclusively that the interest

---

[6] See L. P. Alford, "Technical Changes in Manufacturing Industries," *Recent Economic Changes*, New York, 1929, p. 139. Ruth P. Mack, *The Flow of Business Funds and Consumer Purchasing Power*, New York, 1941, pp. 255–56.

D

rate is largely neglected when investment decisions are made.[7] Also econometric studies have been made to determine the quantitative significance of the different factors affecting investment. Tinbergen found in his investigations that the interest rate is an insignificant variable in the investment equation of his statistical model. The present author has also carried out statistical calculations of the investment equation for the economy as a whole and for various subsections such as agriculture, manufacturing and mining, public utilities and transportation, housing, etc. In few cases has the interest rate, in several trial formulations, proved to be a statistically significant variable.†

Keynes has been consistently in favor of low interest rates in order to stimulate investment activity to a high level. By the time he came to write the *General Theory*, however, Keynes began to have less confidence in monetary policies designed to influence the interest rate. This was evidently just a temporary lapse in his theoretical development, for a few years later he changed his mind again and returned to his former optimistic faiths. Compare for example, the two following statements by him:

> For my own part, I am now somewhat sceptical of the success of a purely monetary policy directed towards influencing the rate of interest. I expect to see the State, which is in a position to calculate the marginal efficiency of capital-goods on long views and on the basis of the general social advantage, taking an ever greater responsibility for directly organizing investment; since it seems likely that the fluctuations in the market estimation of the marginal efficiency of different types of capital, calculated on the principles I have described above, will be too great to be offset by any practicable changes in the rate of interest.[8]

> I am far from fully convinced by the recent thesis that interest rates play a small part in determining the volume of investment. It may be that other influences, such as an increase in demand, often dominate it in starting a movement. But I am quite unconvinced that low interest rates cannot play an enormous part in sustaining investment at a given figure, and when there is

[7] J. Franklin Ebersole, "The Influence of Interest Rates upon Entrepreneurial Decisions in Business — a Case Study," *Harvard Business Review*, Vol. XVII, 1938, p. 35; H. D. Henderson, "The Significance of the Rate of Interest," *Oxford Economic Papers*, No. 1, 1938, p. 1; J. E. Meade and P. W. S. Andrews, "Summary of Replies to Questions on Effects of Interest Rates," *Oxford Economic Papers*, No. 1, 1938, p. 14.*
[8] *The General Theory of Employment Interest, and Money*, p. 164.

a movement from a higher to a lower rate in allowing a greater scale of investment to proceed over a very much longer period than would otherwise be possible.[9]

The relation between the level of investment and the level of real income is, according to theory and observation, such that investment is positively related to income, with the marginal propensity to invest less than unity. In fact, in most dynamical models of the Keynesian system, we find a much stronger condition. In order that the system be dynamically stable the marginal propensity to consume plus the marginal propensity to invest must be less than unity.[10] Extensive calculations of econometric models by the author lead to the conclusion that the relationships of investment and consumption to income satisfy the stability conditions.

The investment function (demand for capital goods), it will be remembered, is derived from the principle that entrepreneurs require the services of factors of production in just those quantities that will maximize anticipated profits over some planning horizon. When the factor of production under consideration is durable capital equipment which will last for a few years in any case, the entrepreneur must try to relate his demand for such equipment to the sales that he expects to make in the next several months. The best objective information concerning these future sales is obviously derived from the level of sales, and possibly their rate of change or acceleration at the time of planning. Statistical approximations of these measures of anticipated sales are found by introducing lagged sales (national income) as well as current sales among the important factors influencing investment.

For many problems we are interested only in the static systems where all lags are zero, but for the general case and especially for the statistical verification of the Keynesian theory, it is important to introduce the appropriate lags. The true relationship between investment and income can be found in the actual data, only if we

[9] See the article by Mordecai Ezekiel, "Statistical Investigations of Saving, Consumption, and Investment," *American Economic Review*, Vol. XXXII, 1942, note 10, p. 283. The quotation in the text is from a letter of Keynes which was quoted by Ezekiel.

[10] Recall, above, the condition that the marginal propensity to consume plus the marginal propensity to save equals unity, by definition.

properly account for the lags that must be present in the investment function.

One of the most important, and unfortunately neglected, factors influencing investment decisions is capital accumulation. This factor has long been stressed by Marxist writers but never adequately incorporated into the models of bourgeois economics, although it is shown in the appendix that the role of the stock of capital in the investment schedule follows logically from a classical theory of the firm based on profit maximization. The influence of capital accumulation on investment must surely be one of the main pillars of the mature economy school, but the supporters and critics of this theory have failed to take sufficient notice of this variable.

Keynes' own treatment of the capital stock was exceedingly superficial. He neglected this variable on the ground that he was dealing with a short-run theory for which the capital stock cannot vary appreciably. He considered capital as given at any point of time by the historical pattern of the system in the past. Thus the stock of capital became a predetermined variable. On the other hand, later Keynesians concerned themselves with the long-run equilibrium, where investment and savings go to zero and the capital stock is introduced as an explicit variable. Such a system is actually given in the appendix. But is there not an intermediate stage which is not a picture of either the long-run or short-run equilibrium, one that has none of the artificialities of these extreme cases?

One of the best arguments for the existence of a mature economy would seem to run in terms of capital accumulation. As a system accumulates more and more productive plant and equipment, the rate of return on new and existing capital becomes depressed.[11] With this lower rate of return on capital in a society of abundance, investment opportunities fade away. Unless higher levels (schedules) of consumption are there to fill the gap, a state of economic stagnation will set in. For example, the housing boom of the 1920's in the United States led to such an accumulation of residential capital that rents began to fall, and new housing investment re-

[11] The theory of the declining marginal efficiency of capital in the Keynesian language or the theory of the falling rate of profit in the Marxian system.

mained low for a long period of time. The same phenomenon occurred in other industries. Unless innovations or some other type of external shocks (*e.g.*, War) are imposed upon the system, the level of investment activity is likely to remain low.

Statistical investigations reveal a very strong negative correlation between investment activity and the stock of capital. This correlation can be readily observed in the economy as a whole and all the major industrial sub-groups.

From the savings-and-investment relationship in the Keynesian system we learn how households and business firms make their decisions about the disposition of their current income. But after people have decided whether to spend or save their income, they must make a further decision. They must decide in what form to hold their accumulated savings. They have, in general, the choice of holding goods, securities, or money. An implicit analysis of the decisions to hold goods has already been given. In the case of business firms, included in capital were both fixed and working capital, so that the demand for investment or producer goods includes the demand for inventories. By cumulating each period's demand for capital and taking account of depreciation there is obtained immediately the demand for total capital assets, including the demand for stocks of saleable goods in the form of inventories. Similarly one may cumulate the households' demand for durable consumer goods in each period and thus find the demand for the stock of consumer goods. Hence it remains to show how the demand for other assets, namely money and securities, gets determined.

Individuals and business firms must possess preference scales or utility functions which tell the relationships between satisfactions and the holding of securities of various types and money. Following the general practices of the theory of consumer behavior, it is necessary to maximize this function, which depends upon the structure of asset holdings subject to the constraint that the total amount of assets and money held by an individual should not exceed an initial endowment plus the accumulated savings over the individual's past history.[12] This maximization process leads immediately

---

[12] In the appendix a more general theory is presented in which the household utility function depends on the consumption of goods and the asset holdings simultaneously.

to the demand equations for money and all types of securities. These demand relations state that the demand for money depends upon all the relative security prices, the price of money (equal to unity by definition) and the constraining factor of accumulated savings. If the aggregation procedures are carried out properly, the community relationships will state that the community's demand for money depends upon the general price of securities and the accumulated wealth of the community. Also, the community's demand for the stock of securities depends upon the price of securities and accumulated wealth. However, there is no need for both demand relations. If the demand for money is determined as opposed to earning assets in the form of securities, then that demand relation alone is enough, because the sum of holdings of money and securities cannot exceed the accumulated savings which has already been accounted for elsewhere in the system. If we know the historical pattern of savings and the current demand for money, then the demand for securities follows directly as a residual. Alternatively, the demand for securities may be introduced as the strategic relationship. Then it will be unnecessary to introduce the demand for money.

Following the practice of Keynes, we use the demand for money instead of the demand for securities as the remaining link in the structure of the aggregative system.

The liquidity-preference equation does not yet look like that of Keynes, although the differences will be seen to be superficial. The interest rate can be written in place of the price of securities, as a variable affecting the demand for money. The price of securities is inversely related to the interest rate, and we may work with one or the other variable at pleasure. The other variable affecting the demand for money is the accumulated wealth which limits the sum of money and securities that may be held by the entire economy. The wealth variable, however, is the total income-producing wealth of the system. This wealth can also be expressed as the ratio of the national income to the interest rate, as is the customary practice in capitalizing an income flow from an asset. Now the demand for money depends upon the interest rate and the level of income. We have reached our goal, the Keynesian liquidity-preference function.

According to the Keynesian motives for the holding of money there are other motives besides the liquidity or speculative motive which lead people to choose between money and securities. There is also the precautionary motive, which is best taken care of by imposing the side condition that cash balances shall not fall below a minimum level which is essential for meeting certain extreme contingencies. Finally there is the transaction motive, which states that, for matters of convenience in carrying out everyday affairs, people hold a certain fraction of their income in the form of cash. It is evident that no new variables affecting the demand for money are introduced by the transactions or precautionary motives.

The demand for money depends upon the interest rate and the level of national income.

This fundamental Keynesian proposition may be derived in terms of real cash balances, in which case the appropriate explanatory variable is the level of real income; or it may be derived in terms of money balances, in which case the money value of national income is used. The interest rate remains the same in either case, since it is a pure number.

The relationship between the demand for money and the interest rate should be negative in the sense that a falling rate should cause an increased demand for money. If the interest rate is high, then it is profitable to hold securities and enjoy a large interest income, instead of holding cash. In the reverse case, with a low interest rate, it becomes more desirable to hold money as compared with securities. But, in addition to stating that the demand for money is inversely related to the rate of interest, Keynes implied that this demand was elastic. He argued that there exists a bottom to the interest rate which is just high enough to cover the minimum costs and risks of making loans. According to his theory, at a sufficiently low interest rate, the liquidity-preference function should become infinitely interest-elastic.

The data show a high negative correlation between time deposits (idle balances) and the average yield on corporate bonds in the United States of America for the interwar period. It can be argued that certain institutional forces have caused the stock of cash balances to increase historically with a steady trend and have simultaneously caused the interest rate to fall with a steady downward trend. Their negative correlation can, thus, be attributed to a common cause rather than the Keynesian theory of liquidity preference. However, it is possible to extract the influence of trend. The data still support a strong negative correlation after the trend influence has been eliminated. The Keynesian theory has a solid empirical basis.[13]

There is, however, not sufficient evidence of the infinite elasticity hypothesized by Keynes. It may exist, but there are not enough observations in the neighborhood of low interest rates to substantiate his claims.

As is to be expected, there is also a close relation between the demand for money and the level of income, after the influence of the interest rate is already extracted. In the case of the transaction motive alone, a direct correlation can be made between the stock of demand deposits, plus circulating cash, and the level of income. There is an extremely tight positive correlation here, and there can be no doubt of the existence of this relationship.

The remaining component of the Keynesian system in its customary formulation is the supply of cash balances. The standard assumption is that the supply of cash balances, in money terms, is autonomously determined by the banking system. All the laws, written and unwritten, with regard to reserve ratios, gold policy, lending policy, etc. which are determined by central bank action cannot be formulated in terms of definite patterns of economic behavior. The supply of money is subject to the decisions of the central bank, which may or may not follow a behavior pattern. Instead of assuming this supply to be autonomous, one could alternatively make it dependent upon the discount rate, but since so many non-economic factors are involved, it seems best to leave this variable unexplained.†

The discussions of Keynesian economics are usually carried on in terms of the consumption or savings schedule, the investment

---

[13] Similar results have been found for England. See A. J. Brown, "Interest, Prices and the Demand Schedule for Idle Money," *Oxford Economic Papers*, Number 2, 1939, p. 46.

schedule, and the liquidity-preference schedule. For many problems this is sufficient. A system in terms of these schedules is complete if stated in terms of money flows. In the short-run theory where the stock of capital is assumed to be given from past history and not an explicit variable of the system, these relations appear:

> *Money savings as a function of the interest rate and income equals money investment as a function of thé interest rate and income.*

> *The autonomous supply of money equals the demand for money as a function of the interest rate and income.*

It appears immediately that there are two equations and two variables, interest and income.[14] After solving this system for these variables it is possible to substitute into the savings function and calculate the value of savings. Knowing savings (= investment) and income, we can immediately determine the level of consumption.

If the model system is written in terms of real quantities, or the wage units employed by Keynes, then this simple system is not sufficient by itself to determine all variables. This is true because the autonomous supply of money must apply only to the level of money cash balances and not to the supply of real cash balances The banking system can determine the number of dollars to be supplied, but cannot necessarily determine the number of dollars in relation to the price level or the wage rate. We need additional information in the form of more relationships in order to determine the absolute level of wages or prices.

However, the situation can easily be remedied by introducing some more equations between our variables, which we have not yet introduced explicitly.

In order to derive the investment function from the theory of profit maximization, we had to introduce the production function which expressed the technological relationship between the total output and the input of the factors of production, labor and capital.

---

[14] We have assumed that the price level does not enter explicitly into the savings function when this function is expressed in terms of money flows.

The process of profit maximization with respect to variations of capital subject to the above technological relation enabled us to derive the investment function. Profits should also be maximized with respect to labor input which leads to the proposition that the average real wage rate equals the marginal product of labor; *i.e.*, the contribution to output of the last man-hour. Thus we have a relationship between the amount of labor and the real wage rate.

> *The demand for labor depends upon the level of real wages.*

For an empirically established form of the production function, one may actually calculate the marginal productivity.[15] It is proportional to the ratio between total output and total labor input. Statistical tests from the data on output, employment, wages, and price, show very clearly the indicated positive correlation between the average real wage rate and marginal productivity, or in the case of the particular production function, man-hour output.

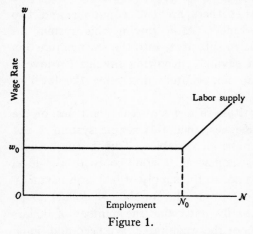

Figure 1.

There is still lacking one relationship, the supply of labor. The supply of labor should be a schedule showing how much of labor's services will be offered at each level of wages. Now comes an impasse. Do we take real or money wages in the supply curve of labor? The classical system would relate the supply of labor to real wages, but Keynes objected to this relation and substituted a supply curve in terms of money wages. This is not the only modification which he has made in the supply schedule, for he has also fixed its shape. He has said that the supply of labor is perfectly elastic at the going wage up to a full employment level.

[15] See the appendix below.

Here w_0 is the going wage rate and N_0 is full employment. This particular supply curve of labor is very important and leads to certain desired results within the Keynesian system which economists thinking along other lines were unable to reach. Realistically, the Keynesian supply curve may be more correct and describe the way workers actually behave. But on a different level of abstraction there is another question to be considered. In a perfect Walrasian equilibrium where the classical supply curve is used, can one get the result of under-employment equilibrium with the Keynesian system? An attempt to answer this question shall be made, and also to show why a classical model must automatically have a full employment equilibrium under such conditions.

It is now possible to add three relationships to the "real" Keynesian system and show at least that there are as many equations as variables:

Output depends upon the input of labor and capital.

The real wage rate equals the marginal productivity of labor.[16]

The supply of labor depends upon the money wage rate.

We now have five equations and five variables which are not assumed to be autonomous: real income, the interest rate, employment, the wage rate, and the price level. The system is complete. The reader should be forewarned that the mere counting of equations and variables is only necessary and not sufficient to complete our economic analysis. The sufficiency conditions shall be examined later.

A SIMPLE MODEL

The set of five relations developed in the preceding section is the complete version of the Keynesian system. There are several mutually interdependent propositions in this system which cannot be easily understood in purely non-mathematical terms. It is

---

[16] In the case of imperfect competition this must be modified for a term involving the elasticity of demand; however, no new variables are introduced, so that determinateness is not affected.

possible, however, to simplify this system even further in order to make the major contribution evident.

We know that Keynes' procedure was to do away with the savings-investment theory of interest and replace it with a savings-investment theory of output. When this had been done the revolution was a *fait accompli*. A simple model, based on the savings-investment relation alone, shows this clearly:

Suppose that savings are completely interest-inelastic; *i.e.*, that the fluctuations of the rate of interest have no influence on the rate of savings. Empirically and theoretically this is a sound assumption. Savings will be taken to depend upon income alone. As income increases, savings will increase, but the increment of the latter will always be less than that of the former — the marginal propensity to save is positive but less than unity. Suppose further that investment is completely autonomous, something unpredictable from the behavior of other economic quantities, but instead determined by forces acting outside the strict economic sphere, like innovations.

The equilibrium condition for this system is that there is an equation between autonomous investment and savings, which depend upon income. This is one equation in one variable, income; hence it is sufficient to determine the level of income. Thus is set up a basic theory which replaces the classical savings-investment theory of interest. Graphically, this Keynesian model is shown in Figure 2.

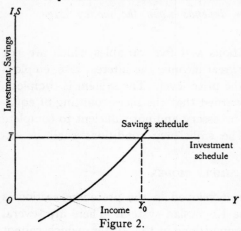

Figure 2.

The curve is the savings schedule. At low levels of income people must dissave or spend more than their income in order to maintain minimum standards of consumption; thus the savings schedule is negative for low levels of income. It slopes upward, showing that savings increase with income. The slope should always be less than unity if the system is to be dynamically stable.

The investment schedule is merely a horizontal straight line at the existing level of autonomous investment, $\bar{I}$. Since investment is autonomous, it does not vary with income, but is constant for each level of income.

Our graphical system says that $\bar{I}$ is that level of investment which offsets just enough savings to generate a level of national income, Y_0. This is the clearest picture of the theory of effective demand. A theory of the business cycle can also be shown in this graph. This theory is based on the idea that the savings schedule is a stable relationship which does not shift very much over time and that the level of investment is extremely volatile, continuously shifting by great amounts. For every different level of autonomous investment there is generated a different level of national income. Fluctuations in investment, superimposed upon a stable savings schedule, determine fluctuations in income — or the business cycle.

This simple model is important for several reasons. While it is not true that all investment is autonomous under ordinary circumstances, there are cases where the assumption of autonomous investment is exactly true. One case is the operation of a socialist economy where all investment decisions are made by the central planning board and are not based on principles like profit maximization which lead to non-autonomous investment under capitalism. Another case where the simple model applies is that of a total war economy.[17] This situation will be discussed at length in Ch. VI in connection with the inflationary gap.

The application of the Keynesian model to the working of a socialist economy is ironic because Keynes was quite outspoken in his distaste for socialism, especially the Soviet system. In fact, while Keynes has been an accurate predictor of many economic events, he has made very poor predictions in the case of Russia. For example he predicted, ". . . if Communism achieves a certain

---

[17] The mere fact that the model of the socialist economy and the war economy have certain formal similarities does not at all mean that a socialist economy must be a war economy. On the contrary, the arguments in the text will discuss exclusively the case of a non-war socialist economy.

success, it will achieve it, not as an improved economic technique, but as a religion." [18] This statement shows a complete lack of understanding of the political, technological and economic basis of the Soviet system. Keynes, glorifier of the bourgeois life, little knew that the arguments why the Russian economy has been and may continue to be one of uninterrupted full employment under socialism follow directly from his own simple model.

For Russia, investment is completely autonomous. The central planning board decides, according to the needs of the people and the political situation of the world, to carry out a certain level of investment activity. The role of the interest rate becomes trivial in this system, and there is little doubt that the savings schedule will be such that savings is simply a function of income. People save in a socialist economy for the same reasons that they save in our system, except for the fact that some of the savings motives are less powerful for them. Inhabitants of a country having a socialist economy do not need to worry about the hazards of old age, sickness, hospital care, etc. Also, the more equalized income distribution should make for a low propensity to save. In the Russian example, the planning board has decreed investment at a high level. The savings schedule has been pushed far to the right; hence out of the savings-investment equation there has been generated a high level of national income. In actual practice, the propensity to save was so small and the level of investment so high that there was an inflationary pressure on prices.[19] This pressure called for the turnover tax, some price control, and rationing in order to prevent inflation. If the planning board has a good idea as to the exact shape and position of the savings schedule, it can calculate easily the necessary amount of anti-inflation (or deflation) measures in conjunction with each level of investment. In any intelligently run socialist economy where there is an abundance of economic resources and a desire on the part of the people to enjoy the fruits of these resources, the central planning board will set the level of investment at that amount which will just offset savings out of a full-

---

[18] *Essays in Persuasion*, p. 305.

[19] Undoubtedly the high level of investment was much more powerful than the reduced savings habits in generating high levels of income.

employment national income. Proper policy by socialist planners can always lead to full employment — this is the superior economic organization which Keynes failed to see in the years just preceding the *General Theory*.†

A simple version of the theory of classical economics can also be given. When this simple model is compared with the simple Keynesian model, it is easy to see some of the important differences in the two systems.

The simple classical model states that savings always flow into investment at the going rate of interest regardless of the level of income, and that the stock of money and the velocity of circulation are given constants. In this system the savings-investment equation determines the rate of interest, and the amount of money and the velocity of circulation serve to determine the value of income (or the price level corresponding to a given real income) via the quantity equation of money. The latter equation states that the amount of money held is proportional to income. If the amount of money and the proportionality factor (reciprocal of velocity) are known, then, obviously, income is known.

Can unemployment exist in this classical system? If there is unemployment, then a cut in wages will always increase employment within the framework of this classical model. Since wages and prices are related by the marginal-productivity theory, the quantity equation can be looked upon as an equation to determine either prices or wages. With a fixed velocity, smaller wages mean that the same quantity of money can accomplish more purchases, and thus restore full employment. The same results can be accomplished through an arbitrary increase in the amount of money by the banking system. If the stock of cash balances is increased, then income will rise. Whatever part of this income is not consumed will pass over automatically into investment. At these higher levels of income, consumption, and investment, more workers will be employed. By an easy-money or flexible wage policy, this classical system can always avoid unemployment.

Keynes threw over the assumptions of this system. He gave up Say's law that makes savings flow automatically into investment regardless of the level of income. He also developed a theory which did not make flexible wages such a powerful tool, always insuring full employment. The incompatibility of the simplest classical system with the simplest Keynesian model shows clearly what is meant by a revolution.

THE COMPLETE SYSTEMS OF MUTUAL INTERDEPENDENCE

The simple models of the Keynesian and classical systems of economics bring out the major differences in the two approaches. More detailed questions can be answered only by considering the complete systems with the demand and supply for labor and the production function as well as the standard Keynesian concepts of liquidity preference, marginal efficiency of capital and propensity to consume.

Before discussing the relationship of Keynesian to classical economics, it will be necessary to state on what grounds the two systems are to be compared. By now, it is well agreed that one of the most pressing economic problems of this country [20] is the problem of unemployment. Economists in this country should operate with theoretical models which are capable of explaining the phenomenon of unemployment. The classical system can explain unemployment which is due to frictions or market imperfections and to unwillingness of workers to be employed. For our tastes this is clearly insufficient, because even a perfectly competitive, frictionless system need not always have full employment.

Keynes thought that it was necessary to develop a new definition of unemployment in order to explain the occurrence of an underemployment equilibrium. He defined involuntary unemployment as that unemployment which could be done away with by cuts in real wage rates. This definition is not entirely satisfactory. It does not admit of the possibility that for some ranges of real wage rates, higher real wage rates will call forth a reduced supply of labor.[21] But more seriously it implies that if workers would offer

---

[20] This is not true of the war-devastated countries of Europe.

[21] The problem of absenteeism during the war production program is good evidence of the existence of a negatively sloped portion of the supply curve of labor in the regions of high wages.

their services according to real instead of money wage rates, there would be no problem of unemployment. It hardly seems possible that Keynes could say that his major contribution to economic theory was to point out a money illusion on the part of workers as the cause of unemployment. Keynes' real contribution, to repeat, has been to show that if savings are not offset by legitimate investment outlets, failure to generate a high level of employment will follow. *Even if the Keynesian supply curve of labor is replaced by the classical supply curve in terms of real wages, there remains the problem of making savings pass into investment.*

A simple definition which would appeal to classical economists would be that employment is full if all who want to work at the going real wage rate are employed. In this case, there is a supply schedule of labor in terms of real wages, and any solution of the classical system for employment which falls along this schedule is a full-employment solution. In classical economics such a solution always occurs in the conditions of full equilibrium. It remains to be seen whether or not analogous results hold for the Keynesian system.

If the classical supply curve of labor is not accepted as being realistic and the Keynesian supply curve is used instead, then full employment is that situation in which anyone who wants to work at the going rate of money wages can find a job.

Other useful definitions of full employment can be formulated in terms of a certain level of output. Full employment, for example, may be looked upon as the long-run potential level of output. The short-run potential may conveniently be called the bottleneck level as distinguished from the full-employment level. There will not be occasion in this chapter to make further use of these concepts. However, they will be helpful at a later stage, in the analysis of the inflationary gap.

Let us first apply our definitions to the complete system of classical economics. In addition to the quantity theory of money and the savings-investment theory of interest, there exists in this system a technological production function, relating output and input of productive factors; a demand schedule for labor as a function of the real wage rate which follows from the theory of profit maximization; [22] and a supply schedule of labor as a function of the real wage rate.

At first glance, the differences between this system and the Keynesian system may seem quite obvious. Some have said that the principal difference lies in the changing of the quantity theory of money into the liquidity-preference theory; others have said that the distinguishing characteristic of the Keynesian system is the substitution of the supply schedule of labor in terms of money wages for the classical schedule in terms of real wages; and still others have been closer to the truth by pointing out that the main contribution by Keynes occurred in the alteration of the savings-investment equation.

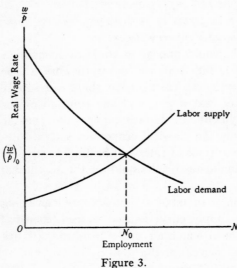

Figure 3.

That the full-equilibrium solution for this system is one of no unemployment, is almost obvious. The demonstration is quite simple. The supply-and-demand equations for labor give the level of employment and real wages, as in Figure 3.

By substitution of the level of employment into the production function, real output can be determined and this output level can be substituted into the quantity equation to get the price level. The rate of interest follows from the savings-investment relation.

The values of output and employment thus determined represent full-employment levels, since this value of employment lies on the supply curve of labor. All who want to work at the going real wage are employed. If any maladjustment occurs within this system so that there is not full employment, a wage cut can always

---

[22] Commonly called the marginal-productivity theory of wages.

restore the economy to its full-employment equilibrium. The competitive bargaining among workers will always be remunerative. Since the amount of money and the velocity are given in the quantity equation, total spending is given. At lower wages certainly more workers can be hired with total spending constant. Wage cutting will continue up to the full-employment level.

With the assumption of various frictions, imperfections and rigidities of the real world, an explanation of unemployment is not difficult, either in the classical or the Keynesian system. But assuming away all such defects, can unemployment exist? Many economists will answer this question today in the negative. Those who pick out the essential, distinguishing feature of the Keynesian system as the assumption of rigidities imply also that they would answer *no* to this question. Unfortunately, Keynes has practically admitted [23] that he, too, would answer *no*. Again, as in the *Treatise*, Keynes did not really understand what he had written, and chose the wrong thing to publicize as his innovation. The Keynesian supply curve of labor and definition of involuntary unemployment were no more important to the *General Theory* than the "fundamental equations" were to the *Treatise*.

Suppose that we live in a Euclidean world in which there exists a perfectly competitive capitalist system. It shall now be argued that this Utopia will not automatically solve the unemployment problem under the conditions of Keynesian economics. However, full employment will always be insured in a classical situation in this world. Now it becomes possible to see the fundamental difference between Keynesian and classical economics.

Let us imagine a model economic system in which there is perfect competition, with no inflexibilities or rigidities.[24] All quantities will be reckoned in terms of wage units.[25]

The background relationships will be those of classical economics, pure and simple; *i.e.*, there will be the production function for real

[23] See "The General Theory of Employment," *Quarterly Journal of Economics*, Vol. LI, 1937, p. 209, where Keynes said that Leontief was correct in pointing out that the Keynesian system differs mainly from the classical system in not being homogeneous of order zero in prices.

[24] See the appendix for the mathematical version of the system.

[25] With the obvious exceptions of price, interest rate, and employment.

output, and the supply-demand relations for labor in terms of real wages. The other relations will be of a general form. There will be savings (dependent upon interest rates and income) equal to investment (dependent upon interest rates and income). Finally the supply of the stock of cash balances (measured in wage units) will be equated to the demand for such balances as a function of interest rates and income.

It might be argued that this is a perfect classical system which represents a perfect equilibrium of perfect competition. Any classical economist would naturally proceed to obtain a solution to this system as follows: From the background relations, as before, find the real wage, the level of employment, and the amount of output. Next, convert full-employment output to income measured in terms of wage units. This can be done by dividing real output by real wages. Substitute full-employment income into the savings-investment relation and get the rate of interest. This gives everything except the absolute level of wages and prices. But the supply and demand for money will produce a solution for these variables. Since the interest rate and income are already calculated, the value to which the supply of cash balances (measured in wage-units) must be equated is known. The stock of *monetary* cash balances as an autonomously given variable is also known; therefore the absolute level of wages can be calculated. Knowing real wages, already, and absolute wages, it is possible to obtain immediately the absolute price level.

But now, let us become Keynesian and see what happens. As before, solve the background equations for real wages, employment, and output. Substitute full-employment income into the savings-investment equation. Is there always a solution for the interest rate? There are as many equations as variables, but does that guarantee an economically possible solution? The answer is that it certainly does not! More must be done than merely to count equations and variables. We must consider the shapes of our functions. The Keynesian Revolution rejected the classical theory of interest. It denied that the equation

$$S_w(r, (Y_w)_0) = I_w(r, (Y_w)_0)$$

need always have a positive solution for the interest rate, r, when $(Y_w)_0$ (income) is given *at the full-employment level*.[26] When the saving process is analyzed, the slope of the savings function with respect to the interest rate might be negative or positive and will probably be small in absolute value. More recently, we have come to believe that the investment function is also interest-inelastic. It is more likely than not that there will be no positive

value of r which satisfies this equation. *Perfect equilibrium of perfect competition is not in general compatible with the system of Keynesian economics.*

A feasible graphic presentation of this situation is given in Figure 4.

When income is at the full-employment level, $(Y_w)_0$, it is both possible and probable that the savings-investment sched-

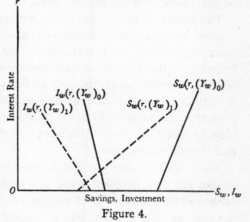

Figure 4.

ules as functions of the interest rate will appear as the two solid lines. The relative positions of the two schedules mean in this case that no matter how low the interest rate is pushed, savings out of a full-employment income exceeds investment out of that same income. It is obvious that this result becomes more possible as the two schedules become more interest-inelastic. If there were unlimited investment opportunities at the going interest rate, the investment schedule would be a horizontal straight line — infinitely elastic — and consequently always intersect with a non-horizontal savings schedule. Many orthodox economists use a model of the latter type, although it does not describe a savings-investment process that could exist in the present world, no matter how perfect the system might be. The case of the horizontal investment schedule and the non-horizontal savings schedule comes in the end to Say's law.

[26] The subscript w represents measurements in terms of wage units.

But there is an adjustment which takes place within the Keynesian system, so that a positive interest rate can be determined. If income falls from $(Y_w)_0$ to $(Y_w)_1$, then the two schedules of Fig. 4 will shift to the positions of the dotted lines. Incomes will have to adjust to that level, $(Y_w)_1$, at which savings out of that income will be equal to investment out of that income. Only after a theory of the adjustment of output is introduced can the rate of interest be determined for the general case.

The principal difference, then, between Keynes and the classics centers around their theories of savings and investment. The multiplier theory, or the theory of the determination of effective demand, is the Keynesian savings-investment theory. The theory of the determination of the rate of interest is the classical savings-investment theory. The money equation merely serves the purpose of determining the level of wages and prices, and does not play an essential part in showing the differences between the new and the old economics.

The principal question which must inevitably arise now is, How do we get any solution from this real, Keynesian system? The answer must be that there can be an equilibrium of perfect competition in this system, but it cannot be a perfect equilibrium; *i.e.*, an equilibrium such that all relations hold simultaneously as they do in the classical case. Something must give way in order that the economic variables can assume some determinate values. It is obvious from Fig. 4 that it will not help matters if the interest rate gives way. Income must be the obvious thing that gives way in order to bring savings and investment into equilibrium. But if income falls from $(Y_w)_0$ to $(Y_w)_1$, then output and employment will be forced to lower levels.[27] But workers will not remain on their supply curve of labor for an amount of employment less than the full-employment equilibrium. The employed workers can always get higher real wages by moving along the demand curve for labor. The final position will be that of Fig. 5, with the supply of labor in excess of the demand at the going real wage rate. The excess of supply over demand $(N_2 - N_1)$ is a measure of unemployment.

[27] See the appendix for a more complete proof.

The superior bargaining power of the employer over the employee explains easily why the supply-demand relation for labor is the one relationship of the system which can have a solution that is not at an intersection point.

The non-Keynesian economists will argue now that if workers compete for jobs and cut money wage rates, full employment will be restored. This proposition is correct only under the conditions of classical economics. In the Keynesian system lower wages need not do any good.

An analysis of the true picture of the economic world shows that interest rates have been pushed to very low levels so that the liquidity-preference function may be interest-elastic. But more important, all statistical information leads to belief that lower interest rates will have little, if any, influence on

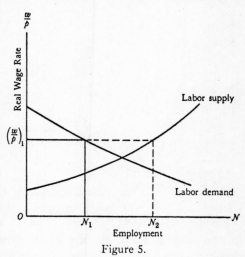

Figure 5.

the rate of investment. The economics of an interest-inelastic schedule of marginal efficiency of capital is an important branch of modern analysis. It is easy to show that if the liquidity-preference schedule is elastic and/or the marginal efficiency schedule inelastic, wage cuts will not raise the level of output and thus employment via the production function.[28] The argument can be conveniently presented on a diagram due to Hicks. On the vertical axis measure the interest rate and on the horizontal axis measure income. The liquidity-preference equation, then, for a given value of cash balances, describes a two-dimensional relation between the interest rate and income. Similarly, the savings-investment equation also gives a curve in the same plane. The intersection of the two curves determines the equilibrium level of income.

[28] A mathematical treatment is given in the appendix.

The curves are drawn in Fig. 6 under the assumption of interest-elastic liquidity preferences and interest-inelastic schedules of the marginal efficiency of capital and savings.

If the two curves intersect so that the Keynesian system yields a solution of an unemployment level of income, will wage flexibility quickly restore economic life to full employment? The most direct effect of wage cuts is to increase the stock of real balances,

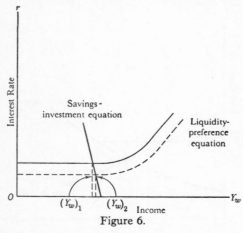

Figure 6.

provided the banking policy is such that the money stock of cash balances is not lowered. This is true, obviously, because real cash balances are the ratio of money balances and the wage rate. Wage cuts, viewed as an easy-money policy, cause a shift in one of the schedules of the system. The liquidity-preference equation now moves to the dotted curve in the above graph. Equilibrium income changes from $(Y_w)_1$ to $(Y_w)_2$, practically no change at all. There are very serious limitations to the employment-creating effects of wage cuts. In the limiting case in which the savings and investment schedules have zero elasticity with respect to interest rates and in which the liquidity-preference schedule has infinite elasticity, there are no employment-creating effects. The savings-investment equation becomes in this case a vertical line, and the liquidity equation becomes horizontal, in the range of low interest rates. But the protagonists will not give up in their argument at this stage. They will say that, disregarding the limiting case, consider the situation where the increase in employment is some small positive amount. Then, since there is no limit to the extent to which real cash balances can rise with a fall in wages, there is no limit to the rise in Y_w. But they have argued themselves directly into a trap. What will be the effects of unlimited increases in cash balances as a result of unlimited wage cuts? The effects will be those of the economics of hyper-deflation and social revolution. If the increase in cash balances becomes large through limitless wage cuts and employment receives only a slight stimulus, adverse expectations must certainly occur. As a result of expectations of further wage cuts, production plans would be postponed. Wages could fall endlessly to zero without any increase in employment, but instead decreases. Undoubtedly, this process would have to stop somewhere before zero. The method of stopping it would be the overthrow of the capitalist system.

Professor Pigou has pointed out that once-and-for-all wage cuts without any expectations of further wage cuts will always increase employment. If the Keynesian functions are such that liquidity preference is interest-elastic and/or marginal efficiency is interest-inelastic, the effect of wage cuts will be slight. But if there are to be no adverse expectations, the extent of wage cuts must also be small (otherwise there will be adverse expectations). The product of two small factors will also be small. It is not possible to abstract from expectations in this problem.

There is, perhaps, some possibility that wage cuts will cause shifts of the savings or the investment functions. In this case, shifts of the schedules do cause great changes in the level of income, but the drawback to this possibility is the limited extent of the shift. If wage cuts have a strong stimulative effect on investment relative to savings then we could greatly expand employment. But there are serious doubts as to whether wage cuts will have any effects on the savings or investment schedules. The reasons for these doubts are discussed more fully in the next chapter.

As a result, it can be stated that unemployment is possible in a perfect system and that perfect equilibrium of perfect competition is not compatible with the Keynesian conditions; whereas the achievement of full employment in the classical world is automatic. In order to show that full employment is not automatic in a perfect world subject to the Keynesian conditions, it is necessary to assume nothing whatsoever about rigidities in the system, but only to make plausible assumptions about the interest-elasticity of certain basic relationships.

The numerous remarks throughout the recent literature that Keynes relied upon wage inflexibilities to obtain his results are entirely unsubstantiated.

But the assumption of rigidities will become very useful in explaining how an under-employment situation can be one of equilibrium. The essential contribution of Keynes was to show that full employment is not automatically assured. One need only look at the real world to realize why unemployment can be a persistent equilibrium condition. Under classical economics wage flexibility leads always to full employment. Within the framework of Keynesian economics wage flexibility does not correct unemployment and leads merely to hyper-deflation if carried to its logical conclusion. But in the real world one observes neither hyper-deflation nor full employment. The explanation is that wages *are* sticky; they are not flexible. The solution to the Keynesian system which gives a value of employment not on the supply schedule persists when wage cuts do not occur. Because workers do not bid against one another, we do not experience the hopeless downward spiral.

When imperfections and rigid money wages are introduced into our model of the Keynesian system, the results of under-employment equilibrium follow quite easily, providing a more realistic picture of how the economic system looks. But it is not true, as many have said, that the Keynesian equations in conjunction with a perfect, frictionless system will always yield a full-employment solution. Unemployment is extremely likely even under perfect competition. It shows clearly that the discussion of the new results of Keynesian economics should not be centered in the price sphere of the economy; rather in the probability, psychological, and expectational sphere of the economy. One should investigate the determinants of the shapes of the Keynesian functions. These are the strategic economic variables. They tell whether or not a full employment solution is possible. The long-familiar observation about the stickiness of wages supplements the results of Keynesian economics and brings the student into contact with actuality.

CHAPTER IV

A POLEMICAL DIGRESSION

For those who feel that the controversies, in the literature, on Keynesian economics have been carried on *ad nauseam*, this chapter will be of little interest. However, economists should be absolutely clear about their theoretical foundations. It is true that some rare individuals have great intuitive insight into economic problems and do not find it necessary to rely on rigorous theoretical analysis, but there is nothing more tragic than an economist floundering in the field of economic policy because his theory is confused. This chapter is designed as an attempt to clear away some confusions in theoretical economics and should be of interest to those who take economics as a serious affair.

REVIEWS OF REVIEWS

Neither Keynes nor his immediate reviewers understood the full implications of the theoretical model of the *General Theory*. Much of the later polemical literature represented wasted paper, but by no means were all the discussions worthless. To those making a survey of the battlefield after most of the shots have been fired, it seems impossible that this theory could have been so little understood, but such a lack of comprehension merely serves to emphasize the revolutionary character of the work.

Two of the well known reviews of the *General Theory* were made by disciples, A. P. Lerner [1] and W. B. Reddaway.[2] Lerner's review was generally cited as an approved, condensed version of Keynes' book. It was a clear exposition of the *General Theory* but made certain arguments in attempted support of the theory which later gave rise to much controversy. For example, there are two Keyneses on the matter of the savings-investment equation. One

---

[1] "Mr. Keynes' 'General Theory of Employment, Interest and Money,'" *International Labor Review*, Vol. XXXIV, 1936, p. 435.

[2] "The General Theory of Employment, Interest and Money," *Economic Record*, Vol. XII, 1936, p. 28.

Keynes maintained the equality of savings and investment in terms of definitions of observable economic quantities, with no refutable hypothesis behind the equation. The better side of Keynes' dual personality stated the savings-investment relation in terms of intersecting schedules of economic behavior, which determine an equilibrium position. Lerner in his review chose the former exposition and has, apparently, never parted with it.† He looked upon savings and investment as identically equal and not brought into equilibrium by any economic process. Here are the beginnings of a controversy which will be discussed at greater length later in this chapter.

Another controversial issue on which Lerner supported Keynes is the question of wage cuts. Lerner attempted to show that whenever there is a uniform money wage cut, prices will fall by exactly the same proportion as wages, thus leading to no change in real wage rates. He then followed Keynes with the proposition that since real wages have not fallen, employment cannot be increased. The doctrine of equiproportional wage and price declines has never been accepted by the classically minded economists who have advocated wage cuts as an anti-depression policy. With regard to this problem of wage cuts, there was also another Keynes. The second personality considered the effects of wage cuts on the structure of the entire determinate system; *i.e.*, upon the shifts induced upon the various schedules of the system. It is a much more fruitful line of attack to inquire as to the possible effects of a wage policy on investment, saving, and liquidity preference.

With the rest of Lerner's article there is little to contend, since it was a straightforward story of the *General Theory*.

Reddaway's article was one of the best reviews of the book. This writer saw clearly the fundamental contributions of the new economics and was one of the first to be able to formulate a mathematical model of the skeleton system. According to Reddaway, Keynes was primarily attacking one of Ricardo's basic assumptions — Say's Law, or the proposition that supply creates its own demand. The incompatibility of Say's Law with the determinate Keynesian theory is great, and it would be hopeless to try to derive the Keynesian results with a theory based on such principles.

Furthermore, Reddaway recognized the fault of the *Treatise*, namely, the study of stability or lack of stability of various price levels rather than the study of the determination of the level of output.

He wrote down the model of the Keynesian system as follows:

Savings which depend upon the level of national income = Investment which depends upon the rate of interest.

The autonomously determined supply of cash balances = the demand for cash balances which depends upon a function of national income plus a function of the rate of interest.

His skeleton is basically the same as the more general model of the preceding chapter, especially when account is taken of the probable shapes of these functions. Reddaway went all the way with Keynes in eliminating entirely the influence of interest rates upon savings. The current fashion is to include interest as a minor variable in this function. Reddaway also omitted income as a determinant of the level of investment. However, today it is recognized that some investment may be passively related to income. The treatment of the liquidity function as the sum of two separate functions is quite all right and is merely a special case of a more general relation, which states that the demand for cash balances depends upon the level of national income and the rate of interest. The split of this function into two parts is an attempt to bring out more strongly the dichotomy in the functions of money; *i.e.*, money as a medium of exchange and money as a store of value. Reddaway's (and Keynes') formulation attempted to maintain the last vestiges of the quantity theory of money.

The reviews of Lerner and Reddaway were hardly typical. The mere fact that personalities were not spared in Keynes' sarcastic attack upon the classical economists would lead one to expect many hostile reviews. Professor Pigou was cited in the *General Theory* as a particular exponent of the theory which Keynes was attacking, since Pigou had formulated most explicitly and elegantly the classical model. Pigou returned the blow with a bitter argument against the *General Theory*.[3] It is not difficult to see

[3] "Mr. J. M. Keynes' General Theory of Employment, Interest and Money," *Economica*, N.S. Vol. III, 1936, p. 115.

that Keynes was the winning economist but the losing gentleman; he hardly observed the rules of the academic game. Nevertheless Pigou's review shows quite plainly the breach between classical and Keynesian beliefs. Comparison with Pigou's later writings on this subject reveals a partial conversion to the new ideas.[4]

Pigou stated that the fundamental charge against the classics was that of the assumption of an equilibrium position built up around an intersection of a real demand and a real supply schedule for labor. He repeated the classical view that unemployment is not an equilibrium position in the classical system because money wage cuts would always lead to a decline in real wages and hence to more employment. What Pigou objected to in Keynes' argument was the claim that a cut in money wages would entail a fall in prices exactly by an amount which would leave real wages unchanged. Pigou may have been correct in disputing this Keynesian view, but he did not consider adequately the effect of money wage cuts on other variables of the system such as interest rates, investment and savings. An interesting point to be noted is that in the world of concrete policy, Keynes and Pigou were not entirely at opposite ends since the latter agreed that there would be many practical difficulties in carrying out a wage cut. But, on the whole, Pigou firmly believed that, with the proper banking policy, wage cuts, in practice, could be relied upon to raise the level of employment.

With regard to the developments which have been stressed in the preceding chapters, Pigou remained quite conservative and refused to give up his older views. He did not look upon saving decisions as complete in themselves; i.e., there has to be a corresponding act of investment to round out the saving process. According to him, the motives behind saving are investment opportunities or possibilities of future consumption. Pigou did firmly believe that a smooth-running saving process which changed only steadily would always be exactly offset by a similar smooth-running investment process. Only when sudden increases occur in the saving process could there be a lag of investment oppor-

---

[4] See especially *Employment and Equilibrium*, Macmillan, London, 1941, and "The Classical Stationary State," *Economic Journal*, Vol. LIII, 1943, p. 343.

tunities. But even this lag was considered temporary and of an entirely different order of magnitude from that which existed in Keynes' mind. Thus Pigou could not see the maintenance of the savings-investment equation as an important economic problem. Like other economists of the day, he was not able to envisage a lack of investment outlets. He made an argument similar to that attributed to Hawtrey in Chapter II [5] when he criticized the use of the multiplier theory on the ground that governmental expenditure for public works would exert an upward pressure on interest rates and thus cut private borrowing for purposes of investment. For the non-Keynesians, private and public investment are always compensating alternatives; any governmental investment will somehow be at the expense of private investment.

Keynes' day of judgment was not a worry for Pigou. If we should ever approach a situation in which people attempt to maintain savings on a high level with a failure of investment offsets (due to a previous exceedingly high rate of capital accumulation), then, Pigou predicted, money wages would be forced down by competition to keep people fully employed.

Finally, Pigou criticized Keynes on minor technicalities some of which are points well taken and some of which represent confusion. For example, Pigou did not understand how Keynes could take the stock of capital as given for the short run and then speak of a non-zero rate of investment. He had in mind the fallacious argument that if capital is regarded as given, then it can have no rate of change other than zero. However, those acquainted with the simplest concepts of the differential calculus know quite well that a variable can be given for each point of time and yet have a positive or negative rate of change over time.† Pigou also objected to the breaking of the liquidity-preference function into two parts, one depending upon income and the other upon interest. His argument here was that the transactions motive for holding cash (the Marshall "k"), which Keynes had not dropped, already depends on the rate of interest and includes the notions of liquidity preference. However, it is questionable whether the classical

[5] See p. 46.

economists, in their discussions of the quantity theory, did regard the transactions motive as a function of the interest rate. It is wrong also to think that the liquidity-preference theory does nothing more than make the transactions velocity of circulation of money depend upon the interest rate. We saw, at an earlier stage, that the argument of the *Treatise* was based to some extent on the proposition that velocity is a function of the rate of interest.

But the two "fundamental equations," which did relate the classical concept of velocity to the interest rate, were not related to the liquidity-preference theory. It was only the theory of bearishness coupled with an analysis behind the various motives for holding cash balances, including idle cash balances, that was related to the doctrine of liquidity preference. The classical treatment which viewed money only as a medium of exchange does not come to the same thing as the modern theory of Keynes even if the velocity (the Marshall "k") is made a function of the interest rate. At any rate, this whole problem has no effect on the Keynesian system, since it is possible in full generality to make the demand for money depend upon interest rates and income, and get all the important economic results. But there was one minor criticism by Pigou which does seem to be a well aimed blow. He did not like Keynes' verbiage on the "own" rates and the money rate of interest, including the involved explanation of the strategic importance of the money rate.[6] Pigou concluded, and correctly, that it makes no difference what standard of value is chosen. *Numéraire* problems are never essential problems in economic theory. One should be able to dismiss the own-rate analysis as one of the "red herrings" of the *General Theory*.

Pigou was not the only follower of classical tradition who felt injured by Keynes' assault. The *General Theory*, more so than any other modern work on economics, warranted a formidable array of reviewers. Professors Knight and Cassel joined the mob in the stoning of the revolutionary dissenter.

Knight,[7] in the first place, denied that Keynes actually refuted

[6] The own-rate of interest is the interest premium calculated in terms of the ratio of future to spot quantities of a particular commodity other than money.

[7] "Unemployment: and Mr. Keynes' Revolution in Economic Theory," *Canadian Journal of Economics and Political Science*, Vol. III, 1937, p. 100.

anything that can be called classical doctrine, in the modern sense. He looked upon the *General Theory* as an attack upon straw men. However, it would be very strange to consider Ricardo, Marshall, Pigou, Wicksell, Hawtrey, Hayek, Mises, Robbins, etc., as straw men! Keynes was revolting against all these theories which did not explain the phenomenon of effective demand. Knight could see no innovation in the Keynesian contribution. For example, in his consideration of the proposition that savings depend upon income in a definite way, Knight concluded that there is nothing new in this result, since it is a familiar point in classical writings that saving is an institutional matter, dependent on social psychology. But he did not bother to mention that whenever classical economists were thinking seriously about the savings-investment process, they worked with the theory of the determination of the interest rate. An appeal to side remarks of classical writers cannot eradicate the major differences between their ideas and Keynes' ideas of the savings-investment process.

Another point made by Knight, which is similar to a remark of D. H. Robertson's, was that the rate of interest can equate more than one set of desires simultaneously; *i.e.*, it can equate the desires for holding cash and non-monetary wealth, and it can equate the desires for lending and not consuming. Robertson criticized Keynes for not leaving more than one alternative open. But what Knight failed to do is to distinguish between a complete, interdependent system and a building-block theory. In working with the building-block theory from which any final construction must be built, we have to pick out the strategic variables in each relation and hold the others constant. Keynes took income to be the important variable in the savings-investment equation, and took interest to be the important variable in the liquidity-preference equation. In the end result of the most general Keynesian system one cannot pick out cause and effect. The interest theory of this system is the solution to the entire set of equations *which is based on the liquidity-preference building block.*

There is further a methodological issue to be settled with Knight. He, implied that there was something asymmetrical in Keynes' analysis due to the assumption first of unemployment and then

E

of the presence of obstacles to a return to full employment. Knight was aware that, historically, full employment has been the most usual state of affairs; therefore he argued that we should not assume unemployment, but instead full employment, and then explain how such a happy situation could end. Does not the multiplier theory work in reverse? If investment opportunities wear out due to a high level of capital accumulation, while saving habits persist, the multiplier equation will be in operation with the multiplicand [8] negative. Income will fall, and employment will decrease. It is as convenient to explain the upper turning point of the cycle with the Keynesian analysis as it is to explain the stagnant trough. One of the major differences pointed out in Chapter II between the over-investment theorists and Keynes was in the analysis of reasons why the boom comes to an end.

Knight claimed that all the Keynesian results follow only from assumptions of unemployment and rigidities. While this book does not deny that the rigidities exist and make the Keynesian analysis simpler, it does deny that they are essential to the theory. In particular, it was demonstrated in Chapter III that Keynes' results are still powerful in a frictionless system. It would be much more fruitful to shift the discussion from the assumptions of rigidities to realistic assumptions about the shapes of the important schedules of the Keynesian system.

Cassel [9] was another who came immediately to the defense of established doctrines. His review brings out very well the fact that Keynesian ideas are not those of classical economics. Cassel began his review with the support of a linear trend extrapolation, so frequent and so disrespected among economists. Past trends showed clearly to Cassel that wealth doubled every twenty-five years, and he firmly expected this trend to continue into the future. Hence he argued that since Keynes' book was primarily an attack on saving, it was plainly wrong in both fact and theory because savers would have a big job on their hands in supplying funds to meet the dou-

---

[8] The multiplicand is the change in investment with which the multiplied change in income is associated. Unlike the multiplier, the multiplicand can be either positive or negative.

[9] "Mr. Keynes' 'General Theory,'" *International Labor Review*, Vol. XXXVI, 1937, p. 437.

bling of wealth of the next twenty-five years. Cassel could not possibly imagine an exhaustion of investment opportunities, and even imagined potential investment outlets as standing in line awaiting satisfaction. He thought that every new amount saved would give rise to new investment, but he saw the savings-investment equation as being maintained solely by the rate of interest. He flatly declared that Keynes was wrong to substitute a theory of effective demand for a theory of interest. Also he was ready to discard entirely the concept of marginal efficiency of capital. For him, nothing but the interest rate could have any relation to investment.

Naturally, Cassel could not put up with the liquidity-preference theory of interest. Interest, according to him, is determined in the savings-investment equation, and the price level comes out of the quantity equation. He envisaged a general equilibrium system in which all relative prices are determined, and then allowed the introduction of a theory of money to determine the absolute level of prices. This system is in equilibrium when the supply of money is so regulated as to stabilize purchasing power. In the light of this background, he regarded Keynes' attempt to revive the Mercantilist ideas of a monetary theory of interest as a complete failure.

Finally, Cassel concluded that there always exists a solution to the general equilibrium equations which gives full employment and that there is no such thing as a general theory of unemployment. The following proof is taken from Cassel: Ideas such as the propensities to save or consume cannot possibly explain unemployment. Suppose the existence of a propensity to save such that there is unemployment. Now if all the unemployed die, there will be full employment and the same propensity to save; *ergo* Keynes is wrong.

The reader should not get the opinion at this stage that all the reviews, other than those by disciples, were made up entirely of destructive criticism. Hicks is an example of a non-Keynesian who gave the *General Theory* a more favorable review,[10] although he was unable to pick out the essential Keynesian development.

[10] "Mr. Keynes' Theory of Employment," *Economic Journal*, Vol. XLVI, 1936 p. 238.

He remarked that the casual reader may take the savings-investment equality to be the innovation of the book. Then he went on to say that this equality depends only upon definitions. Many of us who claim to be more than casual readers of all Keynes' more important works must side with these simple-minded folk and say that the innovation is "$S = I$," but that it is not a matter of definition alone. When one speaks of the equation $S = I$, he is speaking about savings and investment in the schedule sense and not as observable flows. However, we can agree with Hicks that the theory of expectations as put forth by Keynes was a real contribution, although not necessarily the major innovation as Hicks has put it.[11]

In his *Value and Capital* Hicks emphasized strongly the point that Keynes' interest theory and the loanable-funds interest theory come to exactly the same thing. The argument behind this demonstration, which is not entirely satisfactory, was already formulated in his earlier review article. There he said that there was nothing revolutionary about the liquidity-preference theory. It will be better to drop further discussion of this point now and to take it up in a later section on the interest controversy in this chapter.

In his evaluation of the connection between the Keynesian analysis and the real world, Hicks was not entirely an accurate observer. He accepted Keynes' ideas about fluctuations of the marginal efficiency of capital as being the important cyclical element, but he doubted the implied, longer-run prophecies that the marginal efficiency of capital would decline secularly. He considered Keynes' greatest card to be that of a declining population, because of all the things which maintained the marginal efficiency during the nineteenth century — such as population growth, inventions, new lands, confidence, wars — it appeared to Hicks that population was most likely to fail. We find today among the stagnationists that, while declining population growth is important, many other things are more important in depressing the level of the marginal efficiency of capital. Even if population were growing at an increasing rate, unemployment would be a problem.

[11] See also "Mr. Keynes and the 'Classics'; a Suggested Interpretation," *Econometrica*, Vol. V, 1937, p. 147, where Hicks singled out the liquidity-preference theory of interest as the feature which distinguishes Keynesian from classical economics.

There are other authors who are by no means of the Keynesian persuasion and yet who gave reviews of the *General Theory* which were certainly not hostile, an example being Professor Viner.[12] He concluded that the only difference between Keynes and the classical economists, with regard to such matters as the supply of labor and wage rates, was the former's denial that a cut in money wages will reduce unemployment. This conclusion was quite true, although the proper understanding of the difference depends upon one's view of the *modus operandi* of the wage cut as well as the final effect. The discussion built up around the models of the previous chapter was precisely an attempt to show why wage cuts do not assure full employment. The different assumptions about the supply curves of labor are not essential to the argument. Viner was one of the first critics to question Keynes' readiness to follow the classical correlation between real wage cuts and unemployment. He pointed out that this resulted from a too unqualified application of the principle of diminishing returns. However, Keynes would have countered with the argument that somewhere before full employment is reached, diminishing returns must set in, and then there will be the positive correlation between *real* wage cuts and increments in employment. Viner also pointed out at this time a pitfall in Keynes' definition of unemployment. He said that this definition implies a monotonically increasing supply curve of labor, something that can be doubted empirically and theoretically.

In general Viner claimed that he accepted the broad outlines of the Keynesian system but doubted Keynes' description of the working and quantitative structure of the system. Particularly Viner did not agree with the theory of liquidity preference because he thought that the transaction motive has as much influence on the rate of interest as the speculative motive.[13] He was not able to give up the quantity equation and divorce the concept of hoarding from the theory of velocity, being an expert in the relative manipulations of M, V, P, and T. But to show how far Viner

[12] "Mr. Keynes, on the Causes of Unemployment," *Quarterly Journal of Economics* Vol. LI, 1936, p. 147.

[13] This parallels Pigou's contention that the classical economists had already developed the relationship between the demand for cash and the interest rate by making the transactions velocity of circulation depend upon the rate of interest.

was from the Keynesian analysis, he remarked that savers with high hoarding propensities are not the source of trouble, because they ". . . have investment habits, and abhor idle cash as nature abhors a vacuum." He also said, "It would at least be interesting to know whether these are facts or fancies." The events of recent years urge one to wager heavily on "fancy."

Viner believed that Keynes did not actually refute the classical economists but merely pointed out that money wage cuts might lead to adverse expectations and stifle investment. Actually Keynes has enabled economists to demonstrate more than this, namely, that the classical mechanism is not the automatic lever which it was thought to be. Pigou, at least, has admitted that there may be practical difficulties in obtaining wage cuts, and that adverse expectations may set in, but on a higher level of abstraction he has argued that, in the absence of these obstacles, money wage cuts will always lead theoretically to full employment. One who really understands the working of Keynesian economics must dispute the classical point of view.

In conclusion of this review of reviews, it seems fitting to consider the attitudes of a Keynesian convert and a contemporary rival. No better choice could be found for the former category than Professor Hansen, who is undoubtedly this country's most famous Keynesian disciple. As shown above, though, Hansen held many views prior to 1936 which were not in agreement with the developments of the *General Theory*, and when he came to review this work, he was not yet a confirmed Keynesian. In his review [14] Hansen attempted to link up the new theory with Keynes' development. According to Hansen, the theoretical structure of the *Treatise* toppled because of his own and other criticisms. It is true that Hansen pointed out an error in one of Keynes' "fundamental equations," but the *Treatise* by no means stood upon so flimsy a foundation. The pretentious "fundamental equations" were not an essential part of the *Treatise*, and the most that can be said about the recognition of this error is that it was a valid criticism of trivial equations. The theory of the *Treatise* stands or falls on

[14] "Mr. Keynes on Underemployment Equilibrium," *Journal of Political Economy*, 1936, Vol. XLIV, p. 667.

the skeleton model written down in the appendix below. What actually knocked over the theory of the *Treatise* was the replacement of the savings-investment interest theory with a theory of output as a whole, and Mr. R. F. Kahn is responsible for this!

But Hansen did recognize immediately the important contribution of the *General Theory* and saw especially the divergence from the classical system. He pointed out that Keynes' criticism of the classics was not connected with the theory of price or distribution, but with the notion that there is a unique equilibrium point for output — at full employment. He recognized that the classical economists had no theory of output and employment as a whole. He went along entirely with Keynes on the view that the causal forces are found outside the price system in the psychology, expectations, habits and institutions of the population.

Hansen also claimed that it would have been better if Keynes had adopted D. H. Robertson's definitions [15] of savings and investment, because they give a clearer picture of the causal process. With this point of view, we cannot agree at all. The choice between the different definitions depends upon the type of system with which one wants to work — comparative statical or dynamical. If one wants to analyze merely the conditions under which different equilibrium situations exist, the definitions of Keynes are completely adequate. This issue will be taken up at greater length in a later section.

The final review to be considered here is that of Hawtrey,[16] Keynes' contemporary and rival for the leadership of British monetary policy. On the whole, Hawtrey's review was critical but not overly unfavorable. It does seem, though, that he was too preoccupied with a discussion of interest rates. In fact, Hawtrey considered the Keynesian thesis as primarily a revision of the classical interest theory. While this consideration is quite true, its meaningfulness depends upon what Hawtrey thinks Keynes used to replace the classical interest theory. The fact that Hawtrey centered so

---

[15] Robertson's definitions are in terms of arbitrarily defined periods. Savings of any given period equal income of the previous period minus consumption of the current period. Investment of any given period equals income of the current period minus consumption of the current period.

[16] *Capital and Employment*, Longmans Green, London, 1937, Ch. 7.

much of his review upon the Keynesian interest theory seems to imply that he looked upon the Keynesian innovation as the substitution of the theory of liquidity preference for the classical interest equation. If this is what Hawtrey meant, then the present author is not in agreement, but it is difficult to tell from his writing exactly what he did mean.

Hawtrey had some interesting and some confused things to say about the rate of interest. He was of the opinion that in many schemes of new investment the interest rate would play a subordinate role. He did not think that unfavorable interest rates would be an obstacle for promoters of new investment projects where there is competition in the carrying out of new ideas. Furthermore, he considered possibilities of the expansion of demand as a more powerful incentive than interest rates in stimulating investment. Hawtrey's opinions are all in agreement with what have lately been taken to be the structural characteristics of the Keynesian system. But there are two points of confusion with respect to interest rates. He accepted Keynes' idea that in equilibrium the rate of interest would be driven to equality with the marginal efficiency of capital, but his acceptance was too naïve. He thought that lower interest rates would be desirable during a depression; hence he concluded that we should attempt to lower the marginal efficiency in order to lower the interest rate. The Keynesians really want to raise the marginal efficiency of capital far above the interest rate or to lower the interest rate far below the marginal efficiency of capital. They never want to lower the marginal efficiency of capital! Another source of confusion was in the interpretation of the liquidity-preference equation. According to Hawtrey the theory behind this equation involves circular reasoning. He said that the monetary authority regulates the rate of interest through its control over cash balances, and that the demand for cash balances is based on what the public expects the monetary authority to do about the same, but that the authority only determines the rate via the liquidity-preference equation of the demand and supply of cash balances. This argument he believed to be circular. However, we cannot agree with him on this point. The demand for balances is a schedule representing how much idle cash the people will demand to hold at each interest rate, and its shape depends upon the expected future course of interest rates just as an ordinary demand function for a commodity depends upon the expected future price pattern. Once all expectations and psychological behavior are given, the demand function is completely specified.

On the other hand, the monetary authorities make a certain decision as to the supply which is to interact with the demand. This supply schedule is an independent function and depends upon the discount policy of the banking system. The banks autonomously set the rate of discount, which in turn determines the money supply. The discount rate and the market rate of interest are quite different variables, and the banks' control over the former does not involve circular reasoning in the theory of the determination of the latter. The monetary authorities, in their attempt to influence the interest rate, try to guess what is in the public's mind — *i.e.*, what is the form of their demand schedule for balances — and create balances accordingly, but this is not circular. It is merely interaction, typical of all markets in the economy.

In his criticism of the savings-investment relationship, Hawtrey concentrated entirely on Keynes' concepts of observables rather than on his concepts of schedules of economic behavior. However, Hawtrey's substitute definitions practically amount to a use of the terms as schedules. A description of Hawtrey's designed (active) and undesigned (passive) investment can be easily related to the concept of schedules.

A minor point on the matter of policy should be considered. Hawtrey declared that in times of depression it is not the government expenditure which gives rise to employment, but instead the government borrowing. He thought that this borrowing would have the same effect if the deficit were created by a remission of taxation. In the first place, it is the net injection of more purchasing power into the depressed system that gives rise to increased income. Hawtrey's plan of remission of taxes would mean borrowing without increased spending on the part of the government. If the former taxpayers spend their funds which otherwise would have gone into taxes and if the government does not cut down on its spending, then there will be a net injection of purchasing power to raise the level of income. But we can also get beneficial effects of spending without borrowing, for by balancing the budget at a high level the government can also create a net stimulus for the economy. In any case, either the government or private individuals must increase their spending if we are to do away with unemployment.[17]

THE WAGE CONTROVERSY

In the early pages of the *General Theory*, Keynes plunged immediately into the classical theory of wages. The discussion between the Keynesians and non-Keynesians, resulting from this attack, has actually been on two different issues. First there is the issue of the relation between the time paths of money and real wages, and secondly there is the much more important issue of the effects of money wage cuts upon employment.

The spark for the first question was set off by Keynes' conjecture that historical time series would show a negative correlation between the rates of change of money wage rates and of real wage rates. In a later article Keynes revealed the reasoning that lay behind this conjecture of the *General Theory*.[18] The conjecture was based on three general propositions: (1) the added cost of producing an extra unit of output (marginal cost) increases in the short run; (2) for a closed system, short-run marginal costs are not very different from short-run marginal wage costs; (3) prices are governed roughly by marginal costs. Later results have indicated that the short-run marginal cost curve is probably constant in the neighborhood of the existing levels of output and that there is so much imperfection in the system that prices are not at all equal to marginal costs. At any rate, Keynes' conjecture has not been found to be correct in the statistical investigations that have been made.

---

[17] Actually it is very easy to construct plausible models in which the multiplier effect of added government spending is greater than the multiplier effect of tax remission. One such model is that in which consumption or savings depend upon income *after* taxes and investment depends upon income *before* taxes.

[18] See "Relative Movements of Real Wages and Output," *Economic Journal*, Vol. XLIX, 1939, p. 34.

J. T. Dunlop [19] and L. Tarshis [20] both investigated the behavior of the time series of real and money wage rates. Dunlop found that in England increased money wage rates have been usually associated with increased real wage rates, but decreased money wage rates have been associated with both increased and decreased real wage rates. Tarshis' results were for the United States, where he found a high positive correlation between percentage changes in money wage rates and in real wage rates for the period 1932–1938. While these statistical investigations are not of the nature of "rigorous proofs," it appears that Keynes was backing the wrong horse.

Our main concern, however, is not with the empirical problem but with the theoretical relation of wage cuts to unemployment. In the classical models of the preceding chapter, unemployment is not possible as long as there exist wage flexibilities. Time and again in the anti-Keynesian literature we find the claim that if Keynes would have allowed money wages to be flexible downward in his system, an underemployment equilibrium would not be possible. Then these writers have concluded that Keynes' results follow only from his assumptions of rigidities. In addition to the results of Chapter III, above, we should examine more carefully what has come out of the literature on this subject in recent years.

Pigou [21] and Kaldor [22] engaged in the first serious discussion of this question soon after the ideas of the Keynesian system began to take hold. Pigou admitted that he was abstracting from institutional obstacles and from the possibility of adverse expectations. He then, of course, took the position that money wage cuts would lead to more employment. But in order to prove his point he made use of the proposition that the main influence of the wage cut would be on the interest rates. Thus far the Keynesians and the orthodox economists are not at odds. But when one stops to consider the

[19] "The Movement of Real and Money Wage Rates," *Economic Journal*, Vol, XLVIII, 1938, p. 413.

[20] "Changes in Real and Money Wages," *Economic Journal*, Vol. XLIX, 1939 p. 150.

[21] "Real and Money Wage Rates in Relation to Unemployment," *Economic Journal*, Vol. XLVII, 1937, p. 405, and "Money Wages in Relation to Unemployment," *Economic Journal*, Vol. XLVIII, 1938, p. 135.

[22] "Prof. Pigou on Money Wages in Relation to Unemployment," *Economic Journal*, Vol. XLVII, 1937, p. 745.

end result of the reduced rate of interest, the significance of the Keynesian Revolution is quite apparent. Pigou was, according to tradition, using the classical assumptions about the saving schedule; *i.e.*, that interest is an important variable in this function. Kaldor was very ready to point out that the Keynesian innovation was to change this function. If savings are sensitive to variations in the rate of interest, then the classical results become more plausible. If, in addition, we do *not* assume an interest-inelastic schedule of the marginal efficiency of capital or an interest-elastic schedule of liquidity preference, then the classical view is undoubtedly correct. But if we stay close to reality the various elasticities will probably not be of the type to insure the existence of income-creating effects of wage cuts. However, the results of Chapter III agree entirely with the remarks of the Pigou-Kaldor controversy, in that the ultimate effects of wage cuts depend upon the structural characteristics of the entire system.

One of the most important points to recall from this debate is that Pigou has admitted that money wage cuts will not increase employment unless interest rates are reduced as a result of the cut. Furthermore, he admitted that wage cuts and banking policies are merely alternative ways of inducing a change in the interest rate. These admissions show clearly where attention should concentrate when studying wage cuts within the framework of the Keynesian system. It very definitely removes the arguments from the misconceptions of rigidities and perfection of competition to the behavior outside the price system as such, *i.e.*, to the psychological and anticipational attitudes of the population.

While there is a mutual agreement as to the effect of wage cuts upon interest rates, there is not so much accord with respect to the effects upon saving and investing directly. Wages enter as a cost in profit calculations, and thus may have some influence on investment decisions. But wages enter also as a component of personal income, and thus have some influence on the demand for output, which in turn affects the level of investment.

If a wage cut transfers income from the wage earners to the non-wage earners of the population, then consumption will fall and savings will rise. The extent of the rise or fall depends upon the differences in the marginal propensities to consume out of wage income and non-wage income. We know that wage earners, on the whole, occupy the lower income classes where people spend a very large portion of every extra dollar of income. The sector of the population which receives income from dividends, rents, interest, profits, and royalties does not spend as much from each extra dollar of income, because its members are largely in the high income brackets. The initial impact of a wage cut may be a reduction in the level of consumption on the part of the high spenders in the population and an increase in comsumption on the part of the low spenders.

It is sometimes argued by economists that the demand for labor is elastic, *i.e.*, that a cut in wages may increase the total wage payments. If the wage bill is increased, then consumption will rise.

The entire consumption schedule will depend on the distribution between wages and non-wage income. If the distribution pattern is radically altered, a shift can occur in the position of the schedule. In the case where income is transferred away from the wage earners, the consumption schedule will fall and there will be a depressing influence on the level of prosperity. In the other case, the consumption schedule will rise. The end result is questionable.

Since investment depends on so many things other than current demand and costs, it is difficult to see the influence of wage cuts on the investment schedule. In so far as wage cuts set up unfavorable expectations of the future, investment will receive a very adverse shock. The economics of hyper-deflationary situations are very important and should not be ruled out. Large-scale wage cuts intended to alleviate unemployment are likely to cause a postponement of investment in anticipation of further wage cuts. Wage cuts could conceivably stimulate expectations, but such cases are rare.

In order for the net influence of wage cuts on income and employment to be significant there must be a shift of the investment function relative to the savings function. If there is a shift toward more investment but also toward more savings, the two effects may cancel each other. In order to make an unequivocal argument in favor of wage cuts, it will be necessary to show that there would be an upward shift of the investment schedule and a downward shift of the savings schedule. This particular shift pattern seems unlikely, and the present writer must remain unconvinced by the arguments that wage cuts cure depressions.

The famous arguments over the Keynesian proposition, $S = I$, are usually laughingly referred to as wasted hours spent on matters of definition. This attitude misses much of the point. The peculiar thing about this controversy, though, is that its settlement is much more important to theory than to policy. It is undoubtedly true that some of the most distinguished leaders in economic policy are not entirely clear about the savings-investment equation. In contrast, the preceding discussion of the wage question involves a very different situation. It makes a good deal of difference whether one advocates wage cuts or some inflationary measure during periods of unemployment. The theoretical analysis of the effect of wage cuts may have profound influence on the governmental economic policy actually followed.

The entire confusion in connection with the savings-investment controversy can be traced to a failure to distinguish between *schedules* and *observables*. The savings schedule is a relation between savings, income, and the interest rate which gives the amount of savings corresponding to each possible pair of values of the interest rate and national income. The investment schedule is similarly a relation between investment, income, and the interest rate which gives the amount of investment corresponding to each possible pair of values of the interest rate and national income. Suppose, for the moment, that savings and investment are independent of the interest rate. This is a good first approximation. There is then one relationship between savings and income, and an independent relationship between investment and income. If these two schedules are smooth curves, as we believe them to be, there will exist a unique level of national income such that savings calculated from the savings schedule equal investment calculated from the investment schedule. This is the savings-investment equation in the schedule sense.

The term "observable savings" refers to that particular level of savings calculated from the savings schedule from a knowledge of the unique equilibrium value of national income which equates savings and investment. Observable investment is calculated from the investment schedule at the same level of national income. The observable values of savings and investment are single points, while the schedules of savings and investment form continuous series of points along curves.

The economic process is viewed as made up of a series of intersection or equilibrium points of savings and investment schedules. The observed level of national income for each time point can be considered as the equilibrium level of income corresponding to a set of savings-investment schedules. The observed levels of savings and investment are those two values on the schedules corresponding to the observed level of income. All the other values of savings and investment along the schedules are not observed; they are virtual levels of savings and investment corresponding to levels of national income other than that level which actually takes place. The virtual levels of savings and investment are not equal.

Keynes is somewhat to blame for not making the proper distinction himself. Thus he said:

Income = value of output = consumption + investment
Saving = income − consumption
Therefore saving = investment.[23]

Here he was talking about saving and investment as observables. But elsewhere he said, "The traditional analysis has been aware that saving depends upon income, but it has overlooked the fact that income depends on investment, in such fashion that, when investment changes, income must necessarily change in just that degree which is necessary to make the change in saving equal to the change of investment." [24] This latter statement referred to a process of adjustment which achieves an equilibrium.

The same situation occurs in the familiar theory of supply and demand. As observables over time, supply and demand are always equal in so far as they just represent opposite sides of the same transaction. But as static schedules, supply and demand are related

[23] *General Theory*, p. 63.   [24] *Ibid.*, p. 184.

in a genuine equation and are not identical. In the latter instance one can talk about divergences between supply and demand at *virtual, unobserved* prices. Similarly, one can talk about divergences of savings and investment at *virtual, unobserved* levels of income.

It is correct but uninteresting to say that supply and demand or savings and investment represent in each case opposite sides of the same transaction. It follows from definitions and not from economic theory that all demanded goods or invested funds come from somewhere. If we designate "somewhere" by supply in the first case and by savings in the second, nothing has been added to our understanding of the working of the economic system. But if we construct the theories that supply and demand are equal, at the going market price, and that savings and investment are equal, at the going level of national income, then we have some real analytical tools.

The idea of regarding any observed value of national income as the equilibrium value corresponding to an equation between savings and investment, in the schedule sense, is somewhat artificial. A more realistic view is that the observed levels of national income are observed as the result of a continuous dynamical process. Dynamical processes have been long constructed to apply to demand and supply in individual markets. A familiar dynamical scheme runs as follows: Supply depends upon the price level; demand depends upon the price level; and the rate of change of price depends upon the difference between supply and demand such that prices go up when demand exceeds supply and prices go down when supply exceeds demand. It is very simple to form a mathematical model of this market structure and determine the exact time paths of each of the variables involved.[25]

In the above example, price serves as the equilibrating variable which always adjusts so as to bring supply and demand into equilibrium. The analogue of this adjustment process in the Keynesian system can easily be formulated in terms of a dynamical model. In this model, savings depend upon the level of income;

[25] Numerous models have been constructed by P. A. Samuelson, "The Stability of Epuilibrium, Comparative Statics and Dynamics," *Econometrica*, Vol. IX, April, 1941, q.97.

investment depends upon the level of income; the rate of change of income depends upon the difference between savings and investment such that income rises when investment exceeds savings, and income falls when savings exceed investment. In equilibrium, income has a zero rate of change; it is neither rising nor falling. The equilibrium, in this sense, implies that there is no difference between savings and investment. Thus the Keynesian savings-investment equation can be looked upon as the equilibrium solution of a dynamical system. In exactly the same way, the usual supply-demand equation can also be looked upon as the equilibrium solution of a dynamical system.

It is obvious that the behavior of prices in relation to divergences between supply and demand can be succinctly stated in terms of inventory fluctuations, because the difference between supply and demand is defined as the rate of change of inventories. Goods which are supplied but not demanded, accumulate in the form of stocks or inventories. The price adjustment relationship can be restated as: the rate of change of prices varies inversely with the rate of accumulation of inventories. It will now be shown that the savings-investment equation can also be formulated in terms of inventory accumulation. This formulation will be helpful in acquiring an understanding of certain cyclical patterns of national income.

National income as calculated by the Department of Commerce, the National Bureau of Economic Research, and other organizations is defined as the sum of expenditures on consumer goods, expenditures on fixed capital, expenditures on working capital (= inventory accumulation), expenditures by the government on goods and services, and the net foreign balance. Neglect, for expository purposes, the last two items, for they have nothing to do with that which follows.

The expenditures on working capital, or inventories, are of two types. One type of inventory expenditure is made by the business man for transactions, precautionary, or speculative motives. A firm must hold a certain amount of goods on hand to fill orders as they come in; furthermore it may hold goods in anticipation of price rises or liquidate its holdings in anticipation of price drops. In any case, it will demand a certain amount of goods in response to rational economic motives. The other type of inventories which entrepreneurs hold are those that they are forced to hold because the market will not take all their supply at suitable prices. These inventories are stocks of goods that business men hold but which they did not intend to hold according to rational economic calculations based on the transaction or speculative motive. They are unintended inventories.

Now say that investment includes the intended expenditures on working capital but not the unintended expenditures. Then the fundamental definition of national income reads: consumption plus investment plus unintended inventory accumulation is national income. We have also defined savings to be that part of national income which is not consumed. These two definitions lead to the following result: The difference between savings and investment is equal to unintended inventory accumulation.

In the light of this definition of the divergence between savings and investment, let us consider again our dynamical theory. The rate of change of income varies inversely with the difference between savings and investment, or, what is the same, the rate of change of income varies inversely with unintended inventory accumulation. This statement implies a sensible theory of entrepreneurial behavior. When inventories accumulate, entrepreneurs cut production and sell out of stock; when inventories are being depleted, they increase production in order to fill market orders. In equilibrium when incomes are not rising or falling, it must follow that unintended inventories are not rising or falling, and savings equal investment. The equilibrium condition which brings about an equality between savings and investment is that unintended inventories are being neither accumulated nor depleted.

A graphical picture of the savings-investment equation can be presented in terms of the savings and investment schedules directly, as was done in Fig. 1, or in terms of the consumption and investment schedules. The latter exposition is widely used in current discussions involving economic policy.

The straight line which is inclined 45 degrees toward either axis is that line along which the horizontal coordinate is always the same as the vertical coordinate. The curve C is the consumption schedule showing how much the community will spend on consumer goods (vertical axis) corresponding to each level of community income (horizontal axis). We add vertically to each point of the C-curve, the level of investment corresponding to each level of income. The investment schedule is thus the vertical distance between the C-curve and the $(C + I)$-curve, which gives a particular level of investment for each level of income. Savings are given by the vertical distance between the 45-degree line and the C-curve. Savings are negative up to the point where the C-curve crosses the 45-degree line, zero at this crossing point, and positive beyond this point to the right. The value of income, Y_0, has two interpretations. It is the unique level of income such that consumption expenditures

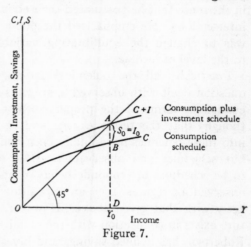

Figure 7.

out of this income plus investment expenditures out of this same income exactly add up to this same income. The equilibrium level of income in this type of graph is always given where the $(C + I)$-curve of total spending (consumption plus investment schedule) crosses the 45-degree line.

The other interpretation of Y_0 is that it is the only level of income such that investment, as measured by the vertical distance between the $(C + I)$-curve and the C-curve, is equal to savings, as measured by the vertical distance between the 45-degree line and the C-curve. The equilibrium level of savings, S_0, equals the equilibrium level of investment, I_0, but both S and I are measured by different schedules.

This graph represents the building block which forms the entire cornerstone of the Keynesian system.

When Keynes answered his critics on the savings-investment

equation, he had in mind the schedule relation.[26] We know this for two reasons. First, he explained the equation by citing the analogy of supply-and-demand equations in ordinary markets. He was thinking of savings-and-investment schedules exactly as we think of supply-and-demand schedules. Secondly, he claimed that he was old-fashioned in postulating the equality of savings and investment. He actually meant that he was old-fashioned in the sense that he postulated their equality as a result of schedule intersections. He emphasized the point that his real contribution was to change the equilibrating variable from the interest rate to the level of income.

Practically all the polemical articles of recent years on this question dealt with observed aggregates and did not get to a discussion in terms of the proper concept of schedules. It seems, though, that the terms *ex-ante* and *ex-post* which were injected into these polemics have finally been boiled down to mean nothing but schedules and observables. If *ex-ante* quantities are taken to be schedules of economic behavior and *ex-post* quantities to be observed aggregates, then an exposition in these terms agrees exactly with that given above. However, a confusion in the literature exists in connection with the definitions of D. H. Robertson.[27] Robertson has defined savings and investment in terms of periods which may be taken to be of some given length. The exact method of choosing the length is not relevant to the current discussion. Robertson defined savings to be income received in the immediately preceding period which is not spent on consumer goods in the current period. He then defined investment to be the income of the current period less the consumption of the current period.

Many writers seem to think that there is some mystical, superior power in these definitions. It is often claimed that these definitions are better because they are dynamic and because they allow one to speak of differences between savings and investment. Both claims are confused. Robertson's definitions are dynamic only in the most trivial sense. They define observed aggregates at different

---

[26] "Alternative Theories of the Rate of Interest," *Economic Journal*, Vol. XLVII, 1937, p. 241.

[27] "Saving and Hoarding," *Economic Journal*, Vol. XLIII, September, 1933, p. 399.

points of time, but they give no functional relations of economic behavior, so that one can solve for each variable in the system as a function of time alone. Robertson did not realize the existence of a consumption schedule, a savings schedule, or an investment schedule. He has set up a few lagged definitions but has presented no truly dynamical relations. Although, if Robertson's lagged definitions are inserted into the Keynesian functions, then a dynamical system can be developed. This can be done as follows:

Savings which depend upon the current interest rate and lagged income = investment which depends upon the current interest rate and current income.

The autonomous supply of money = the demand for money, which depends on the current interest rate and the current income.

This is a truly dynamical Keynesian system, in which one can determine the time path of all variables of the system. To make the system dynamical, it is necessary to postulate that expenditure on consumption is made out of the income of the previous period. Robertson has supplied this idea, but he did not supply a theory of the consumption function which gives a definite behavior relation between consumption and income. As for the other alleged superiority of the Robertsonian definitions, it is not the only formulation which admits divergences between savings and investment. Such divergences are also permitted in the Keynesian definitions — but not at observable levels of income, only at virtual levels. In a static Keynesian system, there can be differences between savings and investment only when the system is not in equilibrium. Similarly, in the static theory of supply and demand, there can be differences between supply and demand only at virtual prices which are not equilibria.

THE INTEREST CONTROVERSY

The phenomenon of interest presents one of the most difficult problems of economic theory. Economists are now, however, coming to the view that the rate of interest is not a very important variable in the modern economic world, but theories of the rate of interest are in a most unsatisfactory state.† Keynes has opened the road, and economists must in the future study more carefully the motives behind the holding of money as against earning assets.

The controversy of present concern is that between the liquidity-preference (Keynesian) theorists and the loanable-funds [28] theorists. There are two questions essentially: (1) Are the two theories the same? (2) If they are not the same, which theory is the better? The answer to the first question would be a simple and straight-forward economic analysis if the loanable-funds theorists would only define precisely what is meant by loanable funds. It shall be shown below that it is quite simple to answer question (1) when certain specific definitions that have been used by loanable-funds theorists are assumed. The other question is less easy to handle, but the liquidity-preference theory is preferable under those definitions where the two theories are not the same.

There have been at least three attempts in the literature to prove that the two theories give identical results, but all three proofs must be rejected as unsatisfactory. The attempt of Hicks was mentioned previously.[29] He argued that interest, like all other prices, is determined as a solution of a general equilibrium system of n equations. He made the old argument that one equation follows from all the rest and that it can be eliminated. As far as Hicks was concerned, this was all the apparatus that he needed to prove his point, since he then had the choice of eliminating either the equation of supply and demand for money or the equation of supply and demand for credit. Depending upon which equation he eliminated, he could be either a loanable-funds theorist or a liquidity-preference theorist. If, as Mr. Lerner has publicly remarked, he had eliminated the supply of and demand for peanuts, what then?†

In this case, he cannot claim to be either a loanable-funds theorist or a liquidity-preference theorist, and yet the rate of interest gets determined. Hicks was quite correct in stating that the same rate of interest is obtained as a solution to the system of equations no matter what single equation is eliminated, but nothing has been proved by this argument. It does not tell whether the rate of in-

---

[28] These theorists maintain that the rate of interest is determined by the supply and demand for loanable funds. The discussion to follow in the text will attempt to point out the various definitions of loanable funds which have been suggested.

[29] See *Value and Capital*, London, Oxford, 1939, Chapter XII.

terest is the mechanism which allocates funds into idle hoards as opposed to earning assets or which brings the supply and demand for loans into equilibrium. It does not tell which building-block should be fitted into a determinate system.

The mere enumeration of equations and variables is misleading. It is necessary to the Keynesian theory that the shapes as well as the number of schedules be taken into account. The liquidity-preference theory, being a genuine part of the completely determined Keynesian system, is always consistent with the conditions imposed upon the shapes of the schedules. Since the loanable-funds theory has never been made part of a completely determined system, there is no assurance that it will be consistent with the conditions of the Keynesian system. In fact, according to certain definitions, the supply and demand for loanable funds reduces in some cases to the savings-investment equation. It was shown in the previous chapter that the savings-investment theory of interest does not satisfy the Keynesian conditions.

Imagine the case where all investment is made from borrowed capital and all funds to finance this borrowing are made from current savings. The supply of loanable funds in some versions of the theory is the same as savings, and the demand for loanable funds is the same as investment. A loanable-funds theory of interest should imply that regardless of the levels of other variables influencing savings and investment, there should always exist a rate of interest which will equate savings and investment. The Keynesian theory shows that there do exist levels of the other variables, namely full-employment income, such that no positive rate of interest will equate savings and investment.

Another reconciliation of liquidity preference with loanable funds was attempted by Lerner.[30] He defined the supply of credit as savings plus the net increase in the amount of money during a period, and the demand for credit as investment plus the net

---

[30] "Alternative Formulations of the Theory of Interest," *Economic Journal*, Vol. XLVIII, June, 1938, p. 211. In a recent article, Lerner has restated his views on interest theory, but there seems to be no change of his position on the consistency of the loanable-funds and liquidity-preference theories. See "Interest Theory: Supply and Demand for Loans or Supply and Demand for Cash," *Review of Economic Statistics*, Vol. XXVI, May, 1944, p. 88.

hoarding during the period. These are precise definitions of the supply and demand for loanable funds, and, moreover, have been approved by an eminent loanable-funds theorist, Professor Haberler.[31] Use of these definitions shall be made. Denote the net increase in the amount of money by ΔM and the net hoarding by ΔL; Lerner's version of the reconciliation has been graphically illus-

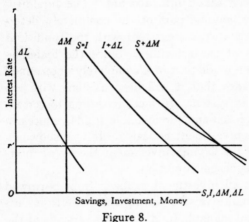

Figure 8.

trated as in the accompanying figure.

Lerner argued that the supply of loanable funds $(S+\Delta M)$ during the current period is brought into equilibrium with the demand for loanable funds $(I + \Delta L)$ during the current period at the rate, r'. He then went on to say that this same rate will equate the demand and supply for money, giving consistency with the liquidity-preference theory. This latter result was achieved by adding a constant, M_0, the amount of money held at the beginning of the period, to both the ΔM and ΔL curves. There is a serious pitfall in his procedure. It was an error to make the savings and investment schedules coincident. If this were the correct presentation of the saving-investment process, then there might not be a determinate system, and the theoretical base might rest upon Say's Law, in the sense that savings are automatically the same as investment without there being a mechanism which brings them into equilibrium. In Lerner's graph, income is treated as an arbitrary constant. Let it be supposed that income is at the full-employment level. Then the S-curve and the I-curve are as drawn in Fig. 4 of the preceding chapter. They do not intersect in the relevant portion of the graph. Consequently when the curves ΔM and ΔL are added to them respectively, the resulting curves will

---

[31] See *Prosperity and Depression*, League of Nations, Geneva, 1939, p. 184.

not intersect along the line r'. We cannot accept Lerner's two-dimensional theorem, which leaves out of account the level of income.

The above demonstration is certainly in agreement with the intuitive idea that the liquidity-preference theory, because it is stated in dimensions of stocks, cannot be identical with the loanable-funds theory, which is stated in terms of flows.

A third attempt was made by Fellner and Somers to prove that the two theories amount to the same thing.[32] Perhaps this attempt was successful, but if it was, then definitions of supply and demand for loanable funds take on some new connotations. Working with a building-block theory and assuming income as given, these writers broke up the liquidity-preference function into three parts: (1) the demand for goods other than claims; (2) the demand by people for their own money; (3) the demand for claims. The entire problem revolves around the definition of claims, for these define the demand for loanable funds in their analysis. They handled this problem as follows:

> The definition of claims is admittedly arbitrary and must depend on what we want to call "the rate of interest" (*i.e.*, on what we want to include, by definition, in the interest structure). But once we have decided on any definition of "claims" we must, of course, be consistent in what we regard as "the rate of interest," since the latter is but a slightly different expression for the price of claims.[33]

It is possible to define claims so that the two theories become identical.

On the supply side they also separated three categories: (1) the supply of goods other than claims; (2) the supply by people of their own money; (3) the supply of claims. Then they took the supply of goods other than claims and the demand for goods other than claims as independent of the interest rate and equal in any general equilibrium situation.[34] Also they used the identity that the de-

[32] "Alternative Monetary Approaches to Interest Theory," *Review of Economic Statistics*, Vol. XXIII, 1941, p. 43.

[33] *Ibid.*, note 13, p. 45.

[34] This is, of course, unsatisfactory because it follows only from the enumerating of variables and equations without considering the influence of the shape and position of all schedule relations.

mand by people for their own money equals the supply by people of their own money regardless of the interest rate. With these two relations, it follows that the sum of their three supply categories is equal to the sum of their three demand categories at the same interest rate for which the demand and supply of claims are equal. The first equality they call the liquidity-preference equation, and the second equality they call the loanable-funds equation, and both equalities lead to the same interest rate. Their procedure, in effect, amounts to defining that part of the equation of the supply of and demand for money which depends upon the interest rate as the supply of and demand for loanable funds. If this is what the loanable-funds theorists mean, then they have a theory which is quite consistent with the liquidity-preference theory, but they cannot characterize the loanable-funds theory in this guise as a theory of flows. Fellner and Somers have defined claims as the stock of earning assets other than that which one supplies and demands of his own earning assets.

If the two theories are stated in terms of stock dimensions rather than flow dimensions, then they will come to the same thing and there is nothing to choose between them. But the more usual treatment of the loanable-funds theory is in terms of flows, while the liquidity-preference theory is unequivocally one of stocks. In the more usual cases there do exist reasons for the superiority of the Keynesian theory. T. de Scitovszky [35] has stated, better than anyone else, the economic reasons why an interest theory should be a theory of stocks rather than of flows.

Scitovszky has pointed out that in ordinary supply-and-demand analysis, price is the allocating mechanism between two flows, and that this approach is legitimate when dealing with commodities for which there are not large stocks or for which the stocks are independent of the price. But in the case in which stocks are significant and are dependent upon price, he claimed that the equation of supply-demand flows may not lead to the correct result. His argument amounts to the following: Suppose that current production and consumption flows for some good are in equilibrium at

---

[35] "A Study of Interest and Capital," *Economica*, N. S., Vol. VII, 1940, p. 293.

the current market price and that this price is also an equilibrium point for the supply and demand for stocks. If now there is a shift of consumer demand for the good, the establishment of a new price at which the two flows will be in equilibrium will be retarded by the adjustment of stocks to the new price. If the shift of demand represents a decrease in consumers' desires for the good, price will tend to fall in order to bring the flow schedules into equilibrium. But then the holders of stocks may want to increase their holdings at the lower price. Hence the stockholder behavior may counteract the flow adjustment and can prevent it from taking place.

It is certainly obvious that money and earning assets are commodities which do possess very large stocks. We know that interest is earned on existing stocks of assets as well as on the current flows. Interest is not the allocating mechanism between the supply and demand for credit flows, rather the allocating mechanism between the holdings of stocks of earning and non-earning assets.

By a very neat argument based on the theories of consumer behavior and utility, Scitovszky was able to show that the demand for the holding of securities is a decreasing function of price. The argument gives a formal substantiation of Keynes' assumptions about the shape of the liquidity function.

In essence, the Keynesian contribution was to point out that people can make two distinct types of decisions. They may decide upon saving or consuming their incomes, and they may decide upon holding idle cash or non-liquid securities. Each decision requires an economic calculation. In the former case, individuals decide on the basis of their incomes how much they want to spend on consumption and at the same time how much they want to save. In the latter case, they must decide on the basis of alternative rates of return (*i.e.*, interest rates) whether they want to hold their historically accumulated savings in the form of cash or securities. The distinction between these two sets of decisions clearly calls for a liquidity-preference theory of interest.

CHAPTER V

ANTICIPATIONS OF THE *GENERAL THEORY*

"Those who are strongly wedded to what I shall call 'the classical theory' will fluctuate, I expect, between a belief that I am quite wrong and a belief that I am saying nothing new." [1] Did Keynes actually say something new? He certainly said something quite different as compared with what most other economists were saying at the time, but it is not difficult to find in the literature of economics many of the same ideas earlier expressed. In fact, somewhere in literature every element of the Keynesian system was at some time discussed. But no single theorist ever worked out a complete and determinate model based on (1) the propensity to consume (save), (2) the marginal efficiency of capital, and (3) liquidity preference.† All the predecessors of Keynes to be discussed in this chapter failed to make use of one or more of the Keynesian ideas. Furthermore, many of these forerunners had not clearly in their minds the theoretical formulations, and it is often necessary to read between the lines in order to reconcile their views with those of today. We shall make no attempt to consider every author in history who discussed economic problems along the lines of Keynesian analysis, but shall merely select some of the better known cranks, heretics, and respectable economists who have concerned themselves with the problem of unemployment.

EARLY IDEAS ON SAVINGS AND INVESTMENT

We saw above that the generalized model of the Keynesian system can be written as a savings-investment equation and a liquidity-preference equation. But since there has never appeared evidence of any previous writer's working with this determinate system, the present study must be confined to one of building-blocks, for these did appear throughout much of the literature.

[1] *General Theory*, p. v.

Nobody, apparently, anticipated both building-blocks, and the writers who are included in this chapter can be conveniently classified according to which building-block they did anticipate. In this section, then, are included those economists who have at some time worried about the problems of saving and investing — the under-consumptionists.

In many cases it is impossible to say whether or not any earlier writers could have had any direct influence on the development of Keynes' ideas. It may be that he always developed his ideas independently, and then pointed out others who had previously expressed similar ideas. But in one instance, we can be reasonably sure that Keynes derived a profound inspiration. T. R. Malthus, a respectable and highly competent economist, was openly admired by Keynes, and, at a time when the revolution was about to be executed. In his *Essays in Biography*,[2] finished by February, 1933, Keynes paid great tribute to Malthus and particularly noted the latter's discussion of effective demand. As was mentioned in a previous chapter, the break between Keynes and his contemporaries can be likened in many ways to the dispute which occurred after the Napoleonic Wars between Malthus and Ricardo. The issues in each case were essentially the same. Malthus and, later, Keynes wanted to replace Say's Law with a theory of effective demand. There can be little doubt that Keynes was aware of this historical similarity and must have profited much from a perusal of the early literature.

Like the Keynesian Revolution, Malthus' contribution to the problem of unemployment was a product of his times. He lived through the prosperous, developmental period of the Industrial Revolution and then the later boom of the Napoleonic Wars. But following the wars was a period of great unemployment and depression without a very rapid recovery. The influence of the socio-economic milieu showed up very much in the Malthusian economics. Malthus was impressed, as were so many economists in the recent interwar period, by the contradictory phenomenon of poverty in the midst of plenty. The prevalent unemployment was all the

[2] *Essays in Biography*, Harcourt, Brace, New York, 1933.

more a problem since it was unnecessary. The economic resources were available and the population desired the fruits of the employment of these resources. But Malthus saw something that those preoccupied with Say's Law could not possibly see, namely, that while the people desired to consume they did not demand effectually to consume. A theory of effective demand was necessary to explain the then current depression.

As is well known, Say, Ricardo, and Mill held that a general glut of the market could not occur. They maintained that maladjustments could occur in specific industries to create temporary shortages and gluts. But in general, they postulated that production regulates consumption via Say's Law. At the market rate of interest, they held that all savings go automatically into investment. This is the doctrine which Malthus denied in his *Principles of Political Economy*, first published in 1820. He, instead, claimed that effective demand determines consumption, which in turn determines production.

If Malthus had developed a complete theory of the determination of effective demand he would have been very close to the present Keynesian system. He knew why effective demand is important, and he knew its true meaning, but he had no adequate theory of how it gets determined. Such has been the case with most of the under-consumption theorists. They have adequately analyzed only part of the process. They understood well the savings-consumption side of the picture, but they usually failed to integrate it properly with the investment side.

Malthus knew that saving is a necessary condition for the occurrence of capital accumulation, but he did not argue that saving must take place at the expense of consumption. He gave a clear explanation of a way in which both savings and consumption could increase in a period of unemployment. He said:

It [saving] may take place, and practically almost always does take place, in consequence of a previous increase in the value of the national revenue, in which case a saving may be effected, not only without any diminution of demand and consumption, but under an actual increase of demand, consumption and value during every part of the process. And it is in fact this previous increase in the value of the national revenue which both gives the great stimulus to accumulation, and makes that accumulation effective in the continued production of wealth.[3]

Here Malthus recognized that savings depend upon income such that an increase in income leads to an increase of savings. Also since we know that he understood the relationship between consumption and savings as alternative ways of disposing of income, it follows from his statement that the marginal propensity to save is less than unity because the increment to income which he envisaged was made up of an increment to savings and an increment to consumption. He was able to imagine a situation in which both savings and consumption could increase only because he did not follow his contemporary classical economists in taking the level of output as given. He spoke over and over of saving habits and attitudes, and provided a basis for the theory of the savings schedule.

In addition to a theory of the saving process, Malthus saw how savings interact with investment, but he never went adequately behind motives for investment. At times he seemed to imply that investment is entirely a function of national income. Consider the following quotation:

. . . but the national saving, in reference to the whole mass of producers and consumers, must necessarily be limited by the amount which can be advantageously employed in supplying the demand for produce; and to create this demand, there must be an adequate and effective consumption either among the producers themselves, or other classes of consumers.[4]

The substance of the above two quotations signifies that Malthus might have been working with the proposition that the equation of savings and investment determines the level of effective demand, but the exposition is not clear-cut. A better analysis of what determines the shape and position of the investment schedule would probably have led to a Malthusian Revolution.

Now that we have in mind some of the major points of the Malthusian theory of employment, let us consider some of the more specific arguments which Malthus made that are relevant to modern economics. In agreement with his views about the savings

[3] *Principles of Political Economy.* Reprinted by International Economic Circle, Tokyo, in collaboration with the London School of Economics and Political Science, 1936 (first published 1820), pp. 365–366.
[4] *Ibid.*, p. 401.

function, he was aware that income and wealth distribution have some effect upon the level of savings. He realized that savings come out of larger incomes or land holdings and that a more equitable distribution of income would stimulate consumption. He said unambiguously that:

> Thirty or forty proprietors, with incomes answering to between one thousand and five thousand a year, would create a much more effectual demand for the necessaries, conveniences, and luxuries of life, than a single proprietor possessing a hundred thousand a year.[5]

Malthus had some enlightened views with regard to the public debt and its effect upon the economy. Being a good theorist, he realized that the public debt is not theoretically a problem, provided the interest burden does not exhaust the national income. But also being alive to the practical issues of the real world, he was against the public debt as an unnecessary evil. He objected to the debt on three grounds: 1. He thought that taxation to meet the interest payments might be an obstacle to production. 2. The mass of population considered the debt to be a bad thing and would be relieved by its liquidation. 3. It would accentuate the evils of inflation and deflation, harming some class no matter which event occurred. It is interesting to see that he linked his theory of employment with the attitudes of the population.

Malthus was disappointing on one question, that of wage cuts in relation to unemployment. We should expect that one who emphasized so strongly the theory of effective demand would not have considered money wage cuts as a stimulus to employment. His argument followed along the strictest classical lines of thought:

> An extension of foreign commerce, according to the view which Mr. Ricardo takes of it, would, in my opinion, place us frequently in the situation in which this country was in the early part of 1816, when a sudden abundance and cheapness of corn and other commodities, from a great supply meeting a deficient demand, so diminished the value of the income of the country, that it could no longer command the same quantity of labour at the same price; the consequence of which was that, in the midst of plenty, thousands were thrown out of employment — a most painful but almost unavoidable preliminary to a fall in the money wages of labour, which it is obvious could alone enable the

---

[5] *Ibid.*, p. 374.

general income of the country to employ the same number of labourers as before, and, after a period of severe check to the increase of wealth, to recommence a progressive movement.[6]

Let us state now a summary of Malthus' view of the cyclical pattern and his positive program for reform. His business-cycle theory was [7] that in prosperity the wealthy individuals save larger amounts out of their increasing incomes, and thereby enable investment and the hiring of productive laborers to take place. As a result of the passage of savings into investment, more goods are put on the market for sale, but since there is a limit to the available number of workers and since it takes time to change consumption habits, the effective demand for consumption does not rise fast enough and there is a glut of the market. The savings of the wealthy thus give rise to a lack of effective demand. The system then goes into a depression, and production falls off. With money wage cuts and more favorable opportunities for profit, recovery is initiated. He advocated as an ameliorative measure the maintenance of unproductive consumption through public-works schemes. The concept of unproductive consumption was Malthus' main contribution to a solution of the economic problem. An unproductive consumer was defined as one who sells services without producing concrete goods for the market in return. Factory laborers sell their services to the employer and produce goods in return. In the Malthusian scheme, they are productive consumers. But servants who sell their services to their master and produce no concrete goods come under his definition of unproductive consumers. Malthus believed that our salvation lay in unproductive consumers since they have purchasing power to clear the glut from the market and do not add anything to the glut as a result of their economic services. In many respects the ideas of Foster and Catchings, to be explained below in this section, were similar to Malthus' ideas built around unproductive comsumption. However, Keynes would have to disagree with Malthus (and Foster and Catchings) and argue that in periods of unemployment a high level

[6] *Ibid.*, p. 393.
[7] See James J. O'Leary, "Malthus and Keynes," *Journal of Political Economy*, Vol. L., 1942, p. 901.

F

of investment, whether it employs productive or unproductive consumers as laborers, would be a net stimulus to the level of income and prosperity.

After Malthus, and some of his contemporaries, the next writers of the under-consumption school did not flourish until the turn of the century, when Hobson was beginning to become prominent. However, we can find in Marx, who followed soon after Malthus, parts of the general under-consumption analysis. It is true, though, that Marx anticipated Keynes differently than did the majority of under-consumption writers. There has been some disagreement among economists on the relationships between Keynes and Marx. D. Dillard, who has done some brilliant work on the relations between Proudhon, Gesell, and Keynes,[8] has argued that since Keynes praised the work of Gesell, the anti-Marxian, disciple of Proudhon, there is probably little substance in the Marx-Keynes comparison. Furthermore Keynes has, wrongly we believe, referred to *Capital* as "an obsolete economic textbook . . . not only scientifically erroneous but without interest or application for the modern world." [9] But the incontrovertible fact stands that some of the modern Marxists who think seriously about economic affairs have supported Keynesian economics. What is there in Keynesian economics that would appeal to a Marxist?

First we should comment on Dillard's reasoning before we consider the above question. As will be shown below, the main contribution of Gesell and Proudhon to Keynesian economics was through the theory of money and the interest rate. These anti-Marxians had comparatively little, indeed, to say about the more important building-block of the system, namely the theory of savings and investment. Say's Law and effective demand were neglected by these two writers, who were purely monetary reformers. On the other hand, Marx was little interested in a theory of the rate of interest. It is very possible for Marx to disagree with Gesell, Proudhon and even Keynes on matters of interest theory or policy

---

[8] "Keynes and Proudhon," *Journal of Economic History*, Vol. II, 1942, p. 63; and *Proudhon, Gesell, and Keynes: An Investigation of Some "Anti-Marxian Socialist" Antecedents of Keynes' General Theory of Employment Interest and Money*, Aug. 1940, Ph.D. Thesis, Univ. of California.

[9] *Essays in Persuasion*, p. 300.

and yet be in agreement with other Keynesian doctrines about the movement of a capitalist economy via the process of sending savings into profitable investment.

In general, we can say that Marx analyzed the reasons why the capitalist system did not and could not function properly, while Keynes analyzed the reasons why the capitalist system did not but could function properly. Keynes wanted to apologize and preserve, while Marx wanted to criticize and destroy.

Both writers looked at the system as an aggregative whole and did not tie themselves up in the hopeless confusion of microstatics, but the methodology of Marx and Keynes was in important respects quite different. Keynes has always been extremely classical in his methods of economic analysis, but Marx was unorthodox. There is an infinite difference between the two propositions:

Constant capital plus variable capital plus surplus value is equal to the value of total output.

and

Consumption, which depends upon income, plus investment, which is an autonomous variable, is equal to the value of national income.

If Keynesian economics were couched entirely in terms of observable aggregates, as in the first proposition, which comes from Marx, the two methodologies would be quite similar. *But all the important Keynesian results were derived from schedules of economic behavior and not from defined relations among observables.* Keynes did, however, speak of and make use of certain historical trends within the capitalist system, and this is where his results dovetail with those of Marx.

With these points in mind, it would seem that the principal relation between Keynes and Marx would be in their respective conceptions of the historical time paths of the marginal efficiency of capital and the rate of profit.

According to Marx, the rising amount of fixed capital in relation to variable capital (organic composition of capital), due to accumulation, pushes down the rate of profit. A gap will be left which consumption will not fill, thus giving rise to a fundamental contradiction within the capitalist process. The theory of the falling rate of profit rests upon the relation; the rate of profit depends, by definition, upon the rate of surplus value (exploitation) and the organic composition of capital.[10]

This dependence is such that the rate of profit varies inversely with the organic composition of capital, if the rate of surplus value is constant, as was assumed by Marx.

Keynes went behind the forces determining the marginal efficiency of capital for any given point of time — he was working with a schedule. Marx went behind the historical forces in a certain social setting which determine the rate of profit. But Keynes and Marx did not reach different conclusions about the time pattern of returns from private enterprise. Both authors predicted a declining trend for this variable due to a high rate of capital accumulation in the past. Keynes gave the basis for the modern stagnation thesis, a thesis not at all unattractive to Marx and the Marxists, who have long predicted the falling rate of profit.

With regard to the savings side of the important savings-investment relations, Marx did not give an analysis comparable to that of Keynes. At most, Marx theorized that capitalists save their surplus incomes and then attempt to invest these savings in profitable enterprises. He, of course, was well aware of the influence of the capitalistic shape of the income distribution on the level of savings.

On the subject of business-cycle theory Marx was too eclectic to be pinned down to a particular idea. It is often claimed that he did support an under-consumption theory partially, but we shall never know what he would have done with the development of this theory had he lived longer. However, practically all the under-consumptionists have germs of the Keynesian system in their theories, and Marx was no exception.

It is worth while to proceed in the spirit of the Marxian tradition and attempt to formulate more precisely the relationships that would go into a Marxian model of effective demand. We can then obtain a better view of the relationship between Marx and Keynes.

Consumption in the Marxian system is made up of two parts,

[10] See Paul M. Sweezy, *The Theory of Capitalist Development*, Oxford, New York 1942, p. 68.

that of the wage earners and that of the capitalist. It is usually claimed that wage earners spend all their income on consumption. This means that their marginal propensity to consume is exactly unity. This extreme view is not supported by data from family budgets and public opinion polls. In the modern world we find that people in the very low income groups save a small part of an extra dollar of income. Their marginal propensity to consume is probably 0.8 or 0.9, rather than unity. At any rate, there is no fundamental change in the structure of the system if the workers' marginal propensity to consume is slightly less than unity.

The other component of consumption, consumption by capitalists, depends upon the income of capitalists such as profits, interest, and rents. The sum of all capitalist income is called surplus value in the Marxian system. The marginal propensity to consume out of surplus value income is small, say 0.1 or 0.2.

Capitalists may spend their surplus value in two ways. They may purchase consumer goods or producer goods. In addition to their propensity to spend on consumer goods, we must account for their propensity to spend on producer goods. The latter propensity is the investment schedule. As was done in the Keynesian system, the propensity to invest may be modified downward by the accumulation of fixed capital.

We may finally round out this system by stating the Marxian proposition that the ratio between surplus value and total wage payments is constant. This is the familiar constant rate of surplus value, an institutional constant of the system.[11]

The complete Marxian system may now be expressed as follows:

Consumption depends upon wages and upon surplus value.
Investment depends upon surplus value and upon accumulated capital.
Wages are proportional to surplus value.
National income is equal to the sum of consumption and investment.
National income is equal to the sum of wages and surplus value.

[11] A rational explanation of this institutional constant can easily be given. If the technological production function is of the linear-logarithmic type used in the derivation of the Keynesian system given in the appendix, then a constant ratio between wages and profits follows by maximizing surplus value subject to the technological constraint. In this formulation, total output is net of the terms in Marx's constant capital — depreciation and raw materials. Total output is defined as net national income.

There are five relationships and five unknown variables — consumption, wages, surplus value, investment, national income.[12] The system is completely determinate if all the schedules are well behaved.

If the marginal propensity to consume out of wage income is actually unity, then the Marxian system places the entire blame for the business cycle and depressions on capitalists, for they are the only people in the economy who save under these circumstances. It is only they who can generate savings which do not get offset by profitable investment outlets. However, if we take the marginal propensity to consume out of wages to be less than unity, the burden of saving is divided between laborers and capitalists. In this formulation, the capitalists cannot be blamed for all the saving, as well as a failure to invest at full-employment levels. They can only be blamed for not offsetting properly the savings of both classes, laborers and capitalists.

We may dynamize this theory in the same way that we dynamized the Keynesian system. We may introduce lags into the investment equation, define investment as the rate of change of capital stock, etc. It is easy to determine the time paths of all variables in the system as a result of these dynamizations. The Marxian theory of the falling rate of profit will then follow directly from the time path of the profit rate in these dynamical models.

Under-consumption contemporaries of Keynes have handed down an interesting body of economic doctrine. Any of these writers could have beaten Keynes to the North Pole had they possessed the faculty of rigorous formalization of their heuristic propositions about the behavior of the economic system. They could see clearly that the difficulty lay in the fact that there was not adequate purchasing power to clear the market during depression; in other words, they saw the failure of effective demand just as Malthus saw it many years before, after the Napoleonic Wars. However, when they attempted to explain the failure of effective

[12] We make the usual assumption that the stock of accumulated capital can be taken as given in the short run. We can generalize by adding the relation: Investment equals the rate of change of the stock of capital. This must be done for the study of dynamical behavior in this system.

demand, they were not entirely correct, because they had no adequate theories of the manner in which the level of effective demand gets determined within our economic system. Usually the under-consumption writers looked at one single feature of the process which seemed outstanding to them and then based their entire program on a correction of the single, supposed maladjustment. They failed to see the more complicated interrelations within the economic system as a whole.

The principal point of all under-consumption writers was that because a fraction of the national income is saved, the demand for finished consumers' goods becomes inevitably too small to clear the market for these goods, and a general glut occurs. Some postulated a periodic appearance of glut and scarcity while others postulated a steady, stagnant glut. The main difference between their theory and the teachings of Keynesian economics is that they looked upon savings as deflationary whether they are offset by investments or not, while Keynes considered as deflationary only savings which do not get invested. Throughout much of the under-consumption literature we find references to the proper balance between the position of zero consumption out of income and 100 percent consumption. Their idea was similar to that, more recently, of Lange [13] — an optimum propensity to consume. As far as we are concerned, the optimum propensity to consume (*in the schedule sense*) is that propensity which interacts with the investment schedule to give a full-employment level of national income, and there are an infinite number of consumption functions which will do this.

The heretic J. A. Hobson was certainly one of the best under-consumption writers and was one of the first to carry on in the tradition of Malthus. Hobson's main point of disagreement with the existing economic order was in the distribution of income. There is much truth in what Hobson had to say, and it may be that he was correct in choosing the most fundamental flaw in the capitalist system as the unequal distribution of income, although this may not be a strategic factor in the determination of output

[13] "The Rate of Interest and the Optimum Propensity to Consume," *Economica*, 1938, p.12.

as a whole. A rough presentation of his argument is the following: The common experience of the real world is a tendency for production to outrun consumption. This situation is caused by the fact that the rich are able to save part of their excessively large incomes and to invest this savings in the construction of capital goods to produce even more consumption goods. In this way, we accumulate more than enough producers' goods to supply the effective demand for consumption. The economic checks of fluctuating interest rates and prices introduce a cyclical pattern sometimes making for a high level of production and employment and sometimes causing depressed levels of production and employment. But no boom can sustain itself, because of the chronic failure of consumption which, in turn, can be traced back to the income distribution. The only permanent remedy envisaged by Hobson was redistribution of income.

It is certainly impossible to refute Hobson's contention that the existing income distribution encourages saving, but we are not ready to assume that over-saving would be impossible in a capitalist society with a perfectly equal income distribution. If an economy were organized according to the principles of theoretical socialism, it is quite conceivable that there would be a much lessened desire to save with an equalized income distribution. In such an economy there are no financial hardships of old age, disability, unemployment, etc. Furthermore there are no opportunities for private capital accumulation. The problem of over-saving would become minimized. But within the capitalist environment, risks of the future continue, and opportunities for capital accumulation exist. Many individuals would save even under capitalism with an equalized income distribution. In fact there is much empirical evidence leading to doubt that the principal motives for saving in this country have been due to the existing distribution of income. There are many reasons to believe that saving has been more closely linked to our institutions, particularly our insurance companies. Furthermore, as was pointed out in the two preceding chapters, the employment-creating effects of income redistribution are limited because the marginal propensities to consume are nearly the same in all income classes up to $5,000 per year.

The real contribution of Hobson to Keynesian economics was his analysis of savings and its effect on the level of economic activity. While Hobson analyzed, in some detail and very brilliantly, the saving process, he failed to give a good account of investment and its determinants. He considered saving to be done primarily for the purpose of capital accumulation, and never mentioned that the problem of making savings flow into investment is really at the root of the difficulty. A high rate of savings which are actually offset by investments provides a net stimulus to the economic system, but Hobson implied that such offsets in both depression and prosperity cause under-consumption and deflation. Had he analyzed more carefully the reasons for scarcity and abundance of investment opportunities, he would have been closer to the true result.

We find that Hobson had a clear picture of what determines the savings schedule. In the first place, he was not in agreement with the classical economists that savings and the rate of interest are related in any definite way. He wrote:

The great bulk of what I call automatic saving will scarcely be affected by a fall in the rate of interest except in so far as this reduces the aggregate unearned incomes. Some sort of conscious thrift, aiming to make a definite provision of income for old age or other future contingency, may even be stimulated, instead of depressed, by a falling rate of interest which demands a larger volume of saving to yield the required income.[14]

Hobson in this quotation was making an argument, familiar today, that the savings function is inelastic with respect to the rate of interest because some saving responses to changes of the rate counteract others. He recognized, throughout his writings, the institutional and automatic character of savings due to the growth of insurance companies and the desires to provide for old age or children. There can be little doubt that he considered personal savings to be a function of the level of personal income as a result of his discussion of the effects of the current distribution of income. It is not a big step from this concept of the personal savings schedule to the aggregative schedules of the Keynesian system.

[14] *The Economics of Unemployment*, 1923, Macmillan, New York, p. 52.

His policy recommendations are also related to those of Keynes. He did not favor a wage cut in order to achieve full employment. In fact, his arguments against wage cuts paralleled closely those of the later Keynesians. He pointed out the institutional obstacles due to the resistances of organized labor. But he was aware of the other difficulties even if this resistance could be overcome. He said:

> The history of "sliding-scales" in wage agreements testifies to the influence of elasticity of wages in aggravating fluctuations of trade by enabling employers to gamble upon future wage reductions.[15]

Thus he too was an inflationist and feared the cumulative, downward spiral of deflation. But in line with his main argument, he was largely interested in the effect of wage cuts on the total wage bill and the distribution of income. The behavior of the total wage bill, he noted, depends upon the elasticity of demand for labor, something which he was not prepared to estimate.

Since Hobson thought the root cause of the difficulty to be the maldistribution of income, his program for reform was to be an attempt to eliminate this cause. He suggested government spending of public credits such that the spending would go as much as possible into wages and as little as possible into profits, rents, interest, and high salaries. He approved unemployment doles as a step in the right direction. But he did not think temporary corrections of unemployment to be an adequate program. What he really aimed at was a permanent redistribution of income in order to get a "proper" adjustment between spending and saving which could maintain permanent prosperity.

While Hobson concentrated on maldistribution of income as the basic flaw of our economy, other under-consumption writers such as Foster and Catchings [16] centered their attack upon methods of business saving and financing. They too were trying to give a theoretical explanation of the reasons why production periodically runs ahead of consumption. All the under-consumptionists observed the same market phenomenon — the availability of more

---

[15] *Ibid.*, p. 91.
[16] See *Profits*, Houghton Mifflin, Boston, 1925, and *Business Without a Buyer*, Houghton Mifflin, Boston, 1927.

goods than consumers could purchase with their money incomes. They tried to explain the deficiency in consumer purchasing power, though, without showing how the level of purchasing power is determined. They were in agreement with Hobson on the proposition of a lack of effective demand, but they did not attach the same significant importance to the income distribution, which they considered to be merely a subsidiary factor.

The argument of these gentlemen was based on the dilemma of thrift. They saw that savings are necessary for economic progress with a growing stock of capital equipment, yet they considered savings of individuals or corporations to generate deficiencies in effective demand. Savings are necessary but are an evil; this was their dilemma. They imposed two conditions for the continued maintenance of effective demand: (1) Business firms must distribute all their profits to consumers. (2) Consumers must spend all their incomes. If by spending they meant spending on consumption, then they were saying that the only salvation for society is an economy of zero net investment and 100 percent consumption. However, this result does not follow from the analysis of the Keynesian system, where we see that, with any given investment schedule, there are infinitely many savings schedules which are consistent with stable full employment.

For them, profits were taken to be the motive behind capitalism. But if the firms who make the profits save some of their net income in order to purchase investment goods (as opposed to consumers' goods), then Foster and Catchings predicted over-production in the sense that consumers could not possibly buy the output at the going level of prices. They argued that the purchase of investment goods would add to the eventual supply of consumers' goods without adding to the demand, but they overlooked the interrelations of our economic system. If business savings are spent on production goods, these liquid funds must be distributed to the workers who produce the production goods, and these workers are in turn consumers. Foster and Catchings concentrated too heavily on the order in which the spendings take place. Their theory stated that funds which are spent more than once in succession on production goods generate over-production. Instead, money must be spent alternatively on production and consumption. They considered the investment of individual savings as pernicious as that of business savings, but they concentrated their argument on the latter because they thought it to be much more important as an aggregate. But Foster and Catchings fell into the same trap which caught most of the under-consumptionists, *i.e.*, they thought that over-saving is evidenced by the investment of too much savings instead of the failure to find investments for all the savings which people desire to create.

Since Foster and Catchings did not look upon the system as constantly in a stagnant state of unemployment, rather as periodically deflated and inflated, it must be explained how there could ever have been full employment because some savings have always been present. They explained our past full employment as the result of acts of God, war, waste, permanent inventory accumulation, business losses. We must agree that these negative items will offset savings to give a high level of employment, but there have been also positive contributions from other offsets which have made our society grow and still have kept workers employed. These two authors saw only part of the picture of effective demand.

They had very little to recommend as to what should be done about the inevitable tendency toward less than full output. They were true to the Keynesian spirit in opposing the deflationary adjustment of falling prices. They argued that theoretically the surplus production with given purchasing power would not be a surplus if selling prices were to fall. But they feared the evils of the deflationary spiral which would lower available incomes very rapidly. The only other policy considerations that they discussed were in connection with the relation of the government finances to under-consumption. While they did not consider seriously the effects of deficit spending by the treasury, they did hint that a possible way out of the dilemma would be for the government to spend newly created money on consumption goods. In this respect they have anticipated the policy measures of Keynesian economics.

Fortunately, the under-consumption writers have had some honest, intelligent, and sincere gentlemen among their ranks. But the colorful crank, Major C. H. Douglas, in England, has done much to lower the scientific achievement of this school. Hobson, for example, was anxious to dissociate his beliefs from those of Douglas.[17] The latter is one of the best examples of an amateur economist supporting a reasonable economic policy on the basis of a nonsensical theory. It is only by stretching the meaning of the Douglas theory that it can be reconciled with the Keynesian system, and let it be made clear that Major Douglas' policy measures are to be considered only in their strictest economic implications. His movement was filled with political dynamite. It was one of those prewar movements with all the trappings of green-shirted legions, anti-labor propaganda, and anti-Semitism. But the demagogues sometimes have important points to make.

Douglas had no under-consumption theory of business cycles. His theory was one of permanent stagnation and more particularly inefficiency. He was interested in poverty in the midst of plenty, with the emphasis on "plenty." Being an engineer, he concentrated his attack upon our industrial efficiency in the light of what we were producing as compared with our potential output. Due to the inability of our economic system to distribute enough purchasing power to enable consumers to clear the markets, he claimed that we would always be producing far below the potential capacity.

The entire theoretical basis for the Douglas under-consumption situation was the famous $A + B$ theorem, an all-time high in economic *un*science. Douglas changed his mind often about the definition of the terms A and B, and this text will concern itself only with the first and last statements. In 1920,[18] Douglas divided total factory payments into two parts, A and B. Group A included all payments made to individuals; *i.e.*, wages, salaries, and dividends. Group B included all payments made to other organizations; *i.e.*, for raw materials, bank charges, and other external costs. Here A represented purchasing power distributed to consumers and $A + B$ represented the total charges made by entrepreneurs necessary for profitable operation of business. He then argued that A, purchasing power, would never be able to purchase $A + B$,

[17] See *The Economics of Unemployment*, Ch. VIII.
[18] *Credit-Power and Democracy*, Palmer, London, 1920, p. 21.

the market value of output, unless extra purchasing power to the extent of the value B should be distributed. The economists' attack on this crude proposition should be obvious. They, of course, pointed out that group B payments should not be added for each stage of the productive process, otherwise there would be much double counting.

The value of output is the value added at each stage of manufacture, which is the same as the total of the A payments. It has been pointed out by H. T. N. Gaitskell [19] that the interpretation of Douglas' $A + B$, the value of output, should be the A payments of the retailer plus the B payments of the retailer. The total A payments of the entire system are obviously not the same thing as the A payments of the retailer; consequently there is no reason why total A payments should be less than the $A + B$ payments of the retailer. In fact, except for time lags they must be equal. But Major Douglas did not quit then; he merely modified his definition of the B payments. He finally, in 1931,[20] limited B to allowances made by business firms for reserves, mainly depreciation. This position, of course, was still untenable, but Douglas was not open to conviction. Keynes correctly remarked that if Douglas had limited the B payments to ". . . the financial provisions made by entrepreneurs to which no current expenditure on replacements and renewals corresponds . . ." [21] he would have been more nearly correct. With Keynes' restrictions on the definition of the B term, he would practically have been saying that the failure of effective demand is due to savings, which are not offset by investment. Hence by the proper twisting of Douglas' remarks, we can find an anticipation of the Keynesian contribution.

As a cure for the chronic illness of our economic system, Major Douglas proposed the corrective of social credit. This was an attempt to make credit freely available and to take it out of the hands of our present financial system, the institution most frequently attacked by Douglas in order to gain a mass following. He proposed that with every purchase. the purchaser be granted a credit

---

[19] "Four Monetary Heretics," *What Everybody Wants to Know about Money*, ed. by G. D. H. Cole, Knopf, New York, 1933, p. 280.

[20] *Warning Democracy*, London, 1931.   [21] *General Theory*, p. 371.

of a certain percentage of the retail price. This was just another way of giving a net inflationary stimulus to the economic system. It should have the same effect in stimulating spending and discouraging saving as many other policy measures which are compatible with the Keynesian analysis. Social credit could be made part of a feasible, anti-cyclical fiscal policy.

Douglas did not give as good an analysis of the savings process as did other under-consumption writers, yet he did see some of the fundamental relations between the volume of savings and effective demand. He had very little to offer, in a constructive way, with regard to investment or interest theory.

Finally in this section on the anticipations of the savings-investment building-block of the Keynesian system, we come to a sadly neglected crank. N. Johannsen, in 1908, published [22] a complete anticipation of this part of Keynes' theory. The only recognition of the works of this author that appears to be available in economic literature occurs in brief footnotes in the *Treatise*, and in W. C. Mitchell's early volume on business cycles. Keynes did not mention Johannsen in the *General Theory*, but actually Johannsen's ideas were much more relevant to the latter book than to the *Treatise*. For those interested in the development of economic thought, the ideas of this brilliant amateur should be studied carefully.

Johannsen wanted to know why crises occur and more importantly why prolonged depressions follow these crises. He admitted that some of the prevalent theories could explain the upper turning point but never the trough, especially the broad, persistent trough, of the business cycle. He wanted only to analyze why the depression takes place, and offered no economic policy as a cure. He began his analysis with the fruitful notion that prosperity is closely linked with a high level of investment.[23] He was observant enough to notice that in the stagnant countries of the world there was little investment except for replacement of the capital stock. His view

---

[22] *A Neglected Point in Connection with Crises*, Bankers Publishing Company, New York, 1908.
[23] He did not speak of investment, rather of new construction and the creation of productive capital or wealth.

of the economic process was that investment funds are supplied by savings, and that so long as the savings are invested in new constructions and enterprises they provide income and employment for workers. The spread of business activity throughout the economic system by the "multiplying principle" generates a high level of prosperity with a high level of investment. But he observed that when savings do not get invested depression will ensue. Thus he directed his attention to an explanation of what happens to savings which are not offset by investment. It should be remarked that Johannsen meant roughly what Keynes meant by savings and investment, but he never defined his terms precisely. The reader of Johannsen must be careful, however, to observe when he meant replacement investment as opposed to net investment or when he did not count dis-savings as negative savings which cancel out positive savings. If we realize the sense in which he used his terms, there is no problem in comparing them with those of Keynes.

A business-cycle theory which he rejected as inadequate was the lack-of-funds theory. This theory claimed that the boom comes to an end because the insatiable demand for new investment exhausts the savings funds of the money market. Johannsen argued that this theory could never explain the continued depression because in the downward phase of the cycle investment opportunities do not press upon the funds of the money market. He was revolting against a theory which is similar to the non-Keynesian theories of the 1930's, namely the so-called over-investment theories which blame the upper turning point on a shortage of capital. The phenomena which he observed in the real world, of a money market with surplus investable funds during depression and little investment activity in progress, he attempted to explain by the failure of investment opportunities. He thought that during prosperity, investment is carried on to such an extent that the demand for capital accumulation becomes satisfied for some time. With the large growth of the capital stock, returns from investment begin to decline and enterprisers develop very poor expectations as to the future returns from investment. Thus he pointed out that people continue to save, but the savings do not get invested. What happens to these savings?

To answer this question he developed the concept of impair savings. Since capital accumulation ceases or falls off during the depression, the outlet for the continuing savings must be in investments which do not enhance the volume of capital stock. These investments he called impair investments. The impair savings which are offset by impair investments are not included in the Keynesian definitions of net savings and investment. To put Johannsen's argument in Keynesian terms, it would run as follows: Investment opportunities begin to fall after a period of rapid capital accumulation. Those who can afford to save, however, continue to do so out of their falling incomes. But since investment outlets fall much faster than these continued savings, the savings do not get invested. Instead they are used to purchase existing assets from or make loans to others in the economy. In essence, Johannsen's impair savings are not offset by the expansion of capital. If he had reckoned dis-savings as negative savings, he would have ended up with the algebraic result that aggregate net savings equals aggregate net investment. The interesting thing about Johannsen's concepts is that they focus attention on the problem of offsets to savings and the relation of the abundance of these offsets to the business cycle. Johannsen was, without a doubt, one of the most unambiguous of the anticipators of the essential points of the Keynesian Revolution.

Let us now examine more carefully some of the specific points made by Johannsen. In the first place, he had a clear idea of the savings schedule. As a matter of fact, he worked with a schedule of the form savings $= (\frac{1}{7})$ income. This schedule, however, made use of his definition of savings. If we reduce his definition of savings to the Keynesian net savings we get a smaller propensity to save. He did not link his savings function directly with the multiplier theory, but the orders of magnitude of his multiplier and its inverse, marginal propensity to save, are not out of line. He estimated that a drop in investment of one billion dollars (*i.e.*, impair investments of that amount) would cut income by five billion dollars. From the savings schedule, his multiplier would be greater than seven. But when he worked out the successive rounds of his multiplier he got lost after a few rounds and merely made a rough estimate. He saw only the rough principle of the multiplier and knew nothing of its formalism. At first, he gave the impression that the "multiplying principle" worked only in one direction — downward, but later in the book pointed out that induced effects worked also on the upswing. He said first:

> One billion dollars of savings, if invested in building up new capital, will augment the country's wealth by $1,000,000,000.
> One billion dollars of savings, if invested in the "impairing form," will not augment the country's wealth but will, according to the figuring above, annihilate the income of the community to the extent of $5,000,000,000.[24]

The first of the two propositions is inaccurate, but it was later not employed by Johannsen in the analysis of the upward phase of the cycle.

He criticized those theories which depend upon the assumption of boundless opportunities for expansion of capital. He was ready to predict that whenever the opportunities should turn up, there would be plenty of savings to supply the necessary funds. His prediction of the outlook for our investment opportunities was slightly premature. He thought, in 1908, that the exceptional investment opportunities that had existed in the United States and Germany in the past would not last long. He did not see then the great automobile and housing expansion of the 1920's that was in store for us.[25] However, he would have been more nearly correct had he made similar predictions for Great Britain. Of course, there is always the possibility that the prolonged depressions which he wanted to explain were somewhat less than ten years in duration and that he looked upon investment opportunities as in a continuous, oscillatory pattern.

According to Johannsen, China had a higher propensity to save than did France, yet China was a much less prosperous country. He explained this situation by pointing out that the Chinese savings were not of a healthy variety because they did not find investment outlets. This failure of offsets to savings, he said, generated poverty

---

[24] *A Neglected Point*, p. 46.

[25] It is possible to argue that we were able to experience a boom as late as the 1920's only because of the fortuitous occurrence of World War I. Such an argument would imply that Johannsen was not predicting stagnation prematurely.

among the masses, unemployment, stagnation in trade, and permanent depression. France, on the other hand, had profitable investment opportunities abroad which offset domestic savings. This accounted for the superior economic status of France. He claimed that if China would save less or invest more, the country would be more prosperous.

In the *Treatise*, Keynes lightly brushed off Johannsen's work with the remark that lower interest rates will always make the available savings pass into investment; a process which Johannsen overlooked. This was hardly a fair or accurate commentary on the latter's brilliant treatment of the savings-investment problem.

MONETARY THEORIES OF INTEREST

The other building-block of the Keynesian system appears much less obviously in the older literature. The principal link that can be found is that between Keynes and Gesell. The latter received great praise in the *General Theory*. Gesell, in turn, belauded Proudhon, Marx's contemporary. In the works cited above, Dillard traced very carefully the chain of ideas from Proudhon, to Gesell, to Keynes, and we shall make use of Dillard's excellent work in what follows.

As far as theoretical economics is concerned, the main relationship among these three writers lies in the connections between their theories of money and interest. These two Keynesian antecedents did not have a theory of the determination of output and employment. They did not see the importance of the savings-investment equation. But all three writers made surprisingly similar value judgments concerning capitalism. Dillard has termed Proudhon and Gesell socialists in the anti-Marxian tradition. Indeed, Proudhon became famous as a result of controversy with Marx. The theme of anti-Marxian socialism has been an attack on rentier income mainly as interest on money and as rent on land. Proudhon and Gesell praised the creative entrepreneur and condemned the rentier. They did not want a collectivist society without private property rights over the means of production, but they wanted purely monetary and land reforms within the framework of capitalism. These value judgments about the socio-economic environment are not far different from those of Keynes. He, too, has opposed the rentier; in fact this opposition has led him to favor inflation over deflation consistently in his writings. Also Keynes has always looked upon the entrepreneur who stimulates capital growth as the prime mover of our economy. The doctrines of the euthanasia of the rentier can be integrated into the writings of all three authors.

Proudhon lived in France during the period before and after the Revolution of 1848. In the years before the Revolution, the Bank of France was the most important financial institution of the country. Small-scale entrepreneurs, who predominated, found it difficult to get bank credit, and this financial situation prompted Proudhon into making his proposals for a cure of the economic ills of the day. He thought that by replacing the Bank of France with his reformed bank of exchange and by reducing the rate of interest to zero (or near to zero), demand would always clear the market of all that could be produced. The purpose of the bank of exchange was to introduce bills of exchange into popular circulation. Producers would make out a bill to consumers; the latter would accept it, and then the producers would take the bill to the bank for discount at negligible rates of interest.[26] The bank would then substitute its own bill, which was to circulate at face value and be irredeemable in specie, for the producer's bill. Proudhon's bank was to insure full employment by making money and credit plentiful. His program was one of purely monetary reform, and left many important considerations in the savings-investment relations of the economy untouched.

Proudhon regarded interest as a purely monetary phenomenon and considered the level of the rate of interest to be determined largely by the available supply of monetary funds. He had the germ of the idea of a liquidity-preference theory of interest, but he had by no means arrived at a complete interest theory. His theory held that interest is a reward that must be paid to the holder of liquid funds so that he will be induced to part with his money in order that it may be used for production. He did not consider all

---

[26] At first the rate would be placed high enough to cover handling expenses.

the psychological and institutional factors which act to determine liquidity preference, but he did see the economic alternatives which interest rates have to allocate.

As in the case of so many of the Keynesian antecedents, there are inconsistencies. These inconsistencies are due to the fact that nobody anticipated the complete, interrelated theory, but only individual building-blocks. Proudhon showed his inconsistency with Keynesian economics by his support of a policy of wage cuts to increase the level of employment. It must be remembered that Proudhon had no theory of employment, only the rudiments of a theory of interest. He gave the well known classical arguments in support of wage reductions. With a given volume of credit, more transactions can take place at a lower level of wages. However, had Proudhon been entirely consistent with his anti-rentier position he would have supported inflationary methods instead of wage cuts in order to alleviate unemployment. Maybe the crucial point in this connection is the fact that Proudhon was not a stanch supporter of organized labor. He was consistently opposed to strikes and unions.

Proudhon's work served as an inspiration for Gesell, but the latter developed many original ideas beyond those suggested by the former.

The basis for the Gesellian theory of interest is the physical difference between goods and money. Gesell was quite emotional on this unfair difference. He said:

The wares which compose supply decay, lose weight and quality, decrease continually in price in comparison with fresh wares. Rust, damp, decay, cold, breakage, mice, moths, flies, spiders, dust, wind, lightning, hail, and earthquakes, epidemics, accidents, floods, and thieves wage war continuously and successfully upon the quantity and quality of wares. . . .[27]

Demand, on the contrary, as we have already shown, is not subject to this compulsion. It is composed of gold, a precious metal which, as the expression implies, occupies an exceptional position among the products of the earth. Gold may be regarded almost as foreign matter intruded upon the earth successfully withstanding all the destructive forces of nature.[28]

[27] *The Natural Economic Order*, Free-Economy, San Antonio, 1934 (?), p. 93.
[28] *Ibid.*, p. 95.

From these two quotations we find the essential element of Gesell's theory of interest — the characteristic of money as a store of value. Money can be successfully held idle without deteriorating physically; therefore Gesell argued that money holders are able to claim a premium for its use. If borrowers refuse to pay a premium, then hoarders have no reason to lend money because it does not deteriorate on their hands. But goods cannot be held indefinitely (except for the pathological cases like wine) without losing their value. Holders of goods would be only too happy to lend out their goods and in the future to receive in return exactly as much as they had lent out, free of deterioration. Gesell would call the repayment of equal quantities of goods by the borrower a repayment at a zero interest rate. However, the lender is getting back more than he otherwise would have possessed if he had elected to hold the goods. It is a real question as to whether or not the premium of non-deterioration is actually interest.

At any rate, Gesell thought that money should be only a medium of exchange and not a store of value. His argument was based on the comparison of the essential differences between a barter and a money economy. He stated that in a barter economy, goods exchange against goods at their face values with no interest charges and that full employment is always achieved. The only reason why money is introduced into the economy is to facilitate the maintenance of efficient division of labor in the economy. He truly looked upon money as a "veil." He was well aware, though, that the world does not behave in this way. Money is not merely a veil. As a result, he attacked the money system in so far as it enables people to earn interest because of the hoardable character of money. He attributed the fluctuations in output and employment to the monetary ills of our economic system.

Gesell's strong points were, of course, interest theory and money. But he did have some ideas about saving and investing. He missed much of the saving-investment problem, but some of his points are worth considering. He remarked:

Interest is, no doubt, a special attraction for the saver. But this special attraction is not necessary, for even without it the impulse of saving is sufficiently strong. . . . It is certainly easier to save 5 dollars from 200 dollars than from 100 dollars. If with 100 dollars wages a man, partly because of the stimulus of interest, deprives his stomach of 10 dollars for his own and his children's benefit, with 200 dollars wages he could probably, from the natural impulse of saving, set aside, if not 110 dollars, at any rate much more than 10 dollars.

Saving is practised throughout nature without the incentive of interest. Bees and marmots save, although their stores bring them no interest and many enemies. Primitive peoples save although interest among them is unknown. Why should civilized man act otherwise? [29]

This is a clear indication that Gesell related savings to the level of income and not to the rate of interest. But investment for him was more closely linked to the rate of interest. He spoke of investment as the disposal of savings. In this connection he wrote:

But no one parts with money savings unless promised interest, and the employer can pay no interest if what he constructs does not bring in at least as much interest as is demanded for the use of savings.[30]

Investors must get a return on their investment if they are to part with savings funds, and borrowers must reap a reward from the operation of the investment which yields a return over and above the interest charge. This is the gist of the latter quotation. But Gesell never attributed our economic troubles to a lack of balance between saving and investing, except to that lack which is introduced by the phenomenon of interest charges. He never got to the heart of the problem, a consideration of the determinants of effective demand.

Although Gesell developed for publication his reform program of economic control long before his theory of interest, his policy scheme can be derived logically from the theory. On the other hand, it is probably true that Gesell, like Keynes, developed his theoretical structure from the observations of the real world of his time and from practical economic policies. His reform measures followed quite naturally from his discussion of the characteristics of goods and money. He wanted to reduce money to the status of goods; *i.e.*, to force it to deteriorate also, so that it would not be profitable to hold money and thereby exact interest. His plan was that of stamped money. He proposed a single type of legal

[29] *Ibid.*, pp. 252–253.   [30] *Ibid.*, p. 114.

tender, irredeemable in specie, and requiring a periodic stamping in order to keep the money at its face value. If every dollar were to require, periodically, stamps which would amount to, say, five or six cents per year, it would be very unprofitable to hold money, and people would prefer to spend in order to hold goods. He thought that he could regulate the price level (at a stable figure) through strict control over the note issue and could speed up the spending of incomes, to prevent hoarding. With this basic reform, he thought that our economic problems would be solved. What Gesell had to say was quite good and contained much truth, but he did not go far enough. He should have analyzed the effect of stamped money on consumption, savings, investment and income. He was preoccupied with prices and interest rather than employment and income. It is probably true that stamped money would be beneficial to spending, both on consumption and investment, in that way generating higher levels of income, but Gesell omitted much about this problem.

As a final thought to conclude this chapter, we should point out that academic economists are ready to ignore the "crackpots," especially the monetary reformers. Johannsen, Foster and Catchings, Hobson and Gesell all had brilliant contributions to make in our day, but could receive no audience. It is hoped that in the future economists will give a sympathetic ear to those who possess great economic intuition.

CHAPTER VI

DEPRESSION ECONOMICS?

All too frequently the charge is heard that Keynesian economics is economics of a depression situation. But the catastrophic thirties were neither the beginning nor the end of periods for which the Keynesian methods of analysis produce useful results. Not only the recent war and postwar period but also the years to come will see fruitful applications of the new methods. It is wrong to think that Keynes' system fails if it cannot predict pessimistic results. The pessimism is not inherent in this system; instead the determinants behind the system make it operate either pessimistically or optimistically, depending on the current state of affairs in economic and non-economic life. That is to say, the Keynesian economic system is essentially a machine which grinds out results according to where the several dials controlling the system are set. The functional relations are the building-blocks of the machine, and the dials are the parameters (levels and shapes) of these functions. The setting of the dials is taken care of by the banking system, the government, the psychology of consumers, the attitudes of investors, the achievements of the technologists, etc. Is it correct to blame the machine if the dials are consistently set at pessimistic levels? If the machine is a true model of the way the system of the real world behaves, then we are not justified in criticizing the machine because other factors set the dials at particular levels. It is just as easy to explain one phase of the business cycle as any other with the Keynesian analysis, provided we take into account the correct structure of the relationships involved during each phase. If the conditions of our time are such that this (the equilibrium solution of the Keynesian system) is not one of full employment, then we must realize this fact and do something about it.

The future may be such that we get a continuously changing structure for the economic model. Without serious modification, this can be incorporated into the theory. There is nothing to make us work with constant, unchanging functional relations. Shifting equilibria and dynamically changing relations can also be ground out of the machine. The principles of the Keynesian Revolution need not be discarded; rather they must receive elaboration and be extended to handle more complex situations.

At any rate, we must be brought to realize that Keynesian economics will admit full employment or over-employment as legitimate solutions to the equations as well as the infinite number of under-employment solutions.

THE INFLATIONARY GAP

The argument against the classification of Keynesian economics as depression economics seems so obvious that it is difficult to do more than shrug shoulders at the charge, yet the other side is never convinced. However, since "the proof of a pudding is in the eating," an example from the actual world of affairs should decide the argument definitively. The example to be used is a happy choice since it also brings the analysis of the results of Keynesian economics almost up to date, showing the extension of the achievements since the *General Theory*.

During the war we were not worried about an immediate deflation. We were living in a period of anything but depression economics. Never before had we experienced such high levels of output and employment. Curiously enough, in this state of the inflationary gap we did not throw over the Keynesian system. Of what use to us was this system of depression economics? The purpose of this section is to analyze the gap problem with those tools which some prominent economists would like to discard during other than deflationary conditions.

The discussion of the inflationary gap, as such, did not attract much attention until the term was introduced in England in the budget speech of the Chancellor of the Exchequer, April, 1941. About one year earlier, Keynes wrote his well known booklet, *How to Pay for the War*,[1] in which he dealt with the inflation problem in very much the same manner as did the later "gapists." He

---

[1] *How to Pay for the War*, Harcourt, Brace, New York, 1940.

stated the inflation problem clearly in terms of national output, war expenditures, and aggregate consumption.

Using rough figures, he put the matter this way: Incomes were being paid out in Great Britain at the rate of about £6,000 million per annum and the taxation was yielding £1,400 million, leaving individuals with spending power of £4,600 million. The government expenditures inclusive of transfer items were reckoned at £2,750 million, leaving a balance of £3,250 million for public consumption. The inflation situation arises out of the fact that persons would have £4,600 million in purchasing power to bid for goods valued at £3,250 million in pre-inflation prices. Of course, we have learned well enough that people do not spend all their income on consumption goods. Corresponding to a disposable income of £4,600 million there would be, according to the existing consumption function, a definite amount which people would want to consume and to save. Only if savings should happen to be as much as £1,350 million out of a disposable income of £4,600 million would there be no inflationary gap. For purposes of illustration Keynes assumed savings of £700 million, which meant that £3,900 million would actually bid for goods valued at £3,250 million. The difference of £650 million can be taken as a particular definition of the inflationary gap. The consumption function and the level of war expenditures by the government interact to determine the level of income. The inflationary gap is then the difference between what the population will try to consume out of this income and the amount available for consumption at pre-inflation prices.

The Chancellor of the Exchequer defined the gap as "the amount of the government's expenditure against which there is no corresponding release of real resources of manpower or material by some other member of the community." [2] An adequate measure of this gap would not be the simple difference between expected governmental expenditures and tax revenues. The lack of balance between expenditures and tax receipts was filled somewhat by the sale of securities abroad, genuine savings of private individuals or

[2] "The First War Budget," *Economist*, Vol. CXL, 1941, p. 475.

corporations, extra budgetary governmental receipts, etc. But with these corrections, there was still ,a lack of balance between what the government wanted to acquire for the prosecution of the war and what the population would give up at current price levels. The government always gets the goods, and the population consumes only what remains, but the important problem is to analyze by what methods the government can get the goods which would not be given up at current prices by the public. There are good and bad ways of doing this. We particularly wanted, during the war, to avoid getting the goods through price rises.

In Keynes' example from *How to Pay for the War*, he demonstrated how the process might work through price rises. A 20 per cent price rise in his case would bring the value of goods available just up to the amount of purchasing power directed at these goods, £3,900 million. But his price rise would increase incomes by bringing a windfall gain of £650 million to sellers of the goods. In the next year, we would then begin with £650 million added to the income stream, and if all other data increased *mutatis mutandis* we would find ourselves confronted with another gap. But Keynes pointed out that it would be very likely that part of the windfall of £650 million would be collected from excess-profit taxes by the government. In this event, there would be an anti-inflationary pressure on the system.

Hence with a given tax schedule, price rises and voluntary savings may be considered as alternative methods by which the government may realize its demands upon national output.

We can conveniently think of two strategic levels of national income, the full-employment level and the bottleneck level. We reach the former level, say, when all who want to work at the going wage rates can find a job. The bottleneck point is reached when plant capacity is fully limited and all increases in money national income become price increases. It is not always certain that full enployment will precede the bottleneck point; much depends on the state of capital equipment. It is quite conceivable that a serious depression could so depreciate the capital stock of an economy that plant capacity would be limited far below the full-employment level of income. Keynes, in the early years of the war, was worried lest the bottleneck point be reached too early.[3] As it happened, in this country we reached full employment and then continued to expand output by inducing new workers into the labor force. Our wartime increments of money income represented substantially more than price rises.

Although we probably did not reach the bottleneck point, we came very close to it, close enough so that for purposes of simplification in the analysis it will be legitimate to assume output as no longer expansible. Increases in money national income thus represent price rises. It is actually nearer the truth to say that increases in money national income represent substantial price rises so that a policy of money income stabilization of our wartime levels of output, in the neighborhood of the bottleneck point, is in the public interest as an anti-inflation measure.

With this background, it will be very simple to go back to our familiar Keynesian model and give an analytical presentation of the problem of the inflationary gap.

During war periods, private investment decisions are practically nullified. In a total war economy, income represents the sum of private consumption plus war expenditures by the government. The latter component is completely autonomous, its size depending entirely upon Congressional appropriation bills. Our simple Keynesian model of this situation is as follows:

Consumption depends upon income after taxes.[4]
Consumption plus autonomous war expenditures = income before taxes.[5]

Out of this model we find a certain value for income, say Y_0, which will be taken as our base quantity. This money-income stream defines a certain price level because output is given at the full capacity of our productive powers. Suppose next, as must inevitably occur in wartime, that war expenditures increase by

---

[3] *How to Pay for the War*, p. 19.
[4] Taxes are also autonomous, being settled by Congressional action. Congress actually sets the tax rates and not the level of taxes. We could equally well add another relation to our model which relates tax receipts to total income, but the parameters of this relation are entirely at the disposal of Congress, and this body can make taxes fall at any level it pleases by appropriately varying the rates.*
[5] We could alternatively write the model as: Savings which depend upon income after taxes = autonomous war expenditures.

some definite amount. In this new situation, a different and higher value for income which we call Y_1 will be obtained from the model. The task of wartime fiscal policy, however, is to prevent Y_0 from rising to Y_1. If under our assumptions all price increases are to be avoided, then we must somehow operate on the relations so that a level of income no greater than Y_0 is generated. Clearly, we can do nothing to war expenditures; so our only hope is to influence

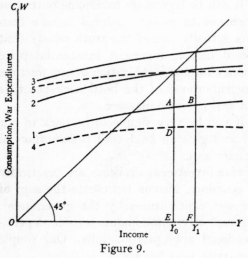

Figure 9.

the consumption function — the task of war finance is clearly set out. At the base prices there is an amount equal to the base-quantity income minus the original war spending and also minus the increased war spending, available for consumers. At the income levels that would be generated out of the new conditions, people will try to consume according to the existing consumption function. But such consumption must be larger than the amount available at base prices. Fiscal policies must be devised to wipe out the gap between these two figures. A diagrammatic exposition, as given in Figure 9, can make the situation quite clear.

At the starting position curves 1, 2 represent the consumption function, and the consumption function plus war expenditures, respectively. The income determined is Y_0. As war expenditures are added we move up to curve 3 by a constant amount. In the first case, consumers want to spend a total equal to AE; in the second case they want to spend the amount BF. If prices are not to rise, the consumption function must be lowered (not necessarily a parallel shift) so that when the spending of the government is added to it, the total will cross the 45° line at $Y = Y_0$. Curves 4 and 5 depict a possible result of the shift of the consumption function. There are infinitely many shifts which would be suitable, but the requirement that must be met is that curve 5 must cross the 45° line at $Y = Y_0$. No matter what shift is imposed upon the consumption schedule, the new amount of goods and services consumed will have to be DE, which is the same for any shift which meets our basic requirement. The vertical distance between the points B and D is the inflationary gap which we face in this situation. Consumers' goods available at the old prices add up exactly to DE, while unrestricted consumer activity would make attempted spending equal to BF, which corresponds to the income level Y_1.

One variant of the inflationary gap would make it the amount of taxes necessary to wipe out the gap. But this is not an unam-- biguous concept. We have worked with the consumption function where income minus taxes is the independent variable. This function is then given as of a certain tax schedule. A particular tax system underlies each possible consumption function. If taxes are changed so as to get more revenue to finance government spending, a new consumption function will come into existence. The change in the tax system needed to close the gap is that change which will push the consumption function downward so that curve 5 crosses the 45° line at the proper point. There is no limit to the variety of changes in the tax system which would accomplish this result. But it is true that no matter what change is made, it will have to sop up an exact amount of purchasing power at the observable levels of income if price rises are to be avoided.

The useful thing about this whole analysis is that it is entirely operational. All that we must know is the equation of the consumption function and possibly the tax function.† War expenditures by the government are announced in advance so that we can have predictable figures for this strategic term. But in making applications to the practical problems of the war we must be careful statisticians and stick to reality. Output never quite reached its maximum in this country. The gap that we want to avoid when output is still expansible, to a limited extent, will be slightly different.

If we take into account the fact that output is still expansible and that small price increases are to be permitted, the problem is not altered in any essential way. In this new case, certain increases in money national income over the base period become permissible, and our policy of shifting the consumption function should still be carried out, but to a lesser extent. The increase in money national income to be expected as a result of an increase in governmental war expenditures can be broken into three parts. One part will be the increase due to the expansion of physical output; a second part will be due to permissible price rises; and the third part, which is to be avoided, will be due to undesired price rises. Given the base year income, the expected expansion of physical output, and the price levels at which stability is desired, we can calculate an exact level of money national income which will lie between the values Y_0 and Y_1 of the preceding graph. Fiscal policy should be directed toward shifting the consumption function to an extent such that this function plus the stated level of war spending cross the 45° line at this unique level of national income between Y_0 and Y_1. The gap will be determined by the difference between the ordinate to the old consumption function at Y_1, BF, and the ordinate to the new consumption function at the value of Y which is calculated between Y_0 and Y_1.

During the war we closed the inflationary gap with relatively small price rises by rationing, price control, taxation, and voluntary saving. All these methods served to depress the level of the consumption function sufficiently to enable us to fill the gap in an orderly fashion. Rationing limited the variety and amount of goods available for consumption; price control limited the amount that we could spend on the reduced amount of goods available; taxation limited our disposable income; and war-bond sales increased our propensity to save. The combined effect of these measures can be readily seen in Figure 10.

On the horizontal axis are measured the actual levels of disposable income that we have experienced in the United States yearly since 1929, and on the vertical axis are measured the actual levels of consumption corresponding to each observed level of disposable income. From 1929 to 1940, all the points fall along a smooth line; this is the statistical consumption schedule for this country in the peacetime years. For each level of disposable income, there was associated a level of consumption approximately along this line. However, as early as 1941 we began to transform to a war economy, and consumption was pushed below this line. We obtain for the period 1941 to 1945 a new consumption function which is substantially below the normal peacetime relationship. This is precisely the theoretical picture that is developed in Figure 9.

There are, however, certain important aspects of the inflationary situation which are not uncovered by the type of analysis of the immediately preceding paragraphs. Inflationary phenomena are highly dynamic, and our methods of comparative statics conceal many important aspects of the process. We learn nothing about the speed of inflation from the analysis of shifting static schedules. In a situation where expectations are so important it tions are so important it

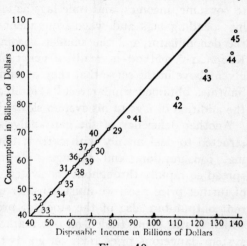

Figure 10.

is not possible to disregard the dynamic influences. The faster price rises occur, the more likely are they to breed anticipations of further increases and develop into an irresistible, cumulative process. Only by dynamizing the Keynesian system can we account for the speed of inflation. The simplest way to dynamize this system is to introduce the important lags that are concerned with the receiving and spending of income, the adjustment of wages to prices, etc. Keynes in *How to Pay for the War* was quick to see the influence of lags upon the system. He regarded lags as an ace in the hole which would tend to be a stabilizing factor. He said:

It is these time lags and other impediments which come to the rescue. Wars do not last forever.[6]

[6] *How to Pay for the War*, p. 66.

G

T. Koopmans [7] and, later, A. Smithies [8] formalized these ideas about the influence of lags and developed from specific models precise relations between the rate of price increase per unit of time and the significant lags. It is seen from Koopmans' article that for the general case the relative rate of price increase is a fraction whose numerator is the governmental expenditures and whose denominator is made up of terms involving marginal propensities to consume, incomes, and time lags as factors. The larger become his spending lags and wage-adjustment lags, the larger becomes the denominator and the smaller becomes the speed of inflation. Koopmans' method is really a generalization of the procedures given above in the sense that they dynamize the shifting equilibria. Smithies obtained similar results for his models, and found that the addition of lags to his system slows the process of inflation.

Another deficiency of the gap analysis is that it has been constructed to deal mainly with current flows of income, war spending, consumption, and savings. However, since inflation can spread so rapidly throughout the system by means of expectations of further price rises, we must consider not only the prices of current output but also of the stock of previously produced output which is still being traded on our markets. There may be in the system dangerous price rises on goods that in no way enter into current output. Also spending in excess of the available quantity of goods valued at base prices may be not only from the current stream of income paid out, but also from idle balances which were a part of the income of earlier periods. The economists of World War I were not entirely wrong in concentrating their inflation analysis on the growth of the stock of cash balances, for that will have some influence on the volume of spending which can be directed against the limited output. Indeed, even the Keynesians of World War II recognize a potential inflationary danger in the postwar resulting from the large amounts of liquid funds now in the hands of the population. We may save part of the flow of

---

[7] "The Dynamics of Inflation," *Review of Economic Statistics*, Vol. XXIV, 1942, p. 53.

[8] "The Behavior of Money National Income under Inflationary Conditions," *Quarterly Journal of Economics*, Vol. LVII, 1942 p. 113.

income year after year in just the right amount so that the gap does not engender a runaway inflation, but these savings may also accumulate as liquid funds for future spenders. The prevention of inflation for any number of years does not insure against the dumping of accumulated funds all at once on the market at a time when output is not sufficiently expansible to counteract spiraling price increases. The gap is related entirely to flow concepts, but the influence of stock concepts cannot be ruled out.

It is of course, quite possible to calculate numbers of gaps within the economy; e.g., the durable consumer-goods gap, the steel gap, the butter gap, etc., all in terms of the difference between expected expenditures on these goods and the amount available, measured at stabilized prices. However, most of the treatment has been in terms of broad aggregates, because here we have more knowledge about the relation of spending to incomes. It is possible that the method of aggregates may cover up some important price increases. While the general price level may be unchanged, there may be such increases in specific bottlenecks of the economy that an inflation may be initiated. It may be said, though, in favor of the aggregative method, that workers and employers in this war followed general price levels surprisingly closely. If bargaining is kept within the methodology of the "Little Steel Formula," then it will not be incorrect to work with over-all consumption functions, war expenditures, and national income.

A review of the economists' writings during World War I on the subject of inflation is enough to convince one that there has been a revolution in the subject of inflation economics. It is not possible to find an analysis during that period which really grappled with the problem, as the gap analysis does, in terms of anticipated expenditures and available goods at a given price level.

Most of the literature of that earlier period dealt with the questions of war finance and inflation from the point of view of the stock of currency, the state of the security markets, and the level of interest rates. There seems to have been little objection to the proposition that the price rises which occurred were due to the increases in the amount of money in circulation or perhaps to the changes in the stock of gold. The quantity-theory explanation was in vogue.

The very prominent discussion of taxes vs. loans as a method of war finance, it might be suspected, would have led to some discoveries similar to those of the current discussion.   But instead of considering taxes and loans with respect to their separate influences on the rate of private-consumption expenditures in relation to available output, the arguments concentrated entirely on the respective burdens which would be left for future generations. The relative efficacies or even possibilities of reaching a solution to the immediate inflationary problem by the two methods was not adequately considered.

A vast difference exists between the current fashions and the more classical methods of 1914–1920, and the principal reason for this difference can be traced to the recognition today, from Keynesian economics, of the interaction between autonomous war expenditures and the consumption function in determining national income.

CHAPTER VII

KEYNES AND SOCIAL REFORM

In the past few years there has grown up a large group of young economists who have accepted the theoretical doctrines of the Keynesian Revolution and who have come into national prominence through their support of an economic policy of full employment. The general public has closer acquaintance with the policy measures of these economists than with their theory, especially since such confused versions of their theories have been presented on a large scale to the public by the opponents of Keynesian economics. The preceding chapters have dealt largely with the historic development of a body of economic thought. We are now ready to conclude this volume with a chapter on the relationship of this new theory to our actual economic life.

KEYNES' SOCIAL PHILOSOPHY

In Chapter I we pointed out some remarks in *The Economic Consequences of the Peace* by Keynes which gave an idea of his appraisal of the capitalist development which preceded World War I. There Keynes viewed the capitalist system as smooth-working except for artificial barriers. He attempted to justify the unequal distribution of wealth inherent in capitalist development. He argued that the conditions of the nineteenth century demanded a large amount of individual savings to support the rapid rate of capital accumulation, and considered the unequal distribution of wealth necessary to maintain the level of savings high enough to supply the abundant demand for capital. But he concluded the *General Theory* with these words:

> Thus our argument leads towards the conclusion that in contemporary conditions the growth of wealth so far from being dependent on the abstinence of the rich, as is commonly supposed, is more likely to be impeded by it. One of the chief social justifications of great inequality of wealth is, therefore, removed.[1]

[1] *General Theory*, p. 373.

The unemployment problem has so greatly influenced contemporary life that economists have been forced to reconsider, in its entirety, their social philosophy. A philosophy appropriate to the conditions of nineteenth-century capitalism is hopelessly out of place today.

Why did Keynes lay so much stress on the problem of unemployment? While this was not the only economic problem, it was certainly one of the most important in the sense that it was at the root of most of the major social ills that plagued the world in the interwar period. For example, Keynes thought that full employment would make for peace. He realized that domestic unemployment caused capitalist nations to adopt beggar-my-neighbor policies in international trade in order to improve their employment position at the expense of the other countries of the world. The competitive struggle for markets among capitalist nations can never breed peace, only armed conflict.

From Keynes' point of view the economic system, as it existed before the war, solved appropriately the problem of resource allocation; it failed only in its solution of the unemployment problem. The line of least resistance seemed, evidently, to be to improve the conditions of employment while still maintaining the capitalistic market mechanism for allocation of economic resources. Thus the Keynesian approach is clearly to modify capitalism so that full employment can be maintained. Any features of the capitalist system which do not interfere with the achievement of full employment may be preserved, according to this position.

There are other reasons why unemployment is such a dangerous social ill, and there are also other methods in addition to Keynes' program of liberal capitalist reform of achieving full employment.

The demagogue thrives on mass unemployment. The psychology of the unemployed worker is such that he is willing to listen to many dangerous arguments if they hold promise of a job. There are not many social conditions that are more depressing than forced idleness and forced abstinence from consumption. If fascistic demagogues can promise jobs, the unemployed workers may follow even if the job is one of producing bullets. It is no accident that the Nazis grew powerful in Germany during times of unemployment and economic dislocation. It is also no accident that native fascists in the United States gained great followings during the decade of the thirties through promises of improved economic conditions. Thus there is one type of solution to the unemployment problem in a capitalistic economy which will be brought about by natural forces if we adopt a do-nothing attitude. There will appear on the scene the fascists, who will bring about full employment by producing armaments in preparation for war. The need to avoid such a solution shows clearly the importance of understanding the problem and of solving it by democratic methods.

There is yet another method of achieving a full-employment economy which is essentially different from fascism and capitalist reform. This is the method of socialization of the means of production. It was pointed out in Chapter III why a socialist economy will always have full employment. There may be serious problems confronting the successful operation of a socialist economy, but unemployment will not be one of them.†

There is a great misunderstanding among the American public that the practical reform measures of the Keynesian economists are leading to socialism. It must be emphasized that the Keynesian reforms do not infringe upon the rights of private individuals to own producer goods. The most important characteristic of a socialist economy is that there do not exist private property rights over producer goods. The Keynesian approach visualizes the state as a balancing force which serves only to supplement the behavior of individual capitalists, while the socialist approach visualizes the state as the sole entrepreneur which replaces, entirely, the individual capitalists. The Keynesian policy is, indeed, a conservative one because it aims to conserve free-enterprise capitalism. Socialism is not conservative; it is radical and aims to change the capitalist system into a completely different form.

Fascism, on the other hand, represents the worst stage of capitalism. It is the form that our capitalist society will acquire unless we are successful in bringing about Keynesian reforms or a socialist economy. If we let nature take its course, the economic law of motion of capitalism will take us down the same road that Germany followed so recently.

PLANNING FOR FULL EMPLOYMENT

It will be instructive to outline a practical program of economic policy which will be necessary in order to reform capitalism to a system of full employment. We shall first consider this program from a mechanical point of view, *i.e.*, the way in which it should operate if it were accepted by the entire society. Then in the next section we shall consider this program in its relationship to the political scene, and try to judge whether or not it is possible.

From the theory of employment discussed in the preceding chapters, the general problem of government economic policy can be very easily stated. It must be such that the government will supplement or stimulate total private spending on consumption or investment by exactly the amount that will maintain full employment. We could also say that private investment plus government investment must be exactly equal to the amount which will be saved by individuals and business firms out of their full-employment income. We must caution the reader to be certain not to believe that this government activity must always be of a positive character. If the particular problem is one of filling the deflationary gap, the government must undertake a program of positive spending activity. However, if the task is to wipe out the inflationary gap, the government activity must be one of negative spending. In any case, the government is to be the balancing agent. An approximate forecast must be made, in advance, of the level of income which will be generated by private economic activity and a normal government budget. The difference between this level of income and full-employment income is a measure of the government's task. If private activity will generate less-than-full employment income, the government must undertake a positive spending program in order to reach full employment. If the forecast [2] shows a level of income above full-employment income, the government must curtail spending and combat inflation.

[2] The problem of our ability to make adequate forecasts is a purely technical one. The author is currently attempting to construct statistical models which will be suitable for such forecasts, and believes that the difficulties of the problem can be overcome. See L. R. Klein, "A Post-Mortem on Transition Predictions of National Product." *Journal of Political Economy*, Vol. LIV, 1946, p. 289.*

In the years before the war, the type of policy needed was one to combat deflation. The depression conditions of the 1930's were never successfully eradicated by government action. Looking back, at this time, on our policy we can easily see why the United States remained in a depressed state for a decade. The size of the deflationary gap was never properly estimated, and the government activity needed to restore full employment was actually much greater than that which was instituted.

The impact of the war on our economy showed clearly that if the government expenditure is sufficiently high, full employment follows automatically. The war activities of the government were, of course, larger than the necessary full-employment activities of a peacetime situation. That is why we experienced an inflationary pressure. But an intelligent politico-economic policy need not necessarily be either too great, or too small. It could be just right.

All during the 1930's our population was growing and our technological productive capacity was growing; consequently the full-employment level of output was also growing. We should have been raising our sights to ever higher levels of full-employment income. Instead, we calculated in terms of 1929 as a norm, and our government economic policy was designed for a world of pygmies when we were approaching life in a world of giants.

The postwar boom in which we are now living is not likely to last long. In the decade of the 1950's (or even sooner), we may be confronted again with the problems of unemployment, unless we take adequate steps to prevent another catastrophic depression.†

Our theory of effective demand demonstrates that there are two classes of policy measures that we can use to raise the level of income in the system toward fuller employment. We can try to stimulate investment by increasing the amount that would be spent on investment out of each level of national income, without at the same time inducing a compensating change in the amount that would be spent on consumption out of each level of national income. Alternatively, we can try to discourage savings by reducing the amount that would be saved (not spent on consumption) out of each level of income, without at the same time inducing a compensating change in the amount that would be spent on investment out of each level of national income. The first type of policy attempts to raise the entire investment schedule [3] (propensity to invest), while the second type of policy attempts to lower the savings schedule [3] (propensity to save). A high-level investment schedule and a low-level savings schedule will generate a very high level of income. These two types of policies are by no means mutually exclusive, but they do have different characteristics.

The level of investment can be stimulated most directly by outright government investment. There are many socially useful projects which need to be undertaken from the point of view of economic welfare of the entire community but which will not be undertaken by private entrepreneurs operating according to the profit motive in a capitalist society. For example, the slums in every metropolitan district of the United States should be cleared away and replaced with modern low-cost dwelling units. Cities should be redesigned to diminish the nuisance of smoke, provide better traffic arteries, allocate space more rationally between dwelling areas and recreation areas, etc. These investment projects have not been and are not being undertaken, yet they are certainly desirable.† They are not carried out by private entrepreneurs because they are risky — if we use a money profit criterion. These projects, if they are to be socially useful projects, must be carried out for the masses of the people who cannot pay high rents. But low-rent housing will pay for itself slowly, more slowly than private capitalists require in the world of today. Useful investment schemes like these must be undertaken by the sole agency which can afford to take the risk of slow or zero return, the government. It is well known that the magnitude of all such building programs that are socially desirable could insure full employment in the United States for several years, at least. Here is an obvious method for stimulating the level of investment; the government directly invests in socially desirable projects which will supplement private investment so that full employment can be maintained. It should be remarked, however, that direct government investment would not be necessary if the private construction industry had sufficient

---

[3] These terms are carefully defined in Chapters III and IV.

capacity to carry out the program, for the government may subsidize private firms to encourage them to engage in activity which would otherwise not appeal to them because of the risks involved. We should not be anxious, though, to subsidize those sectors of our economy which least deserve it.

An alternative method of granting subsidies is to lower business taxes. Economists have recently been arguing strongly in favor of reduced business taxes in order to stimulate investment. However, many of these arguments are not correct. The most frequent suggestion is to lower corporate income taxes. This policy will not stimulate investment in the way in which many people think it will. The theory of investment developed in Chapter III is a theory appropriate to a capitalist economy where entrepreneurs behave in such a way as to maximize their profits. What is the difference between maximizing 60 per cent of profits or 90 per cent of profits? The profit-maximizing relations are absolutely invariant. If the tax rate is changed from 40 per cent to 10 per cent, there is no reason why an entrepreneur who is maximizing his individual profits will directly alter his investment decisions. It is a general proposition that the profit-maximizing decisions of business firms are independent of the income tax structure (progressive or constant proportionality) if the marginal tax rate [4] is always less than unity, as is the case with any reasonable tax system.

These remarks do not mean that variations in business taxes will have no effect on total income and employment, but they do mean that there is not an entrepreneurial behavior pattern such that investment decisions depend directly upon tax rates. If taxes of any variety, personal or business taxes, are lowered, disposable income in the hands of household consumers will be increased. The increased disposable income will cause higher consumption and thus induce, by the familiar multiplier theory, a higher level of income in the system. The induced higher level of income leads to a larger amount of investment, but if there is no change in the basic relationship of investment to income, the process comes to a

---

[4] The marginal tax rate is the amount of an extra dollar of income that is paid in taxes. If the marginal rate is less than unity, every additional dollar of business income will not be paid entirely in taxes.

halt. Hence there may be an indirect effect on investment as a consequence of reduced taxes; the effect, however, is the same for either business taxes or personal taxes.

An exception to the above argument occurs if business savings change when business taxes change. If business savings increase as business taxes decrease, there will be a smaller stimulus from a reduction in business taxes than from a reduction in personal taxes.

There are other types of special taxes which may be directly conducive to investment. It has long been suggested that business firms be taxed on retained earnings which are not used for investment purposes. A satisfactory tax policy along these lines has never been devised, but this is the direction in which we must look for investment-creating tax reforms.

Keynes was long in favor of manipulation of the interest rate in order to stimulate the desire to invest. Such policies are based on the assumption that investment is sensitive to changes in the rate of interest, but as is pointed out in Chapter III, all the evidence, theoretical and empirical, suggests that the investment schedule is interest-inelastic today.†We observed a great decline in the long-term rate of interest from 1932 to 1941, yet we did not observe high-level investment activity. Econometric models fitted to the data of that period show that we would not have noticed high-level investment even if other things besides the interest rate had remained constant.

There may be some fields in which interest policy may have much more than average effectiveness. The government has begun to provide low interest rates on loans for residential building. This policy in itself did not cause a satisfactory upturn from the trough of the residential building cycle in the 1930's, but it may be more helpful in the future. At best, we can hope for a small stimulus in a few isolated sectors of the economy as a result of lower interest rates. Interest rate policy can, in general, be expected to be quite ineffective.

Another reform measure, along more classical lines, which is advocated as a stimulus to investment, is the abolition of certain monopoly privileges. For example, it is often said by critics of both left and right that the patent system which grants at least 17-year monopolies on new inventions serves to decrease the volume of investment by holding back innovations which would otherwise call for increased investment. The innovations are suppressed because they conflict with certain vested interests. It is undoubtedly true that patents are used to suppress innovations in many cases, but it does not follow that patent reform, in itself, would be enough to maintain the investment schedule at a full-employment position. The same can be said of all other anti-monopoly measures. It has been argued in this book that a perfectly competitive capitalist system does not automatically solve the problem of unemployment. In any type of capitalist system which lacks a definite plan to maintain investment and savings in full-employment relationship with one another, there will be economic fluctuations, and there will be periods of substantial unemployment.

Many economists have defended monopoly privileges on the ground that they stimulate investment. They claim that the innovations of our modern industrial society require extensive scientific research facilities which cannot be provided in small firms. It requires, according to their reasoning, corporations like General Electric, General Motors, American Telephone and Telegraph, Du Pont, etc. to furnish adequate laboratories in order to carry out the scientific research underlying innovations. However, when we speak of abolishing or revising the patent system to decrease the power of monopoly interest, we should also include a proposal for the maintenance of scientific research on a large scale in non-profit institutions such as government or university laboratories. A well thought out plan can provide for the abolition of monopolies and maintenance of research simultaneously. An adequate scheme can make for increased investment, but we must still prepare for the contingency of depression or inflation in a competitive system.

Keynes' latest contribution to economics came forth during the war in the form of the Keynes Plan for international monetary stabilization. He was in large part responsible for the work accomplished at Bretton Woods, which may provide an additional stimulus to investment. When there are no profitable outlets for domestic investment, capitalists may look abroad for fresh opportunities. Foreign investments, like domestic investments, also lead to higher levels of national income. The International Bank in the Bretton Woods proposals is a definite attempt to underwrite, in undeveloped countries, investment projects that would not be carried out as part of the activities of the private capital market. All the investment projects supported by the bank will definitely serve to enhance the general level of prosperity, but again the limitation is a quantitative one. We cannot depend on the level of foreign investment to supplement domestic investment just enough to obtain full employment. The resources of the bank may be utterly inadequate to underwrite enough capital exports to fill the deflationary gap in the United States, for example. International investment will help improve domestic prosperity in this country, but it is likely to be on a small scale as compared with the magnitude of our economic problem.

The methods of government investment, tax policy, interest-rate policy, anti-monopoly policy, foreign investment are the principal sources for raising the investment schedule toward higher positions, and we must now turn to the alternative approach dealing with policies directed at the propensity to save or consume.

It must be remembered that a policy to improve the level of employment by acting upon the propensity to save means a policy to change the position of the entire savings schedule; *i.e.*, a policy to change the relation between savings and income. This is something quite different from a policy which merely changes the independent variable (income) of the savings schedule without changing the position of the schedule. For example, a public-works policy which creates direct government investment causes more income to be paid out and thus changes the income variable of the savings schedule. This income change, in turn, causes a change in the observed level of savings, but the propensity to save, the saving schedule, has not changed. We can move to new positions on the savings schedule and thereby alter the observed levels of savings, income, investment without affecting the position of the savings schedule. However, we now turn to policies which attempt to change the fundamental habits of saving and thus change the position of the savings schedule to a lower level.

From statistical data over the last three decades we notice a gradual downward shift in the schedule relation of savings to income. There are certain natural forces which are slowly altering the propensity of the entire community to save. We have moved in the direction of a higher consumption economy, but at the same time we moved much faster toward a low-investment economy; hence the savings schedule in relation to the investment schedule produced unemployment in the 1930's. We had over-savings in relation to investment, but the propensity to save was not increasing temporally.

The natural forces which were lowering the propensity to save were changes in consumer tastes, the growth of the advertising industry, the increasing degree of urbanization, the increase of educational opportunities, the increased use of consumer credit. The first two forces (consumers' tastes and the growth of the advertising industry) are related. Consumers were propagandized by advertisements that the "American Way of Life" called for certain expenditures (two cars in every garage, e.g.) that they had not previously been accustomed to make. The advertising industry has certainly had a bad influence on many aspects of our lives. It has been grossly untruthful; it has caused waste; it has served to support wealthy vested interests; but it has also served to maintain consumption at a level higher than it otherwise would have been. Advertising is not the best way to get a high-consumption, low-savings economy, but it is a way.

More important, though, than advertising has been the migration of population from farms to the city. It is well known from family-budget studies that city dwellers have a much lower propensity to save than do farmers; hence the trend toward urbanization has served to lower the savings schedule.

Education serves to teach people to enjoy the fruits of life. We learn to use complex labor-saving devices in the form of durable consumer goods that increase the propensity to consume or decrease the propensity to save. Along with education, we are more able to pay for these expensive items with a small income augmented by the use of consumer credit, whereby borrowed funds as well as current and past income can be used to purchase these goods.

These forces which tend to lower our propensity to save have evolved naturally in our system, but they can also be incorporated into a consciously directed government policy. We can subsidize truthful advertising and education. We can have government investment projects to mechanize agriculture and get the surplus population off the farms into the city in more productive jobs where these migrants will have a lower propensity to save. We can extend the operations of organizations like the F.H.A. to provide credit for durable consumer goods at low interest rates. All these policies will depress the savings schedule and help to reach a high-consumption economy.

We can attempt to tinker with these trend forces which influence the propensity to save, but we can also attempt to bring about more fundamental reforms which will lower the savings schedule. How are savings habits formed? What are the causes of saving? A basic program should investigate these questions and attempt to influence fundamental habits.

In our modern industrial society built on individualistic principles there are obvious reasons why people save. They save for the rainy day when they will be unemployed, sick, disabled, or too old to work. They will attempt to provide for future outlays to set up a home during married life, to educate their children, to cover the expenses of maternity, to cover funeral expense, etc. These are some of the primary causes of need listed in the famous *Beveridge Report* of 1942. The obvious way to diminish savings on account of these primary causes of need is to have the state provide for these needs at the cheapest possible cost. People now try to provide for some of these contingencies through privately held insurance policies. Every year the American people pour billions of dollars into insurance companies for future contingencies. These companies in turn must find profitable and safe investment outlets for these funds, and this is not always possible. Furthermore, the private insurance industry has not been able to make low-cost policies available to the people so that they can cover adequately these primary causes of need. We need a non-profit institution like the government, which can provide a comprehensive, minimum program of social security in order to reduce the propensity to save.

This program must cover the entire population, and it must cover all those contingencies which cause people to save on a large scale for the future. A program like that embodied in the *Beveridge Plan* or the Wagner-Murray-Dingell Bill in this country is necessary in order to reduce significantly the level of the savings schedule.

A high-level-consumption economy is really the long-run hope for capitalism.† Suppose we rebuild our cities and roads, what peaceful investment project should come next that could be large enough to insure full employment? Maybe there will be something available, maybe not. This question cannot be answered definitely in advance. But if we have reached a position of high consumption, the population will be better off from any welfare criterion and the unemployment problem will be at a minimum. The greatest possibility for reaching high-level consumption appears now to lie in the plans for social security. If we diminish the fear of the unknown future on the part of consumers, they can enjoy the fruits of our economic activity in their youth when it can best be appreciated.

There is at least, one further method of discouraging saving that has already been mentioned in earlier chapters. This method, the redistribution of income, has occurred often throughout the literature. If we redistribute income from the rich, who have a relatively high marginal propensity to save, to the poor, we will decrease the community's marginal propensity to save. Such policies of income redistribution can be carried out by taxing the rich and paying a dole or other types of contributions to the poor. But, as has been remarked in earlier chapters, this procedure will not, in itself, be sufficient to insure full employment. There is a tendency to regard income redistribution as a panacea, but this tendency is misleading. Any program of capitalist reform should include income redistribution, but this program, if it is to be successful, must not rely unduly on this one element to bring about full employment.

One of the major propositions in Keynesian economics is that the savings schedule is stable, changing only gradually as a result of trend forces. On the other hand, it is posited that the investment schedule is extremely unstable and that this instability is responsible for the pattern of the business cycle. The reasons on which the stability of the savings schedule is based give us a hint as to the proper timing of the various steps in a full-employment program. The savings schedule is stable because the decision to save is based on institutions like insurance companies and thrift attitudes that are passed on from generation to generation.† Most children are raised on the virtues of thrift, and high spenders are usually considered to be unworthy citizens. It is difficult to change these fundamental habits, because the action of any single individual has no appreciable influence on the economy as a whole. It is necessary to get mass action; but each individual, thinking in terms of his own action alone, will refuse to participate. Curiously enough, people do not realize their own best interests. It is a theorem of the Keynesian system

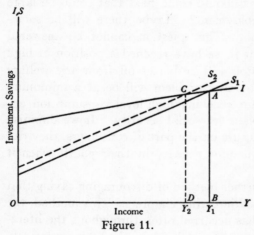

Figure 11.

that if each person tries to save more out of his income than previously was done, the community as a whole will not end up with a greater amount of savings. Consider Figure 11.

If each individual in the community increases his propensity to save, the savings schedule will move from S_1 to S_2. This means that the community will try to save more out of any level of income along schedule S_2 than along schedule S_1. But the equilibrium or observed level of savings will fall from AB to CD. By trying to save more, we actually save less. The people acting on individualistic principles do not know their own best interests. They must be taught to look at the system as a whole. These arguments show why it is difficult to induce the population to lower the savings schedule.

We must resort to indirect methods such as social-security programs which wipe out the need for saving. However, it takes time for these indirect methods to have their full effect, and we cannot rely on them in situations like those that developed in 1931–1933. We must expect the policy measures designed to influence the fundamental savings habits to show their full effects over decades. These policies are the basis for long-run hopes and cannot be used to counteract short, sharp fluctuations in the near future. We should smooth out the latter type of disturbances by government investment projects. A backlog of planned public works should always be ready so that unemployed factors can be immediately put to work on useful jobs whenever the private sector of the economy is unable to carry the ball. Government spending should be very flexible and subject to immediate release or curtailment in just that precise amount which will maintain full employment, no more and no less. But as the economy gradually reaches its position of high consumption as a result of social security, the amounts of government investment needed to counteract fluctuations will be smaller.

Full employment seems to be such a desirable economic policy that we may well be led to wonder why there must be any opposition to it. The major arguments voiced against the Keynesian economic policy of full employment by more conservative economists [5] are threefold: (1) It takes away individual freedom. (2) It leads to inflation. (3) It increases the public debt.

Kalecki, in an informal talk, recently met the first argument very elegantly with the remark that the regimentation of unemployment and poverty is infinitely more severe than the regimentation of economic planning. Which is worse, to tell the rural population of the Missouri Valley that they must use cheap electric power in order to give jobs to the unemployed, or to have the merchants refuse to sell goods to these people because they do not have purchasing power? While some old-fashioned economists may ponder over the answer to this question, we know that the majority of the American people will quickly come forth with support for the first type of regimentation.

Those who fear a revolution of the bondholders in our society

---

[5] The opposition of the left is considered in the next section of this chapter.

warn continuously of the dangers of inflation. They oppose the full-employment program because they believe that it may lead to excesses, to inflation. There does exist the possibility that the plans will be carried to excess, but if the alternative is the misery of the unemployed, then, by all means, let us have a little inflation. In the Keynesian spirit we may always prefer inflation to deflation if the choice must be made, but we also should qualify this preference with the side remark that we should like, even better, to have neither. There is no reason why intelligent economic planning cannot be of just the correct amount, that amount which gives permanent full employment and stable prices.

There are several administrative methods of gaining full employment without inducing inflation. If the economic planners are given complete control over the government fiscal policy so that they can spend when and where spending is needed to stimulate employment and tax when and where taxation is needed to halt upward price movements, there will be no problem of associated inflationary dangers. But in our political society these powers of fiscal policy are given only to Congress. That body must decide on the appropriate spending or taxing program. It is inevitable that the Congressional debating techniques will be much too slow and cumbersome to provide the flexibility needed for fiscal policy in a full-employment program.† An alternative would be to maintain a skeleton O.P.A. always ready to step in when the price level shows inflationary tendencies. The O.P.A. served us beyond all best hopes and wishes during the war, and it did not infringe upon any fundamental liberties, only upon the liberty of greedy profiteering. This organization can serve us also in peace. We found during the war that the truly efficient way of preventing runaway inflation was through direct controls. These controls are also adaptable to a peacetime economy. We must have a planning agency always ready with a backlog of socially useful public works to fill any deflationary gap that may arise; similarly, we must have a price-control board always ready with directives and enforcement officers to wipe out any inflationary gap that may arise. This is the road to the kind of full employment that we need.

The third objection against the full-employment program, the evil of the public debt, leads to a basic matter, the reason why un-employment is a problem in a capitalistic society but not in a social-ist society. We might begin this basic discussion with the rhetorical question, Is not unemployment an unnecessary problem in this country? We should give the self-evident answer *yes* because the people in this country, at our present state of civilization, have vast unfilled desires; furthermore we have the economic resources with which to fill these desires. Why should we not use these re-sources to fulfill these desires? In a socialist economy we would use these resources as fully as is physically possible. We would dig coal, manufacture steel, operate motors, transport goods, as in-tensively and extensively as we have people who wish to carry on these functions at prevailing wages. The socialist planning board would plan to use our resources to that extent, the full-employment extent, as long as the unfilled desires exist. When we reach that blissful state of large-scale satiation of desires, we can use more leisure and less material goods. But things do not happen this way in a capitalistic society. We have the desires, and we have the re-sources, but the people with the desires are often unable to influ-ence the people with the resources. Since the state does not own the resources, it cannot insure that they will be used as much as is physically possible toward the fulfillment of desires. The state cannot insure full employment unless it can somehow control the resources that are necessary to put people to work on socially useful tasks. The owners of the resources do not have in mind a criterion of full employment; they are concerned solely with their individual profits. In addition, they often do not know their own best interests, and fail to see the true relationship between full employment and their own profits.

If the state is to adopt a conscious policy of full employment, it must use some device that will give control over enough privately owned resources to enable it to put the unemployed to productive efforts. An obvious way for the state to acquire the necessary re-sources is for it to borrow funds with which to purchase the re-sources. The state may sell bonds, and with the proceeds of these bonds buy steel, machinery, tractors, and concrete in order that the unemployed may rebuild our cities or work on some other important project. The building up of the public debt to counteract unemployment is inevitable in our society where the means of production (the steel, machinery, tractors, concrete) are privately owned.

Is the public debt an evil? The funds raised by the public debt are used to put otherwise idle men to work, constructing homes, bridges, roads, and schools that make us richer in real terms; this kind of debt cannot possibly be an evil. The debt can become cumbersome, but it need not be evil. The cumbersomeness of the debt arises from the fact that interest on it must be paid periodically, and the government must have a source of funds from which to pay the interest. The source of funds which the government uses is the tax revenue that flows from the periodic income of the nation. As long as the interest charge is a small fraction of the income, the burden is not cumbersome. At present interest rates and debt size, the interest payments are small in comparison to the national income. If income continues to grow secularly as it has in the past, there is little danger that the interest charge on any debt that we are likely to accumulate will become cumbersome.†

People are quick to argue that debts are undesirable for individual business firms and hence must be undesirable for governments. The analogy is completely unjustified. Individuals in a closed system operate in a sea of competitors. If they borrow in this system from their competitors and become unable to repay their debts, they fail because they owe their debts to a competitor outside their individual unit. Our government can borrow for full-employment planning from its own constituents; it does not have to go to outside units for funds. There is no possibility that a competitor can foreclose our mortgage. An internally held public debt can never be a burden, because we owe it to ourselves. The more sophisticated opponents of full-employment planning complain that they are tired of hearing this trite "owe-it-to-yourselves argument." We can only answer that we, too, are tired of hearing the *a fortiori* trite "burden-of-the-debt argument."

Mechanically the debt problem operates as follows: Given a certain debt, we must pay the annual interest charge. From the national income we extract a tax as government revenue, which we then pay out in the form of interest. The debt is held largely by the richer classes; the taxes come largely from the richer classes; the interest is paid largely to the richer classes. We merely extract from the right-hand pocket of the rich and pay to the left-hand pocket of the rich. But if this transfer enables us to command enough resources to achieve full employment, then both the rich and the poor are better off. The poor are better off because they have jobs instead of hunger pains and the nervous frustration of idleness. The rich are better off because they have lost nothing on the transfer and they get larger profits out of the full-employment income than would otherwise be the case.

There is one more commonly made remark that must be disposed of, before we leave the problem of the debt. It is argued that we cannot postpone forever the evil day. The debt must be repaid. Where will the funds come from? Even in a capitalist society we shall not have unemployment forever. Innovations like the railroad, electric power, internal-combustion engine and others do occur and will bring about some periods of prosperity to counterbalance depressions. During these prosperous times, it will be advantageous to fight the danger of inflation by raising taxes and retiring debt. It is possible, though, that some of the debt may fall due at a moment when it is not propitious to raise taxes. If this be the case, then the government merely needs to borrow funds to pay off the debt that is falling due and incur a new debt that exactly replaces the old debt. The government is a continuous institution that does not die when single constituents die. It can keep replacing old debts with new debts of the same size as long as it lives, by transferring a claim from one constituent to another, with the same interest charge. This process, from the point of view of the government, is equivalent to the issuance of long-term debts, say, perpetuities. But from the point of view of the claimant, who is a constituent, the risk is periodically transferred to new shoulders, which is certainly not undesirable.

FULL EMPLOYMENT AND POLITICS

The program outlined in the preceding section sounds reasonable and fits in perfectly with the Keynesian theoretical system, but it may not solve our problems. The full-employment policies which set out to reform capitalism must be considered in reference to the realistic political environment of today.

There are two groups of Keynesian economists today, both of whom accept the logic of the theory. One group supports the program of economic policy, and what is more, has faith that it will be successful; they regard this program as the best solution to the problem of unemployment. The major supporters in this group among the professional economists include Hansen, Samuelson, Smithies, Mosak, Metzler, Hagen, Lerner, and Lange among others in this country.[6] The alternative Keynesian group is much less known but nonetheless correct. The second group holds that there are inherent characteristics developed within the capitalist system which will be insuperable obstacles to the actual carrying out of the necessary measures. This group is composed mainly of Marxists who possess, in addition to a rigorous theory of economic behavior, a theory of social and political development which gives them a basis for judging the practicability of Keynesian reforms. The best known spokesman of this group in academic circles is Paul Sweezy.

We have already outlined the program supported by the first group, and now it behooves us to weigh carefully the judgments of the Marxist group, which puts less faith in the possibility of liberal capitalist reform.

Keynes, it has been stressed, is not a radical. He wanted to reform capitalism in order to make it work better and to preserve it. How is it possible that any capitalist could object to a policy of the preservation of capitalism? The answer is that many capitalists are unaware of the precarious state of the system during a period of serious depression, and do not see the proper relationship between their own position and that of the system as a whole. It is inevitable that most of the effective measures listed in the full-employment legislation above will be strongly opposed by some group of the capitalist population. A few examples will make this point unambiguously.

---

[6] Some individuals in this group would not call themselves Keynesians.*

There are two effective groups opposing the current Wagner-Murray-Dingell social-security bill. This bill is an integral part of a full-employment program because it is the main force to strengthen the propensity to consume. But the insurance trusts and professional medical societies oppose this legislation. The insurance companies are attempting to maximize their individual profits in a capitalist world and cannot assume a social responsibility for full-employment legislation which might impair that profit position. This is a typical example of a special-interest lobby opposing an integral component of a full-employment policy. Such lobbies present huge obstacles to the program of the Keynesian economists. The medical societies cannot oppose social-security legislation on the ground that the aggregate income to the profession will be lowered, because the reverse will undoubtedly be the case. Instead, the medical societies oppose the social-security bills because the income of practitioners will be redistributed in favor of those who have a smaller voice in the established organizations and because the society will lose some of its great powers in controlling the practices in the entire profession. In a capitalist society, powerful groups dislike to lose power as well as profits, and they will fight any legislation that reduces their power. The Marxists will argue that our society is permeated with groups which will act toward other parts of the program just as the insurance trusts and medical societies have acted toward social security.

There is an inexhaustible list of such examples. The electric power companies in the Middle West will oppose a M.V.A. public-works project which would stimulate the level of investment. The banking associations opposed the Bretton Woods proposals because they saw themselves losing power to an international body. Many business men will declare that price control is very important in closing the inflationary gap, but they will declare with renewed vigor that price control should not be applied in their own particular industry. They will oppose any measure that endangers their own profit position even at the expense of social maladjustment. Unless entrepreneurs can be brought to look upon the entire system and their social responsibility toward it, the Marxists will be correct in contending that the Keynesian policies are not politically feasible.

The Marxists do not oppose the Keynesian program. In fact, they will be vigorous supporters of full-employment legislation. But they are not satisfied with full-employment legislation as a permanent solution. They consider it to be in the interests of the common man and therefore support it, but the only smooth-working long-run solution for them is socialism. In a socialist economy there is less of a problem in overcoming the activities of special-interest groups. In such a system there is central planning which coordinates the activities of each individual economic unit with the movement of the system as a whole. This makes for smoothness and lack of friction under socialist planning.

FULL EMPLOYMENT AND THE UNSOLVED PROBLEMS OF ECONOMICS

Our program of social reform must continue even after we have solved the problem of unemployment. Keynesian economics gives us a set of tools with which to work on the unemployment problem, but it does not deal at all with many other important socio-economic questions that also deserve a large share of our attention and study.

Fair employment as well as full employment must become part of our reform slogan. It is true that fuller employment makes for fairer employment, but we cannot relax our efforts to advance the economic position of minority groups with the achievement of a full employment economy. If full employment, with the Negroes in menial jobs, means a national income of $180 billion per year, then our goal should be a national income greater than $200 billion per year, which can be produced in a society where Negroes have exactly the same economic opportunities as everybody else. Just as the existence of unemployment causes disease in our economic system, preparing the way for disaster, so does the existence of unfair employment create an equally serious disease. A complete economic theory must tell us how to get both fair and full employment. We may accept the Keynesian theory as a step toward the formulation of the comprehensive doctrines for which we are now groping.

Secondly, Keynes has shown us a way to get higher levels of income, but he has not assured us that this income will be distributed in an equitable manner. Many of the Keynesian policies will serve to benefit the poor more than the rich. For example, social-security benefits which require a large employer contribution will represent a shift of resources from the capitalist to the working class. But such redistributive schemes are not adequate, in themselves, to prevent the existence of great social injustices. A successful program of full-employment policies in a capitalist environment will still leave us with a highly skewed income distribution. This is another type of economic injustice, like the injustice of unfair employment, which eventually must pass away if we are to have true economic democracy.

It should be recalled that the classical economists assumed away the problem of unemployment in their theoretical system, yet they kept occupied with economic research. How then did they spend their time? They made contributions toward the solution of the problem of allocating resources in a full-employment economy.

We too must study this problem, once we have put all our men and machines to some useful effort. The productive factors must be distributed among industries and occupations in such a way that we get as high a value of full-employment output as is physically possible within our accepted pattern of work and leisure.

The problem of resource allocation was not treated by Keynes, because there were more urgent matters at hand. But resource allocation will again become urgent when the problems that have bothered Keynes are solved.

NOTES TO THE ORIGINAL EDITION

* PAGE 50.   For reconsideration of views held by Ohlin and Frisch, see Chapter VIII.

† PAGE 53.   The reader is particularly directed to the new, private edition of 1958, in which Haberler adds some chapters reviewing the post-Keynesian development of business-cycle analysis.   He shows great lack of sympathy with modern fashions that are largely spurred by the Keynesian development.

* PAGE 59.   Prewar budget studies were severely limited in coverage of higher income classes, where most of the curvature in the consumption function has been found.   More recent studies would suggest that the consumption function is nonlinear and moderately affected by the distribution of income.

† PAGE 60.   More recent work suggests some statistical effect of terms of consumer credit on demand for consumer durables.   In this respect, the assertion of interest inelasticity of consumption must be qualified.

† PAGE 66.   Since the early 1950's when interest rates showed more variation about higher levels, there does appear to be a definite and statistically significant interest effect on investment.   It should be noted, however, that the relevant interest elasticities are not large.   They are nearly all less than unity.

* PAGE 66.   The techniques of conducting sample surveys were considerably improved after World War II, and the results cited here would be deemed suspect on present standards.   Delicate methods of indirect questioning and more intricate survey design would be needed to give more acceptable answers to the question of the role of interest rates in investment decisions.

† PAGE 72.   Current research is being devoted to building models with endogenous money supplies, dependent on bank regulations, conventional ratios, reserves, and interest rates.   This seems to be much more satisfactory and promising than the crude assumption of an exogenous money supply.

† PAGE 79.   This argument is overstated, and Keynesian types of problems may develop for socialist economies, especially through the cumulation of random shocks.   See L. R. Klein, "The Role of Econometrics in Socialist Economics," *Problems of Economic Dynamics and Planning*, PWN, Warsaw, 1964.   See also Chapter VIII.

† PAGE 92.   This is no longer the case.   Lerner's lack of clarity was surely a matter of the promptness with which he was analyzing the Keynesian doctrines.

† PAGE 95.   It might be preferable to say that the stock of capital is treated as exogenous in the analysis of the *static* Keynesian system.

† PAGE 117.   The unimportance of interest rates was probably overstressed in the post-Keynesian development.   There is ample room for dispute over

the desirability of reliance on interest policy, but its importance, though limited, should not be neglected.

† PAGE 118.   As a student, I heard Lerner make this remark at a seminar presentation.   It has become a part of oral tradition, but some writers have been suspicious of its authenticity.

† PAGE 124.   This should be amended to take account of Kalecki's prior, complete model.   See Chapter VIII.

* PAGE 157.   While Congress can do this in principle, it has been found in practice that forecasts of tax revenues when rates are varied can be highly inaccurate.

† PAGE 159.   A useful model on which a government could rely would have to be more detailed and complicated.   See Chapter VIII.

† PAGE 167.   This view needs qualifying.   See L. R. Klein, "The Role of Econometrics in Socialist Economics," *op. cit.* and Chapter VIII.

* PAGE 168.   During the past 20 years, much progress has been made in dealing with the forecasting problem.   Good statements on recent developments can be found in D. B. Suits, "Forecasting and Analysis with an Econometric Model," *American Economic Review*, Vol. LII, 1962, pp. 104-32.   See also the papers by L. R. Klein and T. M. Brown in *Models of Income Determination*, Princeton University Press, Princeton, 1964, pp. 11-96.

† PAGE 169.   After the 1957 recession, unemployment was a persistent problem for the United States.   Were it not for the Korean War, this problem might have arisen sooner.   Although we did not return to the excessive unemployment of the 1930's, we had a significant problem.

† PAGE 170.   Decay of U.S. cities and problems of urbanization have become worse in the past two decades.   More than ever before, we need imaginative public investment on a large scale.   This will simultaneously attack the urban problems and the unemployment problem.

† PAGE 172.   See the argument above that interest movements show renewed vigor in affecting investment in the 1950's, although the elasticity coefficient is less than unity.

† PAGE 177.   The American economy did, in fact, become a high-level-consumption economy and the result has not been entirely satisfactory. The "Affluent Society" has serious side effects.   I would now be more inclined to argue for a combined full employment policy (cyclical) by public authorities and a high savings policy (trend) for growth.   See L. R. Klein and R. G. Bodkin, "Empirical Aspects of the Trade-Offs among Three Goals: High Level Employment, Price Stability, and Economic Growth," *Inflation Growth and Employment*, Commission on Money and Credit, Prentice-Hall, N.Y., 1964, pp. 367-428.

† PAGE 178.   See Chapter VIII for changed views on the stability of the savings function.

† PAGE 180. Congress has stubbornly refused to relinquish its great power over fiscal matters and refused to grant the President (Mr. Kennedy) discretionary authority to vary the rates of income tax.   They were also very slow to act in passing the tax reduction bill of 1964.

† PAGE 182.   The figures in the table below bear out these views on the relative growth rates of income, interest payments, and debt.

	GNP	NET INTEREST PAID BY GOVERNMENT	OUTSTANDING DEBT OF FEDERAL, STATE, AND LOCAL GOVERNMENT
1947	$234 billion	4.4	238
1964	623	9.2	353

* PAGE 184.   Lange is undoubtedly misplaced.

CHAPTER VIII

THE KEYNESIAN REVOLUTION REVISITED*

It is almost twenty years since the preceding chapters were first published. For most of this period, I have concentrated my attention on statistical studies of the consumption, investment, and liquidity-preference functions and on economy-wide models. It is now time to turn this attention, to some extent, at least, toward the interpretation of empirical findings. It is time to reconsider the Keynesian Revolution, and I propose to do so in this chapter. There have been many interpretive articles on Keynes and the *General Theory* — after ten years, after fifteen years, and after twenty years — but I shall approach the matter in a different way, as a summary of years of econometric testing and studying of the accounts of such quantitative work by others in the field.

THE MEANING OF THE KEYNESIAN REVOLUTION

The primary contentions of Keynesian theory as set down in this book can be summarized in a form that gives us scientific agreement on our terms of reference. The Keynesian system is

1. A theory of the determination of total income (output or employment).
2. A theoretical explanation of the possibility of under-employment equilibrium.
3. A group of doctrines in public policy about how to control the economy at desired levels of economic activity.
4. A long-run view on the historical trend of capitalism.

I shall consider all these main contentions of Keynesian theory, but principally, I am concerned with the first and second. I want to re-examine the theory of income determination in the light of our knowledge of the actual functioning of the economy, a knowledge that has been built up by econometric studies.

* Parts of this essay were presented in lectures given at Osaka University, October 1, 1963; Hitotsubashi University, October 9, 1963; and Nagoya University, November 13, 1963. Reprinted from *The Economic Studies Quarterly*, Vol. XV, Nov., 1964, pp. 1–24.

The Keynesian thinking of the 1930's stimulated national income-accounting and related data-gathering activities. These developments might have progressed without the Keynesian influence, but surely not as swiftly. The new developments in statistical annals made available a body of data that is almost ideal for testing the theory. The testing has been done largely by econometricians who build models of the Keynesian type, but with numerical parameters, that are carefully determined by accepted statistical methods. Unfortunately, Keynes was not sympathetic with this approach to the study of his ideas, and the task of checking the theory has fallen to outsiders.[1] People from the "inside" group at Cambridge never followed through with a careful statistical check of the theory, although they would have been eminently qualified to do so.

The close followers of Keynes, in England and America (the neo-Keynesians), have often advocated the implementation of his theoretical ideas in the formation of public economic policy. At an early stage, it was recognized that this policy implementation would require accurate predictions of the macro-economy, and econometric model-building has this goal precisely in mind. After some years of disappointment, Keynesian followers argued that accurate predictions were not needed and that trial-and-error methods would be satisfactory. I feel that this is an extremely dangerous position. There is really no suitable alternative to the econometric approach. Given the slow motions of our democratic legislative processes, which have been amply demonstrated in recent years, we cannot rely on quick decisions for implementing a trial-and-error approach. We need the kind of model-building that the original Keynesians disdained. Built-in stabilizers, such as progressive tax systems and transfer payments, help in the face of slow-moving legislatures, but they are temporary, partial, and inadequate to the whole task of economic stabilization.

The Elements of the Formal Model: The pillars of the model of income determination are widely recognized as the marginal pro-

---

[1] J. M. Keynes, "Professor Tinbergen's Method," *Economic Journal*, Vol. XLIX, 1939, pp. 558–568. See also, Professor Tinbergen's reply, "On a Method of Statistical Business-Cycle Research," *Economic Journal*, Vol. L, 1940, pp. 141–154.

pensity to consume (or save), the marginal efficiency of capital, and liquidity preference. After the interpretations, in consistent mathematical form, by Hicks and Lange, Keynesian thinking settled along these lines,[2]

$$S(r, Y) = I(r, Y)$$
$$M = L(r, Y)$$

where Y is aggregate money income, r is the interest rate, and M is the nominal stock of cash. The three pillars are represented as $S(r, Y)$, the propensity to save; $I(r, Y)$, the marginal efficiency of capital schedule; and $L(r, Y)$, the liquidity-preference function. This is an informative and succinct way of expressing the theory in what I would now like to call a *pedagogical* model. I want to emphasize that this is only a crude framework for thinking and illustrating main ideas. It has teaching attributes but obscures so much of life that it cannot be thought of as a *working* model.

But the very simplicity of this pedagogical model gets us into theoretical difficulty. It is a closed system of two relationships in two unknown variables, r and Y, given exogenous control over M by the monetary authorities. This latter assumption will come under scrutiny and be seriously questioned, but for the moment we shall accept it. The trouble with this simple model is that it cannot be extended from a theory of income determination to a theory of employment without making it more complicated. Furthermore; it violates received economic theory in the matter of money illusion or homogeneity, in a mathematical sense. Aggregate income is defined as *money* income, yet neo-classical theory would suggest that the equilibrium system should be stated in terms of *real* income. Employment is directly related to real income, not money income.

If we were to redefine the income variable as y (aggregate real output) and also recognize the homogeneity postulates, our system would be

$$S(r, y) = I(r, y)$$
$$\frac{M}{p} = L(r, y)$$

[2] Hicks, *op. cit.* Lange, "The Rate of Interest and the Optimum Propensity to Consume," *op. cit.*

H

This may be a more satisfactory version, but it is incomplete because there are three variables to be determined: r, y, and p. We need to close the system by extending it in such a way that the price level is explained. To do this, we shall have to extend the system to include production functions, factor-demand, and factor-supply functions. A proper statement of Keynesian economics must include all these extended relationships. Indeed, Keynes did start out with notions of labor supply and demand in the *General Theory*, but he failed to give a self-contained, explicit, and internally consistent mathematical model of all the relationships. In the many renditions that have been handed down over the past twenty-five years, it has been thought that the three pillars are adequate; but they are not, either theoretically or practically. We cannot escape from thinking in terms of the whole system.

Even the extended system, with production, factor-supply, and factor-demand functions added, is not adequate for serious applications. The system of two equations and the extended versions that include approximately five or six equations have been analyzed over and over again by scholars in the period since 1936, and there is very little that can be added by going over this ground again. It appears to be more fruitful to consider more elaborate and far-reaching extensions of the theory from the realm of pedagogy to that of realism and application.

EXTENSION OF THE BASIC MODEL

How does the system have to be extended before it becomes a useful working tool?

A public sector must be added. The model as stated in pure pedagogical form makes little provision for public economic action. It permits monetary control over M. Government expenditures are frequently added as exogenous investment, and tax-transfer relationships are incorporated. This gives a framework for a multiplier analysis of public policy.

In reality, the public sector is more endogenous than is commonly recognized. Social and educational expenditures depend on population growth and distribution; highways are needed to meet the traffic generated by consumer purchases of cars; public construction may follow movements in interest rates.   There are many ways in which the public sector responds to the economic climate, but, admittedly, national defense and other government expenditures or revenue decisions are exogenous.   Nevertheless, it is a gross and misleading over-simplification merely to add some exogenous government variables to the standard models.

The system must be opened with respect to foreign trade.   The simplest models depict an isolated, closed economy.   They are possibly good approximations for some of the world's large self-sufficient economies, but most nations rely heavily on foreign trade. The available theoretical extensions with foreign-trade multipliers are useful, as steps in the right direction for opening the system, but they are inadequate.   They lead to the general over-all impression that exports are good (employment-creating) and imports are bad (employment-destroying).   This is not generally so.   In large industrial nations that import competitive goods, an expansion of imports cuts into domestic activity.   In some countries, however, imports of raw materials and capital equipment of a non-competitive type help production markedly.   In Japan's economy, for example, imports are absolutely necessary to its functioning at a high level.

A suitably extended open system must allow explicitly for the productivity of imports, the terms of trade, and the balance-of-payments position, in addition to the simple income effects of the familiar foreign-trade multiplier.   To deal adequately with the open economy and to tackle problems that have recently arisen in the foreign sector of many economies, we would have to make a fairly major extension of the simple models.[3]

The system must be made dynamic.   Except for some notes on the trade cycle, the *General Theory* dealt with a static model.   The world is dynamic, and no static model will give a widely applicable

[3] To emphasize that we need to be reminded of the importance of introducing government and foreign sectors into the basic model, I cite a leading textbook on what might be called the neo-Keynesian theory.   See Gardner Ackley, *Macroeconomic Theory*, Macmillan, New York, 1961.   Ackley's book is built essentially around a model of a domestic economy with no government activity.   However, as a result of his later experience as chief economic counselor to the President of the United States, advocating Keynesian-type policies, I suspect that he might want to extend his model in the way indicated for government activity and foreign trade, as payments problems have been ever present in his tenure of office.

representation of it.   There have been interesting dynamizations of
the simple model, but these fail to show the realistic dynamics.   A
suitable lag structure is important in showing the relationship
between the long and short run in this theory.   Without benefit of
elaborate dynamizations, analysts have misjudged the magnitude
of multipliers, especially in the short run.   The empirical studies of
Goldberger and Suits have shown forcefully that short-run multipliers (one year or less) are barely greater than unity.[4]   In the long
run they build up to preconceived ideas derived from static analysis,
but the build-up is slow.

The accounting relationship between capital stock and net investment should automatically introduce trend dynamics into the system.   Keynes circumvented this effect by using the artificial
assumption that capital stock can be treated as constant in the short
run.   This is an extremely curious assumption, because investment,
which is by definition a change in capital stock, occupies a central
role in the theory.   It can perhaps be explained by noting that the
percentage expansion of capital must be tiny in the short run, while
the percentage expansion of investment is not.   If the short run is
taken to mean one, two, or three years this assumption is quite misleading, for capital formation can make itself felt significantly
within one year and decidedly so within three years.   The static
short-run equilibrium model is, thus, an artifact.   At a minimum,
the production function must be generalized to take account of the
productivity of capital, and the marginal productivity of labor is not
a simple demand function because it depends on the level of capital
stock.   The marginal productivity of capital must be properly
linked to the Keynesian notion of marginal efficiency of capital, and
in this way the lack of contradiction between classical real theories
of interest and the Keynesian monetary theory can be made clear.

The system must be disaggregated.   It is useful for teaching purposes to regard the entire producing economy as one huge enterprise

---

[4] A. S. Goldberger, *Impact Multipliers and Dynamic Properties of the Klein-Goldberger Model*, North Holland Publishing Co., Amsterdam, 1959.   D. B. Suits, "Forecasting and Analysis with an Econometric Model," *American Economic Review*, Vol.
LII, 1962, pp. 104–32.   Interestingly enough, Keynes first guessed at a multiplier of
1.5 for the United Kingdom.   In an open economy this may be high for the short run
but not so high as others.   See p. 41, Goldberger.

and develop the analogue theory of the single firm to explain the macro-economy; but the modern economy is too complex to yield to such simplified treatment. Realistic applications will require an explicit recognition of at least a few sectors. The particular sectors displayed and the degree of disaggregation ultimately chosen will depend on the policy objectives to be considered. My main contention is that some form of macro-model is still workable as a useful tool in applied economics. It is much less aggregative than the usual Keynesian models, but it is not nearly as detailed as the theory of Walras or the empirical schemes of Leontief or Orcutt.[5] The extended Keynesian system that has realism may need to have approximately ten sectors and may be enlarged to have as many as twenty to thirty without going to Leontief's detail of 500 industrial classifications or to Orcutt's family-individual firm level. There is still an important role for macro-economics, but the order of the magnitude of detail is considerably above that of Keynes and his immediate followers. A ten-sector system that explains sector prices, wages, employment, investment, and similar variables mushrooms in size rapidly.

A RECONSIDERATION OF THE KEYNESIAN RELATIONSHIPS

When the *General Theory* was first being discussed and intellectually digested, there was a feeling on the part of many scholars that profound truths of an amazing sort were contained in the interrelationships connecting the three pillar functions. I felt at the time I wrote the *Keynesian Revolution* that a full understanding of this simple model had enabled us to interpret economic events of the period since World War I with great insight. My feeling now is that the *General Theory* is an intellectual breakthrough, but that it is too simple for judging the real world. When it was mechanistically and naively applied to events of the period after World War II, for purposes of economic prediction, it was usually found that there were major factors not accounted for in the simple model that had

---

[5] W. W. Leontief, *The Structure of the American Economy*, 1919–1939, Oxford University Press, New York, 1952. G. H. Orcutt, *et al.*, *Microanalysis of Socioeconomic Systems: A Simulation Study*, Harper and Bros., New York, 1961.

determined the course of the economy. The theory must be regarded as a *core* theory with *kernels* of truth. It needs substantial
amplification for reaching the whole truth. Also, it does not rest
on a carefully laid and well-documented statistical base. In terms
of today's standards, it would be classed as containing "casual
empiricism."

It is almost inevitable that the intensive investigation of the consumption, investment, and liquidity-preference functions by an
army of econometrician-scholars would turn up numerous points of
detail that qualify the simple theory based on 2 or 3-parameter
functions. On looking carefully at each of the main functions, from
a statistical viewpoint, I feel that the theory must necessarily be
expanded by a large measure to take into account some neglected
factors.

The propensity to consume or save: The Keynesian idea of the
existence of a basic psychological law establishing a relationship
between aggregate consumption and aggregate income, with slope
less than unity, needs obvious extension to account for taxes, transfer payments, income distribution, lags, relative prices, and possibly
wealth. Keynes was well aware of these qualifications to the simple
relationship implied by his basic psychological law, but he undoubtedly felt that a function

$$C = C(y), \quad 0 < dC/dy < 1$$

was adequate for most situations.

Modification of the consumption function to take taxes and transfers into account is standard procedure in statistical studies, when
disposable income has become the relevant explanatory variable.
This modification comes about once the system is extended to include the public sector, even if in the most rudimentary form.

Income distribution effects were investigated empirically in the
form of Pareto-coefficients as explanatory variables, just after the
General Theory was first published. These effects were generally
dismissed as being of negligible size, although discernible. An
argument in support of the neglect of income-distribution effects was
the linearity of the Engel curves of total spending or saving esti-

mated from family budget studies.[6] More recent studies of sample surveys of consumer budgets have changed this picture. Modern surveys contain many more high-income recipients than did those of the 1920's or 1930's. For scientific sampling reasons, there is deliberate over-sampling in the upper income groups, and post-war prosperity has changed the distribution of income by placing a larger number of persons in the top groups. Curvature of the Engel curve becomes evident in, roughly, the top decile, compared with the bottom 90 per cent; therefore, recent studies reveal a more significant non-linearity in the Engel curves.[7] The revealed non-linearities do not necessarily imply a short-run sensitivity of aggregate consumption or savings to changes in the distribution of income, and most time-series studies with aggregative quarterly or annual statistics show little effect of changes in the (factorial) distribution of income. Over decades and longer stretches of time, changes in the distribution of income may be more significant. For example, it is customarily felt that one of the reasons why Japan has been a high-saving country over the past 100 years is that a highly unequal distribution of income has been maintained. If there is a future tendency toward more equality, this may promote a higher rate of consumption and a lower rate of saving.

The lag structure of economic relationships has become a very popular problem of econometric analysis in recent years. Stock-adjustment forms of relationship have been proposed for a wide variety of types of behavior. In the case of consumption, the lag structure is usually expressed as

$$C = \alpha_0 + \alpha_1 \sum_{i=0}^{\infty} \lambda^i y_{-i},$$

or

$$C = \alpha_0(1 - \lambda) + \alpha_1 y + \lambda C_{-1}$$

This is also the time-series form of Friedman's *permanent-income hypothesis*, although it was in use by econometricians long before

[6] Cf. p. 59 above.
[7] L. R. Klein, "Statistical Estimation of Economic Relations from Survey Data," *Contributions of Survey Methods in Economics*, Columbia University Press, New York, 1954, pp. 189–240.

that consumption theory was proposed.[8]   It is this lag structure that accounts for large differences between long- and short-run multipliers.   This can be seen readily by observing that statistical estimates of α_1 and λ in the preceding relationship give values

$$\text{est. } \alpha_1 \sim 0.65$$
$$\text{est. } \lambda \sim 0.35$$

This gives a one-period m.p.c. of only 0.65 but a long run m.p.c. of

$$\text{est. } \frac{\alpha_1}{1 - \lambda} \sim 1.0.$$

The stock-adjustment form of lag distribution employed is directly applicable to consumer-spending on durable goods, for it was first developed in detail for investment in fixed capital.[9]   This does not mean that the lag distributions do not apply to non-durable consumption, but the parameters of the lag process are probably different for different types of consumer goods.   This suggests the fruitfulness of the disaggregation of total consumption into durables and non-durables — possibly even further.   Such disaggregation is an essential extension of the original and simple Keynesian model.   But disaggregation may have deeper implications than the proliferation of consumption functions with different lag distributions; it may force us to consider the introduction of relative prices.

In the Keynesian system, income effects predominate over relative price effects, and this may be quite plausible as long as a high degree of aggregation is used.   The more disaggregation there is into types of goods and services, the more important relative prices become in some equations.

The one relative price considered by Keynes explicitly is the price of future compared with present goods; in other words, the interest rate.   Although Keynes considered interest effects in some detail, and seemed to attach great importance to the role of interest, the history of subsequent Keynesian analysis (after the *General Theory*)

[8] M. Friedman, *A Theory of the Consumption Function*, Princeton University Press, Princeton, N.J., 1957.

[9] L. M. Koyck, *Distributed Lags and Investment Analysis*, North-Holland Publishing Co., Amsterdam, 1954.   H. B. Chenery, "Overcapacity and the Acceleration Principle," *Econometrica*, Vol. XX, 1952, pp. 1–28.

is one of a minimization of interest effects.   The theory of existence of under-employment equilibirum appears to depend on interest inelasticity of spending decisions.   As far as consumer-spending is concerned, Keynes was truly doubtful about the magnitude of interest effects, and subsequent statistical studies have justified this doubt.   There is no empirical evidence, so far, that shows significant interest effects on total spending or saving by consumers after income effects are taken into consideration.   That is not to say that wide movements of interest rates and relative prices, much wider in the short run than have been observed, will have no influence on total spending or saving.   However, the evidence indicates that fluctuations of the sort that we have witnessed will not have a marked influence.[10]

The influence of wealth has come into the consumption-function discussion in different ways.   Pigou stimulated much interest by his analysis of the effect of real-cash holdings.   This was generalized and elaborated by Patinkin to the real-balance effect, including all consumer wealth and not simply cash wealth.   The same ideas appear in disguised form in Friedman's permanent-income hypothesis.[11]   There is strong evidence for the permanent-income hypothesis, in a *weak* form, as we have shown here in the lag distribution. More direct studies of real liquid assets or total real wealth are somewhat less conclusive.   In America, after World War II, there is evidence of a strong liquid-asset effect, but this influence seems to have diminished of late.   A combination of circumstances — large consumer accumulations of liquid wealth, low consumer stocks of durables, military victory, and a productive system intact — may have been extremely favorable in bringing out an abnormal effect of liquid-asset holdings.

The wealth effects are unusually important because, following Pigou's line of argument, they insure the reaching of full employment in equilibrium and argue against the Keynesian theoretical

[10] In the latter part of the 1950's, interest rates moved to higher levels in many countries than had been observed for two decades.   This induced some significant shifts in portfolio composition, but not in the over-all choice between saving and spending.

[11] Pigou, "The Classical Stationary State," *op. cit.*   D. Patinkin, *Money, Interest and Prices*, Row, Peterson and Co., Evanston, Ill., 1956.   Friedman, *op. cit.*

concept of under-employment equilibrium, a subject to which we shall return.

Many people are impressed with the rise of consumer credit as an institution fostering high-level consumption. Should consumer debt or the state of the credit market for such debt be a particular aspect of wealth or interest that should be introduced as a variable in the consumer function? *A priori*, there is much plausibility in the arguments about the influence of consumer credit, especially on purchases of durables, but most statistical studies have until now failed to uncover a separate effect that is independent of incomes and lag distributions.[12] Consumer credit is usually restricted to a time duration of only twelve to twenty-four months, and it is not impossible for people to accumulate capital values for purchases of consumer durables in that period of time. Credit, therefore, has appeared to affect the time shape of spending much more than its total amount.

Finally, I want to comment on the more general Keynesian philosophical outlook on consumption. It is an implicit supposition in Keynesian economics, especially the business-cycle aspects, that capital formation is volatile (impulsive, dynamic, variable), while consumption is passive (regular, stable, steady). Consumption is seen as adjusting to the macro-environment that is created by investment. This is not to say that consumption remains constant, but that the consumption function does. Consumption moves along the stable function. Statistically, we ought to find a high-correlation function for consumption and a comparatively low-correlation function for investment. That is precisely what we do find; but we also find that, among consumption types, durables have low-correlation equations, like investment functions. The volatility of consumer durables and spending on luxuries, such as entertainment, some personal services, or vacations, have been large enough to make consumption as a whole volatile. The history of the postwar economy, first in the United States, then in Western Europe, and then in Japan, is grossly misunderstood if one fails to

---

[12] Some newer results suggest that characteristics of the consumer credit market (down-payment percentages, contract length, and interest charges) affect car purchases and possibly other consumer durables.

appreciate the autonomous role of consumption.   Many American fluctuations have been offset by contrary movements in consumption.   Katona and his colleagues in consumer-survey research have strongly emphasized this activist role of the consumer,[13] while old-line Keynesians, such as Mrs. Robinson, have continued to place most of the activating stress on investment.   She has argued that investment plays such an activating role that it creates its own profits.[14]   The Keynesian role of consumption is, however, outmoded, and it will not be possible to capture the spirit of the next phases of economic development unless one takes a more balanced view of consumer behavior.

The stable, aggregative, static, bivariate consumption function of the simplest Keynesian model will no longer serve our analysis adequately.   At a minimum, we must allow for taxes, transfers, lags, and some degree of disaggregation.   It is probably true that income distribution, relative prices, or wealth will also be of some significance, and some disaggregated components will have exogenous dynamic impulses that will be propagated throughout the economy as a whole.

The propensity to invest (m.e.c.): Direct statistical testing of the strict form of the Keynesian theory of marginal efficiency of capital (m.e.c.) is very difficult because we cannot find data on *expected marginal profits* associated with an act of investment.   It is difficult to measure profits in any case, but expected profits are subjective, and marginal profits are not generally recorded in business accounts. If the production function is of a specific type, such as the Cobb-Douglas function, it is possible to transform the theory into a testable form using observed data, provided that expected market variables can be approximated by lag values.   The stock-adjustment forms of investment functions,

$$I = \beta_0 + \beta_1 \frac{p_{-1}y}{q_{-1}} + \beta_2 K_{-1}$$
$$K = K_{-1} + I$$

[13] G. Katona, *The Powerful Consumer*, McGraw-Hill, New York, 1960.
[14] J. Robinson, *The Accumulation of Capital*, Richard D. Irwin, Inc., Homewood, Ill., 1956.

are the type that would be implied. I = capital formation, y = aggregate output, p = price of output, q = price of capital services, K = stock of capital. This function can be modified by the inclusion of an interest-rate variable, and if only one price-level variable is used, relative price ceases to be part of the first variable.

The original formulations of the static Keynesian model omitted lags, the stock of capital, and relative price. They included an interest variable, however. Subsequent statistical work showed minor or nil effects of interest on investment. The results of aggregative time-series analysis were fortified by the direct questioning of business respondents about their decision-making process. On reconsideration, I am inclined to attach little significance to the sample survey results obtained in the 1930's.[15] The samples were not well designed by modern standards, and the questions about intricate matters outside the realm of actual business experience were much too direct. Modern survey techniques in sample design, questionnaire structure, and interviewing methods are vastly improved, although they have not been intensively applied to the question of the interest elasticity of investment. Conclusions from the time-series results may have been premature, for results obtained since 1952 in samples that contain several observations at widely varying interest levels show that interest is a significant variable in equations of investment behavior. The new results show statistical significance for interest variables; they do not necessarily show high elasticity.

Other variables of significance in statistical investment functions are business cash flow (gross operating profit), business liquidity, or explicit measures of capacity utilization. The last mentioned can be used as a replacement for the capital-stock variable.

There are two kinds of investment that have proved to be of great importance in recent economic fluctuations; but they received little specific attention from Keynes; they are residential construction and inventory investment. Residential construction merits separate treatment in disaggregation, because it is strongly influenced by its own demographic factors and may receive special forms of

[15] Cf. pp. 65–66 above.

public support. Inventory investment may follow familiar lines of stock-adjustment theories, but its adjustment parameters imply a very different reaction lag, one that gives rise to short business cycles of less than four years' duration. Speculative variables of price-level change and interest-rate change may also be peculiar to inventory investment. These, then, are compelling reasons for some disaggregation of investment beyond that originally given by Keynes. Followers of Keynes were quick to investigate these specific types of investment, but it must be recognized that the theory needs extension to include these in a consistent and fully determined manner.

Another philosophical view found in Keynesian thinking, similar to the passive role attributed to consumption, as discussed here, is the outlook for a long-run decline in the m.e.c. This pessimistic outlook for investment does not appear to be justified by recent events, either in the industrialized economies of the United States and Western Europe or in the newly developing countries. New inventions inspired by the scientific developments of World War II, such as radar, automated devices, and atomic power, were not foreseen. Prospects are that new discoveries will continue to flow; new investment opportunities will continue to arise; and the long-run m.e.c. need not necessarily decline. Who is to say what the economic prospects of the moon are?

Liquidity preference: The doctrine of liquidity preference is developed for an economy in which people make a choice between only two possible types of assets, money or bonds. Furthermore, the bonds considered are best thought of as perpetuities; then bond price and interest rate are connected in a simple reciprocal relationship. The supply of money is considered to be exogenously controlled by the central banking system (the monetary authorities).

The debate between the loanable-funds theorists and the liquidity-preference theorists has led into many blind alleys. In a truly interdependent system it is generally not possible to establish unique lines of causation; we can, however, construct approximate special cases that give the main flavor of the theory. To do this for the Keynesian model so that we have an unqualified liquidity-preference theory, I think we need to construct an artificial economy in which currency and interest-bearing bank accounts are the only allowable assets. All lending for investment is to be made through the creation of bank loans. In this situation, there is no separate price for marketable assets; there is only an interest cost of bank loans or an interest gain on bank deposits. The bank accounts are non-marketable assets with a fixed money price.

This theory can be used only to explain the kernel of an idea; it is not a realistic analysis of a complicated money market. There are three lines of development that need to be followed to make this theory workable: (1) More assets or debt instruments must be considered — bills, bonds, equities, cash, savings accounts, and goods. (2) More classes of holders must be considered — private households, non-financial companies, private banks, non-bank financial institutions, foreigners, central bank, and public treasury. (3) A supply theory of money must be developed.

The modern theories of portfolio selection in which average return and risk are separately considered have been applied by Tobin to the theory of liquidity preference, and this appears to be a fruitful line of theoretical development for rationalizing the liquidity-preference theory in a multiple asset economy.[16] Intellectually it is a more satisfying explanation than Keynes', and it follows in the tradition of time-honored principles of sound investment counseling — diversification of holdings to minimize risk. In view of Keynes' early work on subjective probability theory, we might have expected the master himself to have worked out this line of analysis in liquidity-preference theory, but the inspiration appears, instead, to have come from the work of von Neumann and Morgenstern.[17]

A new development is coming forth in empirical monetary analy-

[16] J. Tobin, "Liquidity Preference as Behavior Towards Risk," *Review of Economic Studies*, Vol. XXV, 1957-1958, pp. 65–86, and "The Theory of Portfolio Selection," *The Theory of Interest Rates*, F. H. Hahn and F. P. R. Brechling, eds., Macmillan, London, 1965, pp. 3–51, See also, D. Patinkin, "An Indirect-Utility Approach to the Theory of Money, Assets, and Savings," *ibid.*, pp. 52–79.

[17] J. M. Keynes, *A Treatise on Probability*, Macmillan, London, 1921. J. v. Neumann and O. Morgenstern, *The Theory of Games and Economic Behavior*, Princeton University Press, Princeton, N.J., 1946. Curiously enough, this part of the von Neumann-Morgenstern celebrated study has made a greater impact on economic theory than the central theories of bargaining and game-playing.

sis, namely, accounts for the flows of funds through the economy.[18] These statistical tables promise to do for monetary analysis what national income accounts have done for real-economy analysis. The flow-of-funds accounts are sub-divided by type of asset-debt holders, and future empirical studies will undoubtedly clarify behavioral patterns in the money market. We do not yet have as unambiguous a statistical pattern of this type of behavior as we do of consumption and investment. There are results, however, that suggest that price-level changes influence money holdings, illustrating that the holding of goods or equities ought to be considered in the portfolio. Profit rates influence company holding of cash; therefore, equity investments are relevant to business liquidity decisions. We have seen strong reactions in recent years, on the part of households, to changes in rates on savings accounts or to potential capital gains in equities. It is quite apparent that the theory must be extended by type of asset and type of holder.

Most of the empirical econometric works that have followed the Keynesian inspiration have achieved the greatest measures of success in explaining the behavior of the real economy. The link between the real and money economy has been poorly established in a statistical sense, and possibly the link is really weak. In addition, the statistical equations of the money market itself are not firmly established. One of the special Keynesian hypotheses, that of the liquidity trap, as shown by a high-interest elasticity of cash holdings at low rates, has been observed in a few instances. But it is not yet definitely established.

If the monetary sector of the Keynesian model is disaggregated by the type of asset holder, as suggested here, there will almost certainly have to be a theory of money supply, because asset-debt decisions of private banks, central banks, and the public treasury will determine money supply. It is the crudest over-simplification to say that the central authorities control the stock of cash balances exogenously. In America they fix discount rates, reserve require-

---

[18] M. A. Copeland, *A Study of Moneyflows in the United States*, National Bureau of Economic Research, New York, 1952, and Federal Reserve staff, *Flow of Funds in the United States, 1939-1953*, Board of Governors of the Federal Reserve System, Washington, 1955. See also, *Federal Reserve Bulletin*, Vol. 45, August, 1959, pp. 828–859, 1046–1062.

ments (within legislative limits), and engage in open market dealings with government securities; in Japan they principally make advances to private banks or the public treasury, control foreign exchange, and watch over reserve positions; in the United Kingdom they fix the Bank Rate, control overdrafts, and control foreign exchange. These are only some principal control activities. Monetary authorities regulate equity markets, co-operate with treasury officials in managing the public debt, fix entire schedules of bank charges or rates, control terms of consumer credit and home-mortgage markets, regulate the financial activities of insurance companies, and engage in a host of other peripheral financial activities. By these diverse means, they hope to control the money supply. Sometimes bank reserves are plentiful; sometimes they are scarce. This provides ample evidence that in the short run the authorities cannot make the money supply just what they want it to be.

An explicit theory of money supply has been developed by Brunner, and new statistical models of this aspect of behavior are being prepared.[19] The parameters will be the actual control magnitudes that the central bank can regulate. As in the case of the real government sector, some of these supply relationships will involve variables from the private sectors; thus, money supply will become an interdependent (partially) endogenous sector of the whole system.

Production and labor demand functions: The Keynesian theory is not wedded to any particular type of production function. It could be consistent with a linear function, a Cobb-Douglas function, the new version of constant-elasticity of substitution (C.E.S.) functions, or other aggregative relationships. The characterization of a particular output level as full-employment output has been pedagogically attractive and popular in rule-of-thumb policy analysis, but it is not satisfactory in its treatment of capital stock. As noted earlier, the artificiality of the short-run static model with given capital stock is inconsistent with the productivity of current investment. Labor-capital substitution and variable capital stock are

[19] K. Brunner, "A Schema for the Supply Theory of Money," *International Economic Review*, Vol. II, 1961, pp. 79–109.

two requirements for a suitable production function in the theory. Productivity parameters are so different among major industry groupings (agriculture, manufacturing, tertiary industry) that disaggregation ought to be as rewarding for production as for consumption functions.

Labor demand is usually thought of as a transformation of the marginal productivity functions for labor. If capital is regarded as a variable in the production function, the marginal productivity function for labor will not generally define employment as a function of real wage alone. It would be necessary to combine marginal productivity functions for all factors to derive an explicit labor-demand schedule of the usual type. Also, if the production function is linear, marginal productivity will be constant, and the labor-demand function will have to rest on different foundations for the macro-model.

The Cobb-Douglas function and the implied constancy of labor's share provide an attractive combination in which the share equation is used for labor demand even though it is not written as a function of employment and real wage alone. This gives, however, an interpretation of an observed empirical regularity within the context of the Keynesian model. The arguments made previously about the necessity of including the production, labor-demand, and labor-supply functions in the model place the equation of labor's share on an equal footing with the consumption function and similar equations of macro-economics. When we take up the question of the applicability of the Keynesian theory to problems of inflation, we shall see more clearly how the equation of labor's share, or other versions of marginal productivity, are used for explaining the absolute price level.

This pair of equations, the production function and the marginal productivity equation for labor, can be given a different interpretation in the Keynesian system. Because aggregate output is basically determined by effective demand through the savings-investment equality, we can look upon the production function as a *labor-requirements* function, given the stock of capital. From the point of view of establishing main lines of causation, this would mean writing the production function in an inverted form. Instead of writing

$$y = f(N, K),$$

we would write

$$N = g(y, K)$$

For some, but not the most general, methods of statistical estimation, this choice is of significance, but for the inherent algebra of non-stochastic models it would not be an essential modification. It is, however, instructive.

Similarly, the marginal productivity equation for the Cobb-Douglas form of production function can be inverted from its usual form as labor's share into an equation of price mark-up over unit labor costs. This is done explicitly in the discussion of inflation that follows. Again in terms of causal interpretation, the equation of marginal productivity can be looked upon as a price-formation equation instead of as a labor-demand equation.

Labor supply and wage determination equations: For a given wage rate (presumably set by trade-union institutions) and labor force, the Keynesian model has proved to be a powerful theory for explaining the determination of total income and employment, in a simplified form as a teaching theory and in an extended form as a working model. For closing the system with respect to wage and price-level determination, however, we need a labor-supply function and a market-adjustment process of wage determination. Also, for investigating the theoretical possibility of under-employment equilibrium, these two relationships are essential.

So far, our main criticism of the Keynesian theory is that it needs extension — disaggregation, more endogenous processes, dynamization, opening with respect to foreign trade, and so forth. On the question of labor supply, however, Keynes was definitely confused and in error. He suggested that labor supply is a function of the money wage and not the real wage. Of course, we can show the possibility of the existence of an under-employment equilibrium if there is an assumed "money illusion" or inhomogeneity in the supply behavior of workers. Schumpeter stressed repeatedly that the challenging theoretical problem was to make all the classical assumptions about behavior under perfect competition and then show the possibility of an under-employment equilibrium. This is the problem that must be faced by Keynesian economics.

The idea of money illusion in labor supply has surely been refuted by behavior during the postwar inflation. No one has been more conscious of the encroachment of rising prices on wage gains than have individual workers and their trade unions. The demand for built in escalation in labor contracts is a supreme recognition of the fact that the wage-bargain and terms-of-employment offer is in real wages and not money wages. Most contracts are finally written in terms of money wages, but the bargaining process is completely alert to the relationship between prices and wages. There is no illusion in behavior. Empirical equations of labor supply have not been satisfactorily established as functions of real wages, but they are no more firmly established as functions of money wages. The supply of male labor in the able-bodied age ranges is so conventional and standardized that it is difficult to obtain good endogenous explanations of macro-labor supply functions empirically. The real possibilities of determining cyclically sensitive labor-supply functions seems to be in the marginal sectors of the labor force — working wives, students, and semi-retired persons. A strong case for demographic disaggregation can be made in this market.

The statistical studies of wage determination have been found to be more fruitful than those of pure labor supply. These relationships take the form of dynamic change in wage rates as a function of excess supply (unemployment) in the labor market. The money wage is the market adjustment variable, but it has been found to be clearly related, with time lag, to price-level changes too. The equation takes the form

$$\Delta w = \delta_0 + \delta_1 U + \delta_2 (\Delta p)_{-1}$$

In this linear approximation, the money-wage rate changes are made a joint function of unemployment and previous price change. The contract is struck in terms of money wage; that accounts for the choice of a left-hand variable. The indicator of market conditions is U (unemployment), and the lag of wage change behind price change recognizes the facts that wages change in contractual displacements and lag behind price changes. There is no behavioral money illusion on the part of workers, but they cannot adjust continuously to price change and tend to lag behind. This is an inhomogeneous equation, but if it is imbedded in a system that is otherwise homogeneous, the complete model has the property that inhomogeneity occurs only for the dynamic variant. [20] When the system is held stationary ($\Delta w = 0$, $\Delta p = 0$), it is homogeneous in the classical sense. The moving or dynamic system thus contains a theory of absolute wage and price determination that is most closely tied to developments in the labor market. By contrast, the classical view is that the absolute price or wage determination would be most closely tied to developments in the money market. If δ_0 is significantly positive, we have a possible position of under-employment equilibrium.

This is a line of argument that seems essential for the Keynesian theory of under-employment equilibrium. Wage-determination equations of the preceding type have recently become very popular and are known as Phillips curves.[21] The investigations by Phillips have established interesting properties of these equations, especially on a long-run basis, but such equations were repeatedly used in econometric investigations long before the researches of Phillips.

SUMMING UP THE KEYNESIAN MODEL

Simple multiplier models or three equation models involving the propensity to consume, the marginal efficiency of capital, and liquidity preference are useful teaching devices. The Keynesian theory, viewed as a model that can explain the determination of output, employment, wage rate, price level, interest rate, and other variables must be larger. In the first place, it must include production, labor demand, and labor-supply functions. Secondly, it must be extended in a number of directions in order to approach

---

[20] If we used percentage change in wage rates, percentage change in price level, and per cent of the labor force unemployed as variable in the wage-determination equation, we would have a form of homogeneity across time periods, but not for any given period, using lagged values as initial conditions.

[21] A. W. Phillips, "The Relation between Unemployment and the Rate of Change of Money Wage Rates in the United Kingdom, 1861-1959," *Economica*, N.S. Vol. XXV, 1958, pp. 283–300.

realism and usefulness. These extensions will involve disaggregation, dynamization, and expansion of the scope of endogeneity. The systems that are now built by econometricians to describe economic activity in the United States, Canada, the United Kingdom, Netherlands, India, Japan and other countries are actually members of the Keynesian family of models, but they do not closely resemble the parent system on the surface. They are much larger and are more complicated. It requires careful examination by consolidation and tracing of main lines of causation to show that they are extensions of the Keynesian system. Most of the extensions are straightforward and can be traced to their Keynesian roots. The effects of real balances on spending and the analysis of wage determination are distinctly different and not simple extensions of the original model.

The main conclusion is that the *General Theory* is all too simple. Knowing what we do now about several aspects of economic behavior, I find it hard to become satisfied with a model couched solely in terms of the three pillars stated in their simplest form; however, it was undoubtedly the simplicity of the final construct that led to such wide acceptance of the theory at an early stage. If it had been stated in terms of a 30, 50, or 100 equation, model such as we use in today's econometric analysis, it is doubtful that many students would have paid close attention to it. Most people would have ignored it, leaving it as a problem of analysis for specialists willing to linger over its details.

AN INTERPRETATION OF THE KEYNESIAN REVOLUTION IN THE LIGHT OF SOME POSTWAR ECONOMIC DEVELOPMENTS

For the most part, our appeal to empirical results in the previous sections was technical and specialized. I was motivated in that discussion by detailed statistical matter, using the most powerful techniques with great care, for the analysis of behavior in one part of the economy after another. The kind of research that underlay the studies mentioned is that required for building a large-scale econometric model to be used in forecasting and policy formation. Now, I want to turn to some looser empirical observations on broader aspects of the Keynesian Revolution. I am not inquiring into the existence of each kind of behavior relation in the system. I am taking an over-view of the whole economy and looking at points of Keynesian policy and philosophy.

In the first years after World War II, it seemed that the problems that gave rise to the Keynesian Revolution, deep depression and large-scale unemployment, had disappeared and that the economic world would have to deal with inflation, dollar shortage, and other new problems outside the scope of the Keynesian analysis. There was a tendency to discredit the Keynesian theory and argue that it had led to incorrect predictions.

In the United States, economic conditions were strongly influenced by the need to meet the backlog of pent-up wartime demand, by the demographic pressures of an increased birth rate, and by large foreign-assistance programs. The Korean War provided another strong economic stimulus at a time when some of these motivating factors were beginning to weaken. In Western Europe and Japan, the main problem was reconstruction and the re-establishment of foreign trade. These influences were bullish for some time.

There are two issues involved in appraising these developments. First, had the typical Keynesian problems really vanished, and were the bullish stimuli temporary? Second, is the Keynesian system capable of dealing with this new variety of problems? In this section, I shall take up only the first of these issues. I shall consider the second one subsequently.

It is true that Keynesians were caught unaware by the inflationary problems of post World War II and that they failed to appreciate the wage and price pressures that were generated by high levels of employment. Having missed the unexpected turn of economic events, several economists over-reacted in the opposite direction and foresaw a long-run problem of inflation and sought new models to analyze it. The permanence of inflationary pressure proved to be as unreal as the persistence of depression. During the latter part of the 1950's, the United States found itself faced with reasonably steady prices, a substantial hard core of unemployment, and excess capacity.

Now, we are faced again with the typical Keynesian problems, and they might have occurred much sooner in the 1950's were it not for Korea, the emergence of new nations from colonial status, and other events not dependent on domestic activity in the United States and other industrial nations. The prevalence for a number of years in America of an unemployment rate in excess of 5 per cent looks very much like an example of the Keynesian under-employment equilibrium, and it does not seem to be explainable by market imperfections. It is, pure and simple, a case of deficient *effective demand*. The United States remained for much longer than desired at such a low rate of activity because of the unwillingness or inability of the public authorities to apply the requisite heavy dose of Keynesian medicine.

The long-run decline in m.e.c., or the American view expounded in the *stagnation thesis*, is not well founded in recent developments. The cyclical and short-run aspects of Keynesian analysis can be interpreted in the light of postwar developments; the stagnation thesis seems to be less plausible. Our recent difficulties with unemployment and excess capacity may be only cyclical and not secular. Technological change and its influence are too uncertain for us to make a premature judgment about very long-run developments.

Two points of Keynesian policy doctrine that seemed quite acceptable until a few years ago have sadly disappeared with the emergence of political conservatism. Keynes taught us (1) that inflation is better than deflation[22] and (2) that sound domestic economic policy in support of full employment should not be sacrificed to the vagaries of international trade and finance.

The rise of conservative governments in the United States and the United Kingdom in 1952 led to an abandonment of these principles and a return to orthodox monetary policy. The campaigns to save the pound (£) and later the dollar ($) were important steps in the departure from Keynes' views. Both governments were quite successful in holding prices steady, breaking away from cheap money, and keeping exchange rates constant at the expense of unemployment and low growth rates.

Domestic economic policy in the United States is always constrained nowadays by the balance-of-payments situation. Public

[22] Cf. p. 4.

authorities have proposed a Keynesian-type remedy that they think will be compatible with our external position and steady prices. They proposed the celebrated tax cut of 1964. This was a massive dose of the Keynesian medicine already mentioned and has generally been considered an unusual triumph of the new approach in economic stabilization. The tax cut of 1964 worked much as Keynesian economic analysis would have led us to believe it should work. It improved the level of economic activity, but it was not large enough to restore full employment. More of such cuts or other stimulative policies would be needed to bring about full employment, but these would probably endanger price stability and worsen the balance of payments; therefore, we find no rush on the part of authorities to extend these policies all the way to full employment.

An examination of the conditions leading to the tax cut of 1964 is revealing, for Keynesian economists argued in 1962 and 1963 that such a stimulus was needed. Timidity, or inability, or lack of insight restrained public authorities from enacting tax reductions while the economy lost potential output and employment for many months. Furthermore, this large-scale experiment gives us a good opportunity to judge the order of magnitude of multiplier effects. In the first year or two of this cut, it appears that real G.N.P. is higher by approximately the real value of the cut. This multiplier is nearly unity (in absolute value). It is smaller than the expenditure multiplier by a factor that equals the marginal propensity to consume in simple models. Generally speaking, these multiplier values are properly modest in size and much in line with econometric studies of Keynesian-type models. As previously mentioned (cf. p. 41) Keynes had good intuitive guidance in working with a conservatively valued expenditure multiplier of 1.5.

Once the tax cut was passed by the United States Congress and its effects became visible, it was accepted by people of widely differing shades of economic opinion. However, the discussion and political process leading to the cut were cumbersome and slow for the efficient working of the new methods of stabilization policies. Some discretionary authority on the part of the executive branch of the tripartite American system is needed. complete reliance on the slow-moving fiscal powers of the Congress may prove inadequate to the full implementation of Keynesian doctrines.

EXTENDING THE SCOPE OF THE SYSTEM — INFLATION, FAST GROWTH, AND UNDER-DEVELOPED ECONOMIES

Inflation: Whether the postwar inflation problem is merely a cyclical phase or a secular trend, we want a system of analysis that is capable of dealing with this problem as well as that of deflation. It is my contention that the system is fully capable of dealing with inflation if generalized in the way I have emphasized in this chapter. The price level or wage level is as much an endogenous variable in this generalized system as is national income, aggregate employment, or the interest rate.

The inflation problem has been studied in terms of the quantity theory of money, the inflationary gap, and wage push (more generally cost push or administered prices). The generalized Keynesian model contains all three kinds of inflation analysis simultaneously. I would not like to base my analysis on any one approach alone, least of all on the quantity theory of money. I think that the generalized system takes parts of all three and uses them in an interrelated way without imparting a unique casual influence to any one.

The Keynesian doctrine of liquidity preference can be looked upon as a generalization of the quantity theory of money. In place of writing

$$\frac{M}{p} = ky,$$

where

$$k = \frac{1}{v} = \text{constant},$$

we write

$$\frac{M}{p} = k(r, \Delta r, \Delta p)y$$

In these equations M = stock of cash balances (nominal), p = price level, y = aggregate output, k = Cambridge constant, v = velocity, r = interest rate.

The approach here is only symbolic; it does not go into the complications of asset types and different groups of asset holders. It shows that M and p are not strictly proportional as the quantity theory suggests, but that they are closely related depending on how $r, \Delta r$, and Δp affect k. In the strict quantity theory, y is fixed at its full-employment level. In the Keynesian system, full-capacity output is not necessarily reached at all times; therefore, the money equation is only a partial system by itself. However, because the Keynesian system includes the quantity equation as a special case, there is no incompatibility involved.

Keynes, in *How to Pay for the War*, initiated the inflationary-gap analysis. The primary variables considered in this approach are savings and investment. If at full-capacity output, investment exceeds saving, there is an inflationary gap, and if saving exceeds investment there is a deflationary gap. Graphical analysis of these situations are only first approximations because the price level is not explicitly determined in simple savings-investment models. Full-capacity output, as distinct from the concept of full-employment output, cannot be determined unless the dynamic relationship between capital and investment and capital-labor substitution are brought into the analysis. In spite of these complications, the savings-investment balance is an important criterion for the determination of inflationary pressure. During World War II, this method of analysis was popular, but emphasis gradually shifted to the concept of cost-push, or wage, or administered price inflation.

The analysis is simple enough. Prices are determined as mark-ups over prime costs, especially wages. If trade unions establish abnormally high wage rates, prices will be marked up over these, resulting in an upward inflationary movement. Import prices for the open economy are also prime costs giving rise to the same kind of inflationary push. Administered prices are those of giant cartels or monopolies, whose products might be used as materials and, therefore, prime costs, in other industries — giving rise to inflationary pressure.

The mark-up of prices over wages finds expression in a transformation of the equation of labor's share. From

$$wN = \alpha py$$

we can write
$$p = \frac{1}{\alpha} w\left(\frac{N}{y}\right)$$

This is Weintraub's formula, which he proposes as a simple substitute for the classical quantity equation in explaining inflation.[23] In place of k or $1/v$, he uses the constant α (labor's share) as the strategic parameter. This equation establishes a proportional relationship between p and w, given the reciprocal of productivity N/y. Productivity is assumed to grow along a smooth trend.

The equation of labor's share, it was noted, enters the Keynesian system as a form of the marginal productivity of labor or the demand-for-labor equation. This treatment of the inflation problem is, therefore, already contained in the Keynesian system. The position is not changed if the coefficients are modified by monopoly elements (administered prices) or the inclusion of imports as productive factors and prime costs. The Keynesian theory takes no special stand on the presence or absence of competition; it can deal with monopolistic elements. It can also be extended to encompass foreign trade.

Some of the arguments about administered price inflation have been concerned with key sectors of the economy. In America the bellwether steel industry and other particular oligopolies are singled out, and the macro-economic Keynesian models fail to treat relative prices in inter-industry relationships. In this sense, some inflation problems escape the usual Keynesian tools, but there always will be errors of aggregation, and these are no more peculiar to inflation than to deflation.

Newer work on the dynamized Keynesian models containing Phillips curves carry the wage and labor-market analysis of inflation a step further. The wage-push theories are interesting in shifting the focus of attention in treatment of the inflation problem from the money market to the labor market, but they are one-sided in their view of the causal mechanism. They imply that trade unions promote high wages and that these costs lead to high prices. This single cost-push equation is only one in a larger system, and the Phillips curve says that the state of the labor market, *which is derived from the state of the goods market*, affects wage movements. There may also be an effect from previous cost-of-living advances.

[23] S. Weintraub, *A General Theory of the Price Level, Output, Income Distribution and Economic Growth*, Chilton, Philadelphia, 1959.

These may be classified as, at least partly, demand-pull aspects of inflation.   The whole group of equations in the labor market — labor demand, labor supply, and wage determination — together with savings-investment and money-market equations, jointly determine the absolute levels of prices and wages.   The extended Keynesian system, thus, is capable of dealing with the inflation problem in many ways; through study of the money supply and credit, through consideration of savings-investment balance, and through the state of the labor market.   There is no justification for doubting the applicability of the extended Keynesian model to the problems of inflation.

Fast growth: Economists in fast-growing countries — Japan being a typical example — may feel that the forward momentum of their present development will carry them upward at such a pace that they should not use the Keynesian model for analysis.   They may feel that the Keynesian system is well suited only for depression economics, and that they have no foreseeable possibilities of depression.

Just as we have argued here that the Keynesian model lends itself well to the analysis of inflation, so does it lend itself well to the analysis of growth.   Inflation and growth may seem to go together, but actually they are quite different processes.   On a country-by-country basis, there is little correlation in the world economy between growth rate and price change.   All combinations seem to be equally frequent.

The Harrod-Domar model of growth is really an extended version of the Keynesian system.   It extends the model by bringing in the relationship between capital stock and investment in an essential way.   It bases the analysis on the Keynesian concept of savings-investment balance, but it is an extremely simplified version of the theory because it has no price level, wage rate, or interest-rate analysis.

Important ingredients of the modern Japanese growth rate are a high rate of investment, a willingness of the population to save, and the importation of capital.   These are all revealed in an extended Keynesian model.   The interaction of recent Japanese inflation and high growth rate is better understood if the consumption function is extended to allow for the effects of income distribution and a general upward drift.

Just as American economists have often incorrectly projected a few years' experience into future decades, it is possible that economists in Japan and other fast-growing countries are too optimistic about the future. A slump could occur through the building up of excess capacity in certain lines. The safety margins of the Japanese economy are thin in some areas, and Keynesian analysis of other cycle phases may well be a problem for the future.

The socialist economies are special cases of growing, underdeveloped economies, and I think that it would be unfortunate if they were to be dogmatically doctrinaire in overlooking the possible contributions that Keynesian economics could make to the solution of their problems. Investment may be purely exogenous in fully planned socialism, but its level and sector distribution must be decided upon in an economically efficient manner. The Keynesian aggregative theory will help decide upon the level because it is not appropriate to push capital formation to any extreme whatsoever. There is a best level consonant with stable growth without cycles and severe inflation. Central planners must understand and appreciate the propensity to consume, and failure to do so has, in fact, caused economic trouble for some socialist countries. For public finance under socialism, planners must appreciate saving motives and asset preferences. A truncated Keynesian system with consumption (savings) and liquidity preference treated in some detail would seem to be a natural tool of analysis.

Socialist planners claim that they have eliminated the business cycle. As we know it, the familiar capitalist cycle has not appeared in socialist economies, but there may well be fluctuations. These may come about as the result of the cumulation of internal mistakes in the planning operation or as the result of external disturbances. It is well known, from the great Russian theorist, Slutsky, that random error can easily cumulate into cycles.[24] There will

---

[24] E. Slutsky, "The Summation of Random Causes as the Source of Cyclic Processes," *Econometrica*, Vol. V, April, 1937, pp. 105–46. See also my paper in the Kalecki anniversary volume, "The Role of Econometrics in Socialist Economics," *Problems of Economic Dynamics and Planning*, PWN, Warsaw, 1964.

probably be inventory cycles in a socialist economy, and the Metzler extensions of the original Keynesian model would seem to be relevant.[25]

Socialist fluctuations or cycles may exhibit themselves as pauses in upward development or even as downturns. I am not suggesting that there will be a business cycle like ours, but I do argue that a proper understanding of Keynesian economics would help them achieve a smoother growth path.

Under-developed countries: Keynesian-type econometric models that have fit data well in developed industrial countries have also been estimated for India. There may be estimated models for other under-developed countries too, but the Indian case may be typical of what to expect. Trade equations are important for India. On the side of export, the demand for basic Indian materials in the world economy dictates the form of the relationship. On the whole, these are specialized goods, and income effects dominate price effects. The same is true of imports; these are largely non-competitive with domestic production, and income effects are the most important among explanatory variables.[26] Thus, the theory must be extended to include foreign-trade multipliers, but the productivity of imports should be explicitly displayed.

Consumption and investment functions exist for India as well as for the advanced countries. The main difference, however, is quantitative. The marginal propensity to consume is much higher for the under-developed country. The investment functions of the stock-adjustment or flexible-accelerater type seem to fit well, but we should be very cautious about accepting statistical correlations showing the effect of capacity accumulation or utilization on investment in an under-developed country. There are so many needs for capital formation that it is hard to envisage an influence of excess capacity on investment. Excess capacity, however, must be understood in an economic and not in an absolute sense. There can be too much industrial capacity in the aggregate to be supported by

[25] L. Metzler, "The Nature and Stability of Inventory Cycles," *Review of Economic Statistics*, Vol. XXIII, August, 1941, pp. 113–129.

[26] M. Dutta, "A Prototype Model of Indian Foreign Trade, *International Economic Review*, Vol. V, January, 1964, pp. 82–103.

the effective demand of the whole economy or for a predominantly rural sector. Also, there can be partial effects of excess capacity through over-expansion in some area or industry relative to the whole economy.

There is also an asset-preference decision in an under-developed country. Studies of Indian liquidity preference yield relations like those in the United States, but for the great mass of individuals there is no possibility of choice. There may be an abnormal preference for gold, other precious metals, and jewels in an under-developed country. This would affect the parameters of the function but not its existence.

The wage and price mechanism is likely to be different in under-developed countries. With so much disguised and structural un-employment, it is unlikely that the state of excess supply in the labor market will be a big factor in short-run wage determination. Some form of the quantity theory and the savings-investment gap analysis would seem to be more relevant. Import prices are obviously major determinants of the domestic price level.

In fine, a multi-sector Keynesian-type model (agriculture, manu-facturing, tertiary, for example) can fit the data of India and other under-developed countries. Parameter values and other structural characteristics will be different, but the same general class of models can be expected to apply.

SUMMARY

I look upon the Keynesian theory as essentially a system of equations. While I may have once been satisfied with the explana-tory value of a small version of that system expressed in just two or three equations, I now feel that intelligent discussion cannot be car-ried on unless this system is expanded to include fifteen to twenty or even more equations. In current econometric model construction, I am working with some macro-systems that have more than 100 equations.

These larger systems, extended along the lines indicated in this essay, may not be easily recognized as the Keynesian theory, yet I feel that they surely are. They are manifestations of points I have reached, in collaboration with many colleagues, after starting out from the simplest forms of the Keynesian Revolution and working systematically through econometric studies of available data. They are, in a real sense, just extensions of the Keynesian theory in a natural way.

The new versions must have some relative prices, a good theory of price-level determination, dynamic features, a government sector, a trading sector, an effective link to the monetary sector, and a more detailed money market. I think that new advances will be made in these directions and that they will be econometrically based.

A postscript on the role of Keynes in the *Keynesian Revolution* may be in order. Would the Revolution have taken place without Keynes? In the same way that I feel we are now evolving a system, a natural course of intellectual development follows from Keynes' original model. I think that the Keynesian system as a mathematical model would have come into being without Keynes, as a natural outgrowth of the economic discussions of the 1930's.

The dramatic weight of Keynes' personality undoubtedly added much to the speedy acceptance of the theory and was responsible for the philosophical and policy aspects of the *Keynesian Revolution;* but the cold analytical theory would probably have come in any case. The Kalecki model of the business cycle really sets down all the essential ingredients of the simple model, and makes it dynamic in the bargain.[27] Kalecki's mathematical paper in *Econometrica* attracted little attention compared with Keynes' splash, but eventually the theorists would have seen through the matter and given Kalecki's pre-*General Theory* model its full due.

Pronouncements by Frisch and Ohlin on policies for meeting the economic collapse of the early 1930's show clearly that analysis of the situation was congealing along lines that would have led to the same kinds of theoretical models. It was as though these two scholars were interpreting the periods' events in terms of the saving-investment theory of income determination. By a slower, more gradual process their ideas would have merged with Kalecki's

[27] M. Kalecki, "A Macrodynamic Theory of Business Cycles," *Econometrica*, Vol. III, July. 1935, pp. 327–344. Cf. L. R. Klein, "The Role of Econometrics in Socialist Economics," *op. cit.* Compare also Joan Robinson's contribution to the Kalecki Anniversary Volume, "Kalecki and Keynes," *Problems of Economic Dynamics and Planning*, PWN, Warsaw, 1964, pp. 335–341.

formal model into something that is not fundamentally different from the Keynesian system.

Frisch delivered a radio address in 1932 on current economic conditions and took up clearly the role of savings and investment, as separate economic decisions that were interacting to determine the level of economic activity. It is evident, however, that he did not have a closed system of income determination, but he did favor policies that would follow along Keynesian lines.[28]

In 1934, Ohlin reported to the Swedish Unemployment Commission where he outlined a policy to deal with the problems of depression and at the same time presented an analysis of the macroeconomy and business cycles.[29] As in Frisch's analysis, Ohlin gave a clear explanation of the paradox of thrift and the nature of the two-sided savings-investment process. He went further in defining the propensity to save. His theory was not complete enough to develop a well-defined multiplier from a closed system, but he did see the stimulus that would come to economic activity from a rise in either consumption or investment demand. In addition, Ohlin argued against a general wage reduction because of the notion that wages have both cost and demand aspects. He was not like Keynes on the question of wage cuts as a means of alleviating unemployment, but he had good intuition on this subject.

Generally speaking, Ohlin and, possibly, Frisch were more reserved and timid than Keynes on policy recommendations to fight the depression, but they were consistently pointing in the right direction and undoubtedly would have become bolder and more forceful as the magnitude of the world-wide problem became more apparent and persistent. They had substantial pieces of the Keynesian system in their grasp but not a well-articulated complete system that was capable of mathematization. In this respect, Kalecki was far ahead of the Keynesian precursors.[30]

These concluding remarks are not intended to detract from the

[28] Frisch's ideas were published, belatedly, in *Noen Trekk av Konjunkturlaeren*, Aschehoug, Oslo, 1947.

[29] B. Ohlin, "Monetary Theory, Public Works, Subsidies and Tariffs as Means of Unemployment Policy," Stockholm, 1934 (tr.).

[30] Compare Joan Robinson, *op. cit.*, both on Kalecki's position and on that of the Swedish school.

I

remarkable Keynesian contribution; they are primarily meant to give proper credit to other scholars and to give comfort in the feeling that good ideas will eventually predominate regardless of any single personality.

CHAPTER IX

THE ECONOMETRICS OF THE *GENERAL THEORY*

The point has been made that the modern econometric extensions of the Keynesian analysis, to what I would call the development of the theory to its highest degree, have produced systems that appear to be substantially more complicated than the simple Hicks-Lange mathematical versions of the *General Theory*. In this chapter, I propose to analyze a numerical-statistical version of one of these models from the point of view of Keynesian economics. My purposes are to see the sense in which these systems can be called versions of the *General Theory*, to see the ways in which they might be used to implement the teachings of the Keynesian Revolution, and to show the universality of the new approach to economics. In a sense, the econometric analysis that has gone into the construction of models like that presented here has produced a test of the theory because the models are based on a fit to actual data and are tested by application (forecasting, simulation, multiplier calculation, and so forth) to realistic situations. Speaking very generally, I would say that the *General Theory* meets econometric test criteria admirably and emerges as a validated theory in many parts of the world.

AN AMERICAN MODEL

Tinbergen first brought his powerful new ideas to bear on model-building for the Dutch economy, but a greater application was found in his time-honored study for the League of Nations on the American economy.[1] From that point, I was stimulated by J. Marschak to build a Tinbergen type model for the United States economy, just after completing the original version of *The Keynesian Revolution*. This work led me through a succession of United States models — some annual, some quarterly, some small, and some

---

[1] J. Tinbergen, *An Econometric Approach to Business Cycle Problems*, Hermann et Cie., Paris, 1937; and *Statistical Testing of Business-Cycle Theories*, Vol. II: *Business Cycles in the United States of America, 1919-1932*, League of Nations, Geneva, 1939.

large. For the example to be dealt with here, I choose an annual model of the American economy of intermediate size. This model is large enough to show how the Keynesian system must be extended and generalized to make it usable, but it is not too large to be dealt with and comprehended in a single chapter. By contrast, my latest and most highly refined work in modeling the American economy (in collaboration with an entire research team) can only be fully explained in a large volume.[2] The model chosen can be considered to be an up-dated and revised Klein-Goldberger model.[3] That model has enjoyed a certain amount of success in forecasting and simulation. It has been extensively reviewed and analyzed for multiplier properties. In this sense it is a familiar and well-tested model, but it is outdated by this time. In order to test various statistical methods of estimation it was revised (improved) and brought up-to-date.

In a later section, some attention will be paid to the applicability of the Keynesian theory to other countries, but here I might point out that similar models have been built for Canada, Holland (an extension of Tinbergen's original work), the United Kingdom, India, Japan, Greece, Italy, Germany and other countries.[4]

A Revised Klein-Goldberger Model: The Klein-Goldberger model contains sixteen equations with statistically estimated coefficients and four definitional equations (identities). The equations have been estimated from annual time series of the United States economy, 1929 to 1962, omitting 1942 to 1945. In this chapter, the statistical estimation techniques used will not be discussed. Attention will be concentrated on the economics of the final results.[5]

---

[2] *The Brookings Quarterly Econometric Model of the U.S. Economy*, J. Duesenberry, G. Fromm, L. R. Klein and E. Kuh, eds., Rand McNally, Chicago, 1965.

[3] L. R. Klein and A. S. Goldberger, *An Econometric Model of the United States*, 1929-1952, North-Holland Publishing Co., Amsterdam, 1955.

[4] See M. Nerlove, "A Tabular Survey of Macro-Econometric Models" *International Economic Review*, 1966.

[5] See L. R. Klein, "Problems in the Estimation of Interdependent Systems," paper delivered to the Entretiens de Monaco, May, 1964, for a fuller discussion of estimation procedures and problems.

The variables of the model are:

* C_d	Consumption of durables, billions of 1954 dollars.
* Y	Personal disposable income, billions of 1954 dollars.
* C_n	Consumption of non-durables and services, billions of 1954 dollars.
* I	Investment in plant and equipment, billions of 1954 dollars.
* X	Gross national product, billions of 1954 dollars.
W_g	Government wages and salaries, billions of 1954 dollars.
* r	Average yield on corporate bonds (Moody's).
* R	Residential construction, billions of 1954 dollars.
* r_s	Yield on prime commercial paper, 4 to 6 months.
* H	Stock of inventories, billions of 1954 dollars.
* I_m	Imports, billions of 1954 dollars.
p_m	Implicit price deflator for imports, 1954 = 1.00.
* N_w	Wage and salary workers, millions.
N_g	Government employees, millions.
N_e	Self-employed workers, millions.
* h	Index of hours worked per week, 1954 = 1.00.
* W	Wages and salaries and supplements to wages and salaries, billions of 1954 dollars.
* w	Index of average hourly wages.
N_L	Total labor force, millions.
* p	Implicit gross national product deflator, 1954 = 1.00.
* S_c	Corporate saving including inventory valuation adjustment, billions of 1954 dollars.
* P_c	Corporate profits including inventory valuation adjustment, billions of 1954 dollars.
T_c	Corporate profits taxes, billions of current dollars.
* $\Pi - P_c$	Proprietors' income, billions of 1954 dollars.
* Π_r	Rental income and net interest, billions of 1954 dollars.
* D	Capital consumption allowances, billions of current dollars.
D_u	Dummy variable, 0 for 1929-1946, 1 for 1947 to 1962.
r_d	Average discount rate at Federal Reserve Banks.
R_e	Average percentage of required reserves held as excess reserves.
G	Government expenditures, billions of 1954 dollars.
E	Exports, billions of 1954 dollars.
T_i	Reconciling item between net national product and national income, billions of 1954 dollars.
T_p	Personal taxes + contributions for social insurances − government and business transfer payments − interest on government debt and inventory valuation adjustment.

The variables marked with an asterisk at the left are endogenous variables; that is, those explained by the model. The tax and other reconciling items are endogenous for a given specification of the laws of government revenue collection and public-assistance disbursement. These laws have changed so much during the sample period that T_i, T_c, and T_p are treated as exogenous variables, although in any particular application they are endogenously analyzed through the receipt and disbursement functions that characterize the period of specific analysis.

The estimated equations are:

(1) $C_d - .7(C_d)_{-1} = .330\ (Y - .7\ Y_{-1}) - .319\ (C_d) - 6.114$

(2) $C_n = .223\ Y + .754\ (C_n)_{-1} - .767$

(3) $I - .95\ I_{-1} = .0596\ (X - W_g)_{-1} - 2.156\ r_{-1} - .552\ I_{-1} + 9.943$

(4) $R = .0496\ Y - .343\ (r_s)_{-1} + .431\ R_{-1} - 3.32$

(5) $H = .140\ (X - \Delta H) + .379\ H_{-1} - 25.289$

(6) $I_m = .0386\ X - 16.07\ (p_m - p) + .241\ (I_m)_{-1} - 1.317$

(7) $r_s = 1.142\ r_d - .0101\ R_e + .432\ D_u - .384$

(8) $r = .158\ r_s + .844\ r_{-1} + .302$

(9) $X - W_g - .95\ (X - W_g)_{-1} = .196\ (I + R) + 5.359\ [(N_w - N_g - N_e) - .95\ (N_w - N_g + N_e)_{-1}] + 224.62\ (h - .95\ h_{-1}) - 13.405$

(10) $h = - .563\ \Delta w - .03719\ (N_L - N_w - N_e) + 1.180$

(11) $W - W_g = .377\ (X - W_g) + .349\ (W - W_g)_{-1} - 9.838$

(12) $\Delta w = - .0418\ (N_L - N_w - N_e) + .733\ (\Delta p)_{-1} + .234$

(13) $S_c = .894\ (P_c - T_c/p) - .661\ (P_c - T_c/p - S_c)_{-1} - 1.508$

(14) $\Pi_r = .0435\ (I + R) + .380\ \Delta r + .965\ (\Pi_r)_{-1} - .559$

(15) $\Pi - P_c = .0150\ X + .817\ (\Pi - P_c)_{-1} + 2.042$

$$(16) \quad D = .0514 \sum_{i=1}^{20} p_{-i} (I + R)_{-i} + 7.917 D_u - 1.622$$

$$(17) \quad X = C_d + C_n + I + R + \Delta H + G + E - I_m$$

$$(18) \quad Y = C_d + C_n + I + R + \Delta H + G + E - I_m - D/p \\ - T_i/p - S_c - T_c/p - T/p$$

$$(19) \quad \Pi = C_d + C_n + I + R + \Delta H + G + E - I_m - D/p \\ - T_i/p - W - \Pi_r$$

$$(20) \quad pW = whN_w$$

Let us consider each of these equations in turn for their interpretation as elements of a complete (extended) Keynesian system.

(1) and (2): These are consumption functions in which the Keynesian aggregate propensity to consume has been split into two parts — durable and non-durable. There are compelling reasons for making this split: Consumer durable goods behave more like capital formation and are more likely to have active movements that do not passively follow general income fluctuations. Non-durable consumption is more closely associated with the Keynesian concept of a stable, dependable consumption function that follows but does not initiate general economic fluctuations. Equations (1) and (2) extend the original Keynesian formulation in two specific directions: They are dynamic and imply definite lag structure in the income-consumption response pattern. They take account of taxes and transfers by using a disposable income variable, defined in equation (18). These ideas were explained in Chapter VIII.

Relative prices would ordinarily be thought to be relevant for the explanation of the separation of consumption between durable and non-durable goods. However, in order to keep this system at a manageable size, we have disturbed matters a bit in approximation by using only one price level in the entire system. It is also worth pointing out that equation (1) can be written in a transformed way to bring out more clearly the influence of capital accumulation on the demand for consumer durables. It is equivalent to the following equation:

$$(C_d)_t = \alpha_0 + \alpha_1 \, Y_t + \alpha_2 \sum_{i=1}^{\infty} \lambda^{i-1} \, (C_d)_{t-i}$$

where

estimate $\alpha_0 \, (1 - \lambda)$ = $- \, 6.114$

estimate α_1 = 0.330

estimate α_2 = $- \, 0.319$

assumed value λ = 0.7

We fixed $\lambda = 0.7$ in order to have consumer durables depreciate at a geometric rate with a lifetime of twelve years (approximately). In the transformed form, we have the stock of consumer durables, expressed as

$$\sum_{i=1}^{\infty} 0.7^{i-1}(C_d)_{t-i}$$

in existence at the beginning of a year acting as a depressant on further consumer spending on durables.

To get the equation form used in the model from the preceding form, we delay the expression by one period and multiply both sides by λ, to get

$$\lambda \, (C_d)_{t-1} = \alpha_0 \lambda + \alpha_1 \lambda \, Y_{t-1} + \alpha_2 \sum_{i=1}^{\infty} \lambda^i \, (C_d)_{t-i-1}$$

By subtracting this equation from the previous equation, we have
$$(C_d)_t - \lambda(C_d)_{t-1} = \alpha_0(1 - \lambda) + \alpha_1 \, (Y_t - \lambda \, Y_{t-1}) + \alpha_2 \, (C_d)_{t-1}$$
which is the form used in the numerical model.

(3), (4) and (5): These equations describe the investment processes for private fixed capital, residential construction and inventory change. They are all variations of some form of lag distribution and stock adjustment. The first two can be written as lag distributions in the following way:

$$I_t = \beta_0 + \sum_{i=0}^{\infty} \mu^i[\beta_1 \, (X - W_g)_{t-i-1} + \beta_2 r_{t-i-1} + \beta_3 \, I_{t-i-1}]$$

where

estimate $\beta_0 (1 - \mu) = \quad 9.943$

estimate $\beta_1 \qquad = \quad 0.0596$

estimate $\beta_2 \qquad = \; - 2.156$

estimate $\beta_3 \qquad = \; - 0.552$

assumed value $\mu \quad = \quad 0.95$

$$R_t = \gamma_0 + \sum_{i=0}^{\infty} \nu^i [\gamma_1 \, Y_{t-i} + \gamma_2 \, (r_s)_{t-i-1}]$$

where

estimate $\gamma_0 (1 - \nu) = \; - 3.32$

estimate $\gamma_1 \qquad = \quad 0.0496$

estimate $\gamma_2 \qquad = \; - 0.343$

estimate $\nu \qquad = \quad 0.431$

The latter equation is more easily interpreted. It implies that the residential construction expenditure depends on the long-run past history of disposable income and interest rate. For simplicity of estimation, it is assumed that long-run formulations of Y and r_s from past values fade away (geometrically) at the same rate. There is, however, a pure lag in r_s, while contemporaneous values of Y may affect construction-expenditure decisions. Interest obligations become contractually fixed at the time of the initial decision, but income fluctuations can alter behavior as the work progresses.

The short-term rate is not used here as a direct estimate of the mortgage rate. It is used, instead, as an indicator of the general state of the credit market and may be more sensitive for use in the residential construction decision.

The fixed investment equation is written as a lag distribution of a linear combination of past private real output $(X - W_o)$, the long-term interest rate, and past investment. It could also be written as

$$I_t = \beta_0 + \beta_1 \sum_{i=0}^{\infty} \mu^i (X - W_o)_{t-i-1} + \beta_2 \sum_{i=0}^{\infty} \mu^i r_{t-i-1}$$

$$+ \beta_3 \sum_{i=0}^{\infty} \mu^i I_{t-i-1}$$

In this form, we have a version of a stock-adjustment theory that says that investment depends on long-run real output $\Sigma \mu^i (X - W_o)_{t-i-1}$, long-run interest rate $\Sigma \mu^i r_{t-i-1}$, and the stock of fixed capital $\Sigma \mu^i I_{t-i-1}$. By using the same decay factor, μ, in all these long-run, distributed lag expressions, we simplify the estimation procedure.[6] Other parametric formulations of this fixed investment function were estimated, but the one presented here seemed to give the best statistical results.

Finally, let us consider equation (5), the inventory investment equation, which is also a lag distribution of the form

$$H = \delta_0 + \delta_1 \sum_{i=0}^{\infty} \rho^i (X - \Delta H)_{t-i}$$

where

estimate $\delta_0 (1 - \rho)$ = 25.289

estimate δ_1 =   0.140

estimate ρ =   0.379

The equation could also be written as

$$\Delta H = .140 (X - \Delta H) - .621 H_{-1} - 25.289$$

where inventory investment is made a function of sales and accumulated stock.

Keynes really devoted explicit attention to an investment equation such as (3), as it was mathematically expressed by his interpreters — Hicks, Lange, Kaldor, and Kalecki. Inventory dynamics and residential investment were not considered in any detail, yet they are essential ingredients of any theory or model that jointly tries to encompass short and long cycles. In this sense the model extends the Keynesian theory to include all private investment.

---

[6] New non-linear methods are being developed that enable us to drop this restrictive assumption.

(6): The closed Keynesian model surely could not have been expected to apply to the case of the United Kingdom but was, until recent years, thought to be suitable for an analysis of the American economy. It is, however, commonly accepted that propensities to export and import should be added to the statement of the Keynesian model, and that is what has been done by the inclusion of equation (6), the propensity to import. Imports are made a function of real output, relative prices (actually price spread, $p_m - p$, to keep linearity where plausible), and a distributed lag effect. In the latter respect, this equation is much like equation (4), the demand for residential construction.

While an income variable is used in the housing and consumption equations, an output variable is used here in the import equation because imports are widely used in the production process, although some are intended for final consumption. The distinction between national product in the import or fixed-investment equation and disposable income in the consumption or housing equations is fairly subtle and technical. Distinctions like these are important in the building of realistic models that can be usefully applied to actual data and economic policy. Such refined distinctions do not usually appear in the pedagogical models of the *General Theory*. They might cover up an understanding of some fundamentals. Moreover, these distinctions change from country to country, while the underlying theory might remain transferable. That is why I choose to devote so much attention to the relationship between the theory of the Keynesian model and its empirical manifestation in the form of aggregative econometric models.

The import equation has a relative price (price-spread) variable in the form of a domestic and a foreign price comparison. Because the domestic price is represented by our single-price variable and the foreign price is exogenous, we have no need of extra-price equations in this formulation. Exchange rate and tariff policies are hidden in the measurement of p_m. A more detailed model with specific treatment of types of imports would require more price variables.

Exports depend largely on world trade, which we are assuming to be exogenous to this model, but the price relative between United

States exports and competing world prices would be relevant. This would have required the specific endogenous treatment of United States export prices, and we did not want to take up this matter in the present model; therefore, exports are made exogenous here. Admittedly, this is an over-simplified treatment, but it does give minimal extension of the *General Theory* to cover trade and the open economy.

(7), (8): The first six equations cover consumption, investment, and net foreign demand in the total of Keynesian *effective demand.* Except for detail and disaggregation as noted, they use the usual pillars of the Keynesian system. The other pillar is reflected in equation (7), which is effectively a transformation and consolidation of the liquidity-preference doctrine. That theory tells us that the rate of interest is determined by the supply and demand for money. Because the supply is made exogenous, there is only the demand to consider. I have argued against the over-simplification of treating money supply as exogenous and have tried to introduce some of the relevant supply factors, together with the demand side in equation (7). The equation says that the short rate follows the Federal Reserve discount rate but is adjusted for the level of excess reserves. Excess reserves represent, in a rough sense, the balance between supply and demand forces in the money market. On the supply side they are capable of being affected by Federal Reserve open-market operations and reserve requirements. These two policy instruments, together with the discount rate shown in the other variable, constitute the most important instruments of monetary control from the supply side of the market. The demand side also affects excess reserves; therefore equation (7) represents a supply-demand balance as it determines the short rate.

One can go much further in the econometric specification of the money market and interest-rate determination, but the only generalization attempted here is to recognize that public authorities control specific factors in the money market without going to the extreme position that the total supply of money is exogenous.[7] More strategic specification of liquidity preference would involve an investigation of the existence of a "liquidity trap." That particular

[7] See the chapter by Frank de Leeuw in J. Duesenberry, *et al., op. cit.*

functional form is not necessarily implied in equation (7) but is being investigated econometrically.[8] The "dummy variable" D_u in this equation simply represents a break in money-market control and behavior between the pre- and post-World War II periods.

Equation (8) is introduced to show, in a simple way, something about the interest-rate structure — at its simplest level the structure of long and short rates. Transforming this into an explicit lag distribution, we find

$$r_t = \epsilon_0 + \epsilon_1 \sum_{i=0}^{\infty} \sigma^i (r_s)_{t-i},$$

where

estimate $\epsilon_0 (1 - \sigma) = 0.302$

estimate ϵ_1 $= 0.158$

estimate σ $= 0.844.$

In this form, the long rate is expressed as a moving sum of past (expected) short rates.

The theory of liquidity preference has often been criticized for dealing with "the" interest rate. This is an index problem much like that of dealing with "the" price level or "the" wage rate in any macro-model. A concession is made here by distinguishing between two rates, but larger models go much further in this direction.[9] Another, more compelling, reason for making the distinction between the two interest rates in this model is that the lines of control from public authorities to the money market travel via the short-term rate. In fact, an alternative to the assumption that money supply is exogenously determined is that the short-term rate is exogenously determined. This was the case in Lange's original formulation of the Keynesian theory. On the other hand, a relevant variable for the long-term planning of fixed investment is the long rate. We, thus, need two interest-rate equations. Although it might be contended that equations (7) and (8) do not faithfully reproduce all important aspects of the doctrine of liquidity prefer-

[8] K. Marwah, "Yet Another Look at the Liquidity Trap," paper presented to the meetings of the Econometric Society, December, 1965.

[9] See de Leeuw, *op. cit.*

ence, it must at least be admitted that the main channel of interest-rate determination is in the money market.   Thus, we are in keeping with the Keynesian notion that interest is a monetary phenomenon.

(9), (10), (11), (12): The Keynesian system that includes price and wage-level determination requires an extension of the model to cover the laws of production — technology, marginal productivity, and wage determination.   Equation (9) deals with technology.   It is a version of a production function written, in linear approximation, as

$$(X - W_o)_t = \zeta_0 + \zeta_1 (N_w - N_g + N_e)_t + \zeta_2 h_t$$
$$+ \zeta_3 \sum_{i=0}^{\infty} \pi^i (I + R)_{t-i},$$

where

estimate $\zeta_0 (1 - \pi)$ = -13.405

estimate ζ_1 =   5.359

estimate ζ_2 =   224.62

estimate ζ_3 =   0.196

assumed value π =   0.95.

To give simplicity to the form of this marginal productivity relationship, we ought to have made the production function of the Cobb-Douglas type.   However, to simplify some of the estimation and application problems of this model, we made a linear approximation.   This is done in two ways: In the first place, all variables are introduced linearly instead of logarithmically, as in the Cobb-Douglas formula.   In addition, the variables representing employment $(N_w - N_g + N_e)$ and hours (h) are not combined into man-hours $[h (N_w - N_g + N_e)]$, but are approximated as separate variables with constant coefficients.   This is done for some delicate matters of econometric simplicity and has little direct bearing on matters of interpretation of the Keynesian system.[10]

[10] See fn. 5.

The assumed geometric coefficient, 0.95, is the same parameter as that used in the investment function. In the context of production functions, it serves as an ingredient of a measure of the stock of capital

$$\sum_{i=0}^{\infty} \pi^i (I + R)_{t-i}$$

in vintage models of the type developed by R. Solow.[11] Each vintage of capital

investment of t	$(I + R)_t$
investment of t − 1	$(I + R)_{t-1}$
investment of t − 2	$(I + R)_{t-2}$

receives a particular weight π^0, π^1, π^2, and so forth, that falls geometrically; thus, the latest and technologically superior capital receives the greatest weight, as long as $0 < \pi < 1$. We have, therefore, a linearly approximated vintage model of the production function.

Equations (10) and (11) are associated factor-demand equations for h and $N_w - N_g$. The number of self-employed, N_e, is assumed to be exogenous. Because these endogenous decisions are assumed to be centered in the private economy, we measure output as $X - W_g$, G.N.P. originating in the private sector, and labor input as $N_w - N_g + N_e$, the number at work in the private sector.

Equation (11) is variously written, as mentioned in the previous chapter, as a factor-share equation, a labor-demand equation, or as a price mark-up equation. Since (10) and (11) represent demands for labor factors — men and hours — we must account for fixed-capital demand. This is accomplished in equations (4) and (5).

We have not taken up an explicit labor-supply process in this model. That variable is treated as exogenous, but, as in the money market, we have a market-determining equation balancing supply and demand. In this case, market prices determine the wage rate in a form of Phillips equation (12).

[11] R. Solow, "Technical Progress, Capital Formation, and Economic Growth," *American Economic Review, Papers and Proceedings*, Vol. LII, May, 1962, pp. 76-86.

(13), *(14)*, *(15)*, *(16)*: These equations close the system, but they all do so on the side of factor-income payments. Most Keynesian models are fairly detailed on the expenditure side of the national accounts. Total effective demand is made up in this way. The basic national accounting identity, however, relating the income and expenditure sides requires a similar adding up of the components of income. In a highly simplified model, we might get by with just explaining wage income and letting the national accounting identity determine profits as a residual; however, we need more than just two income items for this model. The institutional characteristics of the corporation in a private-enterprise economy require some particular consideration. The accepted version of disposable income, Y, for the consumption-function demand variable excludes corporate saving. An assumption is made that retained corporate earnings are not available for consumer spending.[12]

Personal income minus personal consumption gives a measure of personal saving to satisfy our basic identities; therefore, equation (13) is the corporate-savings equation. The logic underlying the equation is that dividends, D_v, satisfy

$$(D_v)_t = \eta_0 + \eta_1 \sum_{i=0}^{\infty} \chi^i \, (P_c - T_c/p)_{t-i}$$

where

$$D_v = P_c - T_c/p - S_c.$$

This transforms into equation (13) with

estimate $- \eta_0 (1 - \chi) = - 1.508$

estimate $(1 - \eta_1) \quad = \quad 0.894$

estimate $\chi \quad\quad = \quad 0.661$

Another kind of income, in a way very precious to Keynesian thinking, is *rentier* income, but it usually does not get separate treatment in Keynesian models. Because it is tied to interest-rate

---

[12] The influence of capital gains on personal consumption behavior may lead one to dispute this view, but there are no convincing empirical studies that persuade me to revise the definition of disposable income.

developments, just as there are two sides to the wage issue, I have explicitly introduced it here as being determined in equation (14). It is assumed that rentier income moves with a capital base and interest rate. Its movement, however, follows a steady trend.

Another consequence of the institutional nature of the corporate structure of industry is that there are other entrepreneurial incomes not covered by corporate profits. These are self-employment incomes. Equation (15), then, serves to determine these from the movements of G.N.P. in a distributed lag scheme.

A final, reconciling item appears in equation (16). It is depreciation (book value), which is necessary to satisfy the basic social-accounting relationship between G.N.P. and (net) national income. Equation (16) assumes that capital is depreciated at a straight-line rate, based on original cost, over a twenty-year life, with a change upward in the postwar period. Allowable rates of depreciation were revised upward after World War II. That accounts for the dummy variable in equation (16).

(17), (18), (19), (20): The system is closed by accounting identities. The first defines G.N.P. as the sum of consumption expenditure, investment (including all inventory accumulation), the net foreign balance, and government purchases of goods and services. The second identity starts with the value (in constant dollars) of G.N.P. determined in the first identity and subtracts depreciation, corporate savings, taxes less transfers, and other reconciling items to reach a figure for disposable income. The next identity, equation (19), is the basic income-product (or expenditure) identity that equates the calculation of G.N.P. on the expenditure side with factor incomes and reconciling items on the income side. Essentially, this is the residual equation for profit in the economy as a whole. Finally, we have the identity that makes wage income a product of wage rate, hours, and employment.

For different periods of application, we would add to this system such equations as

$$T_i = f_1 (pX)$$

$$T_c = f_2 (pP_c)$$

$$T = f_3 (pY).$$

These would incorporate, on an aggregative basis, the laws of indirect taxation, corporate-income taxation, personal-income taxation, social insurance, and transfer payments.

SOME REMARKS ON THE FUTURE OF KEYNESIAN ECONOMICS

This is a minimal system that can serve to interpret the Keynesian ideas in the light of the actual data of the modern economy and at the same time be a useful system around which to organize thinking on matters of economic policy. Even at this minimal level, the reader might not, at first glance, recognize the Keynesian content of this model. That is why the explanatory paragraphs of the preceding section were necessary. And the research approaches that were spawned by the Keynesian Revolution are bound to take us even further from the initial formulation into systems that will need more and more interpretation to show the original ties. The extent to which Keynesian thinking stimulated econometric research of the type mentioned in this chapter and the extent to which such research was formalized as a test of the Keynesian theory are now being forgotten. The present objective is simply to build a good and highly informative model that gives the best possible description of the economy's structure. Where Keynes is relevant and useful, his ideas will be drawn upon, but there is no necessary link between econometric model-building research and the Keynesian Revolution. That link was a matter of motivation and stimulus in the past, and the econometric research will now go forward on its own.

Tests of the Keynesian Theory: Apart from such casual remarks as the recognition that the United States tax cut of 1964 stimulated the economy as Keynesian thinking said it should have, do we have carefully and rigorously tested evidence of the validity of the Keynesian theory?

An important affirmative answer comes from econometric research. I have made my case, in some detail, as to how I interpret the preceding American macro-model as a statistical representation of the (extended) Keynesian system. The original Klein-Goldberger model and its successive modified forms have been subjected to a number of tests by simulation and forecasting. The econometric models are dynamic and give more business-cycle understanding than the *General Theory*. Viewed as a dynamic system, the Klein-Goldberger modeling of Keynesian economics has been put to severe simulation tests by Mr. and Mrs. Adelman.[13]   Their findings show that this model, in stochastic form only, propagates shocks through the dynamic structure in a way that closely reproduces the business-cycle history of the United States.   The mean duration, the length of cycle phase, and the lead-lag structure of the cyclical series implied by the model closely fit the historical facts. This is a severe test of the model.

Secondly, it has been used to make annual short-run forecasts of economic activity.   A number of these forecasts have been presented in comparison with actual data on activity by D. B. Suits.[14] Except for 1955 and 1959, the forecasting record has been admirable, 1953 to 1965.   Thus, we have a model, or family of models, that can track the short-run movements of the economy and reproduce its cyclical history.   It is in this sense that we have a careful statistical test of the underlying Keynesian theory.

Future Models: This is a workable and just-usable model.   Although it has been good in forecasting, its annual basis is not adequate for use by public authorities in policy decisions.   To follow through with Keynesian policy, we need a sound forward look from quarter-to-quarter or month-to-month.   We must be prepared to anticipate the effects of alternative actions and to know where the economy is headed at all times so that appropriate action can be taken.   We are now engaged in the supplanting of the Klein-Goldberger-type model by quarterly models, and these are inevitably larger and more complicated.   Eventually, we shall turn to monthly models.

But models must also be larger with much more detail by sector, and here we will part company with the Keynesian system.   We may not overthrow what is learned from that system, but we need so much more detail than is covered by that system that we can receive little more in the way of guidance from the *General Theory.*

---

[13] I. and F. L. Adelman, "The Dynamic Properties of the Klein-Goldberger Model," *Econometrica*, Vol. XXVII, October, 1959, pp. 596–625, reprinted in *Readings in Business Cycles*, R. A. Gordon and L. R. Klein, eds.   Richard D. Irwin, Inc., Homewood, Ill., 1965.

[14] D. B. Suits, "Forecasting and Analysis with an Econometric Model," *American Economic Review*, Vol. LII, March, 1962, pp. 104–132, reprinted in *Readings in Business Cycles, loc. cit.* See also, *Survey of Economic Models for Analysis of Disarmament Impacts*, U.S. Arms Control and Disarmament Agency, Washington, D.C., 1965.

Here are some recent policy problems and associated econometric needs of the American economy:

Problem	Econometric studies needed
1. To achieve a better balance of international payments and stabilize gold holdings.	a. Detailed commodity equations of import and export demand with both price and income elasticities.
	b. Equations of demand for services — tourism, shipping, finances.
	c. Equations to determine capital flows — short and long.
2. To reduce unemployment and achieve a better distribution of employment by age and race.	a. Equations showing the relationship of wage movements to the composition as well as the level of unemployment.
	b. Relationship between the distribution of unemployment and the over-all level.
	c. Improved estimates of technical change.
3. To predict the effects of excise-tax cuts.	a. Demand equations, with relative price effects, of goods subject to excises.
	b. Relationships showing amounts of cuts to be passed on to consumers or retained by producers.
	c. The effect of profits from excise cuts on investment.
4. To revise agricultural policy toward more rational use of labor in farming and better control over agricultural stocks.	a. A complete model of the agricultural sector by major types of farming.
	b. Agricultural inventory functions especially needed beyond those used in complete model of agriculture.
	c. Equations of labor mobility between farm and industrial sector.

These are only some of the problems that now confront the American economy, but little guidance will be forthcoming from Keynesian economics, strictly interpreted.   On the other hand, the larger models being generated from the Keynesian Revolution are being geared to tackle these problems.[15]

The effects of the 1964 personal income-tax cut and many other problems can be dealt with in simpler models.   The Keynesian system can take us that far, but we are now seeking to enter new territory.   We have realistic multipliers of the economy and a good impression about main parameters that arise in simple Keynesian systems.   The way of the future will, however, be different by orders of magnitude.

THE UNIVERSALITY OF THE KEYNESIAN REVOLUTION

The General Theory was conceived in England and was obviously greatly influenced by developments in the economy of the United Kingdom during the 1920's and early 1930's.   But the Great Depression and economic dislocations following World War I were world-wide.   While many parts of the *General Theory* were directed at the English consumer, the English investor, or City speculator, they were thought to be truths applicable to most of the market economies of the capitalist world.   In today's economy, we are most interested in examining Keynesian theory in relation to the Western World, Japan, and Oceania.   For short, we shall refer to these areas as the West.   I have argued in the preceding chapter that in other parts of the world, covering the socialist and emerging economies, parts of the Keynesian analysis are also relevant, but here we shall concentrate attention mainly on countries in the West.

There is as stable a consumption function in Japan, the United Kingdom, or Canada as in the United States.   Models such as the one described here for the American economy have been fit to similar data in other countries, and an econometric examination of some of these results will serve to illustrate the universal scope of the Keynesian system.

---

[15] The Brookings model is already being used to study excise tax cuts, but it will have to be elaborated and extended before it can deal with the other problems cited here.

Consumption function: We shall not present complete models for different economies because that would be too lengthy an exposition. We shall instead show salient examples of the more important parts of econometric models drawn from a world-wide collection.

Japan
$$C/N = 0.055 + .230\ Y/N + .576\ (C/N)_{-1} - .0191\ P/W$$
(1934–36 yen per capita)

Israel
$$C/N = 168.52 + .706\ Y/N + .13\ (C/N)_{-1} - 107.24\ D$$
(1955 Israeli pounds per capita)

Netherlands
$$C = 4.10 + .90\ W + 0.40\ P$$
(billions of guilders)

United Kingdom
$$C = 775 + .429\ Y + .315\ C_{-1} - 271\ Q_1 - 75\ Q_2 - 42\ Q_3$$
(non-durables only)
(Millions of 1958 pounds)

India
$$C = -17.1 + .836\ Y + .222\ L_{-2} + .0545\ N$$
(billions of 1953 rupees)

Here we have a collection of Keynesian consumption functions, each representing some aspect peculiar to the economy being studied but all within our expanded scope of the Keynesian system — taking Keynes' own reservations about his simple formulation into account.

Japan[16] — This is a distributed lag form, but there is an additional effect of income distribution, between wage and non-wage income. This equation lends support to the generally accepted view that income inequality stimulated savings historically in Japan and enabled her to industrialize without too much reliance on imported capital.

---

[16] Taken from L. R. Klein and Y. Shinkai, "An Econometric Model of Japan, 1930-59," *International Economic Review*, Vol. 4, January, 1963, pp. 1–28.

Israel[17] — Again we have a lag distribution, but there is an added dummy variable,

$$D = 1 \qquad 1951$$
$$= 0 \qquad 1952\text{--}1963$$

This variable is needed to explain the abnormally low consumption in the early reconstruction years following the war and statehood in 1948.

Although the sum of the income and lag-consumption coefficient is nearly the same in Israel and Japan, the latter is characterized by a slow decay of distributed lag coefficients

$$Y/N + .576\,(Y/N) + (.576)^2\,(Y/N)_{-2} + (.576)^3\,(Y/N)_{-3} + \ldots,$$

while the former is characterized by a fast decay

$$Y/N + .13\,(Y/N)_{-1} + (.13)^2\,(Y/N)_{-2} + (.13)^3\,(Y/N)_{-3} + \ldots.$$

These are realistic differences to be expected within the Keynesian framework.

Netherlands[18] — This equation is not estimated in a per capita form, but it has a direct effect of income distribution on consumption.   It places the marginal propensity to consume from *disposable* wage income at 0.90 and from disposable profit income at 0.40. This equation form gives expression to an observation about the Kalecki model, antedating the *General Theory*, namely, that the m.p.c. from wage income is not unity, but it is high.

United Kingdom[19] — In the study from which this result is extracted, a distinction is being drawn between durable and other (non-durable goods and services) consumption.   The stated function excludes durables.   There are two other distinguishing characteristics: Disposable income is deflated by the price index of non-durables, thus giving rise to some relative price influence at this sub-aggregative level, and quarterly data are used, necessitating the introduction of seasonal variables Q_1, Q_2, Q_3.

[17] Taken from unpublished studies of L. R. Klein and M. Kurz.
[18] Taken from C. A. van den Beld and P. de Wolff, "Exercise in Medium Term Macro Forecasting for the Netherlands Economy," paper delivered to the Entretiens de Monaco, May, 1964.
[19] Taken from unpublished studies of R. J. Ball and L. R. Klein.

$$Q_i = 1 \text{ in the } i\text{-th quarter}$$
$$= 0 \text{ otherwise}$$

India[20] — Like the industrial countries, India too has a propensity to consume function. Its distinguishing characteristic appears to be the relatively high marginal propensity to consume, but this is not unusual for a poor, developing country. This equation is somewhat different from the others in that the income variable represents national income and not per capita disposable income. Population growth, which ought to be an important factor in aggregate Indian consumption, is introduced as a separate explanatory variable: A stable empirical consumption function could not be obtained from per capita data. A liquid-asset variable, L, is also introduced in this equation to show some wealth effect. L, as defined here, includes currency, demand deposits, and time deposits.

This brief collection is far from comprehensive. We could find more studies of the same countries and many more studies along these lines for consumers in other countries. Nevertheless, we do make one point here, that the Keynesian propensity to consume is a functional relationship, with variants, that can be applied to a wide-ranging group of economies throughout the world. All these equations fit the observed sample data very closely. Possibly, a stable function exists for the centrally planned economies as well.

Investment function: Depending on the economy studied and the degree of available statistical material, investment has been studied in great detail — sometimes for individual industries and sometimes for types of investment (public, private, fixed capital, working capital, residential). We shall focus attention on total private investment, but in some cases inventory change and residential construction will be excluded.

Japan

$$\frac{I}{K} = -.005 + .478 \frac{P}{K} - .678\,r + .056\,D$$

(billions of 1934–1936 yen, ratio)

[20] Taken from K. Marwah, *An Econometric Model of Price Behavior in India*, Ph.D. dissertation, University of Pennsylvania, Philadelphia, 1963.

Israel
$$I = - 47.4 + .332X - 1.62\ r - .083\ K_{-1}$$
(millions of 1955 Israeli pounds)

Netherlands
$$I = .85\ P$$
(billions of guilders)

United Kingdom
$$I = - 177 + .088X - 2.6\ r_{-1} - .0050\ K_{-1} + .825\ I_{-1}$$
$$- 61.4\ Q_1 - 20.7\ Q_2 - 38.2\ Q_3$$
(millions of 1958 pounds)

India
$$I = - 6.27 + .089X + .739\ I_{-1}$$
(billions of 1953 rupees)

Japan[21] — This equation gives the rate of total private investment, expressed in terms of the rate of expansion of the stock of capital, as a function of the rate of profit and the rate of interest. The other variable, D, attempts to account for the difference in pre- and postwar behavior.[22]

$$D = 0 \qquad 1930\text{--}1936,$$
$$D = 1 \qquad 1951\text{--}1958$$

In a sense, this formulation attempts, crudely, to express the idea behind the theory of the marginal efficiency of capital by indicating that entrepreneurs compare the rate of return, P/K, with the interest rate. A better expression for *expected* rate of return, than that afforded by P/K, is needed, however. During the postwar phase of rapid growth, Japanese investment has exceeded that predicted by this equation. The permanence of this departure from the function, however, is not certain.

Israel[23] — The Israeli investment equation cited here covers only private fixed investment excluding residential construction and, of course, inventory change. There is a substantial element of public investment in Israel, and the full picture of the role of capital forma-

[21] Klein and Shinkai, *op. cit.*
[22] See the critical remarks of T. Blumenthal, "A Test of the Klein-Shinkai Model of Japan," *International Economic Review*, Vol. VI, May, 1965, pp. 211–228.
[23] Klein and Kurz, *op. cit.*

tion in the expansion of the economy is not given by the process covered in the equation. This, however, is indicative of the problem of applying Keynesian economics to the developing economies of fast growth, particularly when there is a large underlying socialist sector, as in Israel. This is a problem that is less apparent for consumption than for investment.

The contrast between the Israeli and Japanese equations is also of interest in distinguishing the profits and production principles of investment. The Keynesian macro-system could be carried through with either formulation, but the profit variable, P, seems more appropriate to the Japanese capital market, while the output variable, X = G.N.P., seems more appropriate to Israeli conditions. Both economies are high-interest areas. The Japanese values for r vary between 6 and 9 per cent, while the Israeli values fall between 12 and 18 per cent. These are not the kinds of rates (or economies) that Keynes had in mind when he discussed the role of interest in the *General Theory*, yet they seem to be relevant as explanatory variables in aggregative investment functions of the Keynesian type.

Netherlands[24] — This is a very simple proportional investment function dependent on gross profits for the economy as a whole. This simple function appeared to serve its authors well in trend projection, but for a short-run explanation of investment other variables would be needed.

United Kingdom[25] — This equation, covering only non-residential and non-inventory investment, is a stock-adjustment type depending on output, X, lagged interest rate, r_{-1}, and seasonal indicators, Q_1, Q_2, Q_3. It differs from some stock-adjustment models in having both K_{-1} and I_{-1}, simultaneously. The effect of total capital K_{-1} is very small. The inclusion of both lagged terms, K_{-1} and I_{-1}, makes the lag distribution of output and interest effects more complicated than the schemes of simple geometric decay. Basically, however, this equation comes from the same family of investment functions as that used in the other examples cited here.

[24] van den Beld and de Wolff, *op. cit.*
[25] Klein and Ball, *op. cit.*

India[26] — This is purely a distributed lag in X, real national income. Attempts to introduce interest-rate variables for this capital-short economy have produced puzzling results, with significant positive effects. This anomalous result may be rationalized in terms of making more financial capital available for ever-present investment opportunities at higher rather than at lower interest rates, but we have preferred to portray Indian investment behavior as dependent on output, and its lagged values alone.[27] Also, the depressing effect of capital accumulation should be less pertinent for the Indian than for industrially mature economies. The stock of capital has not been included.

It is small wonder that there is less uniformity and more difficulty of construction in the process of fitting Keynesian investment functions around the world. Differences in institutional structure, especially in the degree of public control or influence, have a larger bearing on the investment-decision process. Also, as has been noted earlier, Keynes was in the tradition of business-cycle theorists who attached great importance to the volatility of investment. While I do not want to relegate consumption to a purely passive role, and I refrain from placing the whole burden of dynamic force in the economy on the investment process, I do recognize much in the Keynesian position and find it to be responsible for relatively greater difficulty in finding a universal pattern of investment behavior.

Liquidity preference: The Israeli and Dutch models were both constructed as real-economy models with little explicit attention paid to the money market. While this is incomplete treatment, it is an empirical fact that one can go far in the statistical explanation of economic activity by concentrating attention on the real as opposed to the monetary economy. The neo-Keynesian development has been largely a real-economy analysis centered on the savings-investment process of income determination. We do have some findings, however, on money market equations of the Keynesian type in different countries.

[26] Marwah, *op. cit.*
[27] The perverse interest effect on investment has been noted, at times, in a segment of the United States capital formation market — namely, housing financed by F.H.A. and V.A. mortgages.

Japan

$$\frac{M}{pX} = .229 - .000867\,(p - p_{-1}) - .214\,Dr$$

(billions of current yen, ratio)

United Kingdom

$$r = 2.97 - 1.77\,M/pX + .121\,r_B + .714\,r_{-1} + .207Q_1$$
$$+ .244\,Q_2 + .321\,Q_3$$

(per cent)

India

$$M = -2.62 + .175\,pX - 1.002\,r + .073\,p_{sh}$$

(billions of current rupees)

Japan[28] — The Keynesian theory can be formulated as making velocity a function of interest rate and other speculative variables. That is done in the Japanese equation, where the reciprocal of velocity is made to depend on price change and the interest rate. The variable D is the pre–postwar dummy variable; so interest has an effect only in the postwar period.

United Kingdom[29] — This equation has the long-term interest rate varying inversely with the velocity reciprocal and positively following bank rate, r_B, and its own lags. The use of bank rate here is similar to the use of the discount rate in the United States model. The Q_i are seasonal indicators.

India[30] — This equation is written in the more standard form, expressing cash balances as a function of the interest rate, r, and the share price, p_{sh}; we have a negative association between cash holdings and the rate of return on share alternatives. In this equation, M is measured differently from L in the Indian consumption function. Since many Indian savers use time deposits as a principal instrument of savings, and save more in this form as interest rates rise, M has been defined to include only currency and demand deposits.

Other relationships: All the equations cited here for different countries were extracted from complete models, and we are only sampling the universal structure of the Keynesian system. We

[28] Klein and Shinkai, *op. cit.*
[29] Klein and Ball, *op. cit.*
[30] Marwah, *op. cit.*

could continue to present import and export propensities, production functions, labor-share equations, wage-rate formation equations, and so forth. These exist as stable functions in many different economies. The extended form of the Keynesian system has a wide field of applicability, and its teachings have already permeated world-wide econometric research. The next step is obviously to construct a world model rather than mere national models. Such a move has already been made on a small scale by Polak and Rhomberg.[31]

[31] J. J. Polak and R. R. Rhomberg, "Economic Instability in an International Setting," *Readings in Business Cycles*, by R. A. Gordon and L. R. Klein, eds., Richard D. Irwin, Inc., Homewood, Ill., 1965, pp. 584–592.

TECHNICAL APPENDIX

A MATHEMATICAL MODEL OF THE *TREATISE*

In order to get a comprehensive picture of the structure of the *Treatise*, we can best formulate a simple model of the complete system. For easy reference, we define again all the relevant variables:

I is the market value of investment.

S is the value of savings.

Q is the windfall profits.

r is the interest variable.

$\bar{r}$ is the market rate of interest.

O is the physical volume of output.

R is the physical volume of consumption.

C is the physical volume of investment.

E is the incomes paid out to the factors of production.

Π is the price level of output as a whole.

P is the price level of consumption goods.

P' is the price level of investment goods.

M_3 is the stock of savings deposits.

M_2 is the stock of business deposits.

M_1 is the stock of income deposits.

V_1 is the income velocity of circulation.

Wicksell defined the natural rate of interest as either that rate which achieves price stability or that which equates savings and investment. Keynes applied this idea to his definitions of savings and investment to get the equation

$$S(r) = I(r)$$

whose solution in r determines the natural rate of interest. Actual or observable savings-investment which occurs in the market may be quite different from that calculated by substituting the natural rate in the savings or the investment function. Observable investment would be

$$S(\bar{r}) + Q(\bar{r}) = I(\bar{r})$$

where $\bar{r}$ is the market rate, of course. Wicksell considered $\bar{r}$ as given by the banking system within limits; *i.e.*, he stated that the banks were

255

free to determine $\bar{r}$ as long as their reserve position enabled them always to supply the proper amount of credit corresponding to the rate set.

Keynes also assumed that the banks could determine the market rate of interest at $\bar{r}$. Furthermore he thought that they could control the volume of savings deposits, $\overline{M}_3$. These controls are certainly questionable, but let us follow the mechanical procedure of going where his assumptions lead us. The interest equation along with the others discussed in Chapter I and certain obvious relations can be written as follows:

$$I(r) = S(r)$$
$$Q = Q(r)$$
$$r = \bar{r}$$
$$\Pi O = E + Q(r)$$
$$PR = E - S(r)$$
$$M_3 = B(P')$$
$$M_3 = \overline{M}_3$$
$$O = \overline{O}$$
$$M_1 V_1 = E$$
$$V_1 = \overline{V}_1$$
$$M_1 = \overline{M}_1$$
$$C + R = O$$
$$P'C = I(\bar{r})$$

In order, we have the savings-investment equation, the profit function, the autonomously set market rate, the "fundamental equation" for the determination of Π, the definition of savings (or, alternatively, our version of the "fundamental equation" for the determination of P), the bearishness function, the given stock of savings deposits, the given output, the definition of income velocity, the given velocity, the given stock of income deposits, the division of output into consumption goods plus investment goods, and finally a definition of the market value of investment. We now find ourselves with as many equations as variables when we distinguish between the natural and market rates as distinct variables.

The first equation can be solved for the natural rate of interest, say, r_0. Substituting the market rate in $Q(r)$, we next calculate the windfall profits. Adding the observable savings and the windfall profits, we get the actual level of investment, $S(\bar{r}) + Q(\bar{r})$ or $I(\bar{r})$. The equation of bearishness yields a solution $P' = P'_0$; furthermore the ratio $I(\bar{r})/P'_0$ gives C_0, the volume of real investment. From the equation

$$C_0 + R = \overline{O}$$

R_0, the volume of consumption, can be calculated. We are now left with three equations

$$\Pi\overline{O} = E + Q(\bar{r})$$
$$PR_0 = E - S(\bar{r})$$
$$\overline{M}_1\overline{V}_1 = E$$

to get the three variables Π, P, E. The weak point in this system is the most important element of later-Keynesian economics, namely, a theory of effective demand. A quantity equation is Keynes' sole theory of the determination of E, and the validity of this theory depends upon the assumption that the banking system can determine the stock of income deposits $\overline{M}_1$, as well as the total stock of money. Elsewhere, Keynes also put forth the "theory of effective demand" that $E/\overline{O}$ is institutionally given as efficiency earnings.

It is interesting to see that even if the "fundamental equation" for the price level of consumption goods be left as Keynes wrote it in the *Treatise*, the system does not become more or less determinate. This equation can be written, with the unwarranted assumption, as

$$P = \frac{E}{O} + \frac{I' - S}{R}$$

where I' = the cost of production of investment goods. The assumption

$$I' = E\left(\frac{C}{O}\right)$$

merely adds another equation to determine the one new variable, so that the determinateness of P is, in a sense, unaffected.

Keynes did not recognize $Q \neq o$ as an equilibrium situation, and for the case $Q = o$ we do get a more consistent, although strictly classical, theory. For the equilibrium position he did support the quantity theory, as the quotation in Chapter I shows. The model would now become

$$I(\bar{r}) = S(\bar{r}) \qquad\qquad \Pi\overline{O} = RP + S(\bar{r})$$
$$\overline{M}_1 = \left(\frac{1}{\overline{V}_1}\right)\Pi\overline{O} \qquad\qquad C + R = \overline{O}$$
$$\overline{M}_3 = B(P') \qquad\qquad P'C = I(\bar{r})$$

In this case we have enough equations to determine all the free variables. If we consider only the following self-determined part of the system,

$$I(\bar{r}) = S(\bar{r})$$
$$\overline{M}_1 = \left(\frac{1}{\overline{V}_1}\right)\Pi\overline{O}$$

K

we see that Keynes was as classical as he could possibly be. At the going market rate of interest, all savings flow unobstructed into investment, and the amount of money determines the price level. Full-employment output is taken as given because it comes from the background equations of the complete system.

MATHEMATICAL DERIVATION OF THE SYSTEM OF THE
GENERAL THEORY

The Consumption Function and Liquidity-Preference Function. Consider an individual household trying to maximize its utility function, which depends on the consumption 'of present and future commodities, and its structure of assets in the form of money and various types of securities. The maximization process is not unrestricted. We must impose a restraining condition which states that holdings of liquid assets at the beginning of any given period plus the interest earned on securities held during the period plus other income not spent on commodities during the period (savings) equal the liquid assets held at the end of the period. In other words, this condition requires that the rate of change of the stock of liquid wealth shall equal savings or that the stock of liquid wealth shall equal historically accumulated savings. We ignore the possibility of holding goods (inventories) on the part of the household, but this type of behavior will be included under the investment activity of business firms.

Let us write

$$(1) \quad u = u(x_{11}, \cdots, x_{n1}, \cdots, x_{1T}, \cdots, x_{nT}, \ b_{11}, \cdots, b_{s1}, \cdots, b_{1T}, \cdots, b_{sT},$$
$$m_1, \cdots, m_T)$$

$$(2) \quad m_{t-1} + \sum_{i=1}^{s} (1 + r_{it})b_{i,\,t-1} + y_t - \sum_{i=1}^{n} p_{it}x_{it} = m_t + \sum_{i=1}^{s} b_{it}$$
$$t = 1, 2, \cdots, T$$

where u = utility of a particular household, x_{it} = consumption of the i-th commodity in the t-th period of the future; b_{it} = the holding of the i-th security at the end of the t-th period of the future; m_t = the holding of cash balances at the end of the t-th period of the future; r_{it} = the interest rate corresponding to the i-th security at the end of the $(t-1)$-th period of the future; y_t = the non-interest income of the t-th period of the future; p_{it} = the price of the i-th commodity in the t-th period of the future; T = the last period of the time horizon over which utility is maximized.

Our problem now is to maximize (1) subject to (2). First we form the function

$$\Phi = u + \sum_{t=1}^{T} \lambda_t [m_{t-1} + \sum_{i=1}^{s} (1 + r_{it}) b_{i,\ t-1} + y_t - \sum_{i=1}^{n} p_{it} x_{it} - m_t - \sum_{i=1}^{s} b_{it}]$$

Next, we derive the necessary conditions for a maximum:

(3) $\dfrac{\partial \Phi}{\partial x_{it}} = \dfrac{\partial u}{\partial x_{it}} - \lambda_t p_{it} = 0 \qquad i = 1, 2, \cdots, n; t = 1, 2, \cdots, T$

(4) $\dfrac{\partial \Phi}{\partial b_{it}} = \dfrac{\partial u}{\partial b_{it}} + \lambda_{t+1}(1 + r_{i,\ t+1}) - \lambda_t = 0 \qquad \begin{array}{l} i = 1, 2, \cdots, s; \\ t = 1, 2, \cdots, T \end{array}$

(5) $\dfrac{\partial \Phi}{\partial m_t} = \dfrac{\partial u}{\partial m_t} + \lambda_{t+1} - \lambda_t = 0 \qquad t = 1, 2, \cdots, T$

$\lambda_{T+1} = 0$ by definition.

The set of equations (3), (4), (5) along with the constraints in (2) enable us to solve for all the x's, b's, and m's in terms of the prices, interest rates, incomes, and the initial conditions. These solutions are the demand equations for the flows of commodities and the stocks of liquid assets. We write them as

(6) $x_{it} = x_{it}(p_{11}, \cdots, p_{nT}, r_{11}, \cdots, r_{sT}, y_1, \cdots, y_T, m_0, b_{10}, \cdots, b_{s0})$
$$i = 1, 2, \cdots, n$$
$$t = 1, 2, \cdots, T$$

(7) $b_{it} = b_{it}(p_{11}, \cdots, p_{nT}, r_{11}, \cdots, r_{sT}, y_1, \cdots, y_T, m_0, b_{10}, \cdots, b_{s0})$
$$i = 1, 2, \cdots, s$$
$$t = 1, 2, \cdots, T$$

(8) $m_t = m_t(p_{11}, \cdots, p_{nT}, r_{11}, \cdots, r_{sT}, y_1, \cdots, y_T, m_0, b_{10}, \cdots, b_{s0})$
$$t = 1, 2, \cdots, T$$

The form of the constraints (2) are such that the separate variables y_1, m_0, b_{10}, $\cdots$, b_{s0}, r_{11}, $\cdots r_{s1}$ always occur in the particular form

(9) $m_0 + \sum_{i=1}^{s} (1 + r_{i1}) b_{i0} + y_1$

Our model is dynamic because it represents a maximization over a future time period. The whole complex of future prices, interest rates, income, etc., must be based on the personal anticipations of the individual household. We shall assume that the anticipated future time pattern of any variable is a function of the past and current history of that variable. In a discrete model this historial pattern can be represented by a function of all the lagged values of the particular variable in question. A model with lagged variables will give us a dynamic

Keynesian system, but for our purposes of comparative statics we shall assume that all the lags are zero and hence work only with current values of all the variables; hence let us rewrite (6), (7), (8) statically as

(10) $x_i = x_i(p_1, \cdots, p_n, r_1, \cdots, r_s, y, a)$ $i = 1, 2, \cdots, n$

(11) $b_i = b_i(p_1, \cdots, p_n, r_1, \cdots, r_s, y, a)$ $i = 1, 2, \cdots, s$

(12) $m = m(p_1, \cdots, p_n, r_1, \cdots, r_s, y, a)$

where [1]
$$a = m + \sum_{i=1}^{s} b_i$$

Define consumption as

(13)
$$\sum_{i=1}^{n} p_i x_i = c$$

and total security holdings as

(14)
$$\sum_{i=1}^{s} b_i = b$$

If we have a suitable aggregation procedure, we can write

(15) $c = c(p, r, y, a)$

(16) $b = b(p, r, y, a)$

(17) $m = m(p, r, y, a)$

in which r and p are the interest and price aggregates respectively. If we further impose the customary homogeneity conditions on our demand equations, they become

(15a) $c/p = c^*(r, y/p, a/p)$

(16a) $b/p = b^*(r, y/p, a/p)$

(17a) $m/p = m^*(r, y/p, a/p)$

Suppose that these equations are linear, as family-budget data suggest.

(15b) $c/p = d_0 + d_1 r + d_2 y/p + d_3 a/p$

(16b) $b/p = e_0 + e_1 r + e_2 y/p + e_3 a/p$

(17b) $m/p = f_0 + f_1 r + f_2 y/p + f_3 a/p$

The community [2] demand functions follow by summation over all individuals. Consider (15b), for example, with all variables pertaining specifically to the individual household marked with a subscript i.

[1] The appropriate variable is a because the only component of (9) which does not involve anticipated values is $m_0 + \sum_{i=1}^{s} b_{i0}$.

[2] The reader should remember that we have been dealing with the individual household thus far.

$$(18) \quad \sum_i c_i/p = \sum_i d_{0i} + \left(\sum_i d_{1i}\right)r + \frac{\sum_i d_{2i}y_i}{\sum_i y_i}\frac{\sum_i y_i}{p} + \frac{\sum_i d_{3i}a_i}{\sum_i a_i}\frac{\sum_i a_i}{p}$$

$$C/p = d_4 + d_5 r + d_6 Y/p + d_7 A/p$$

where

$$d_4 = \sum_i d_{0i}; \; d_5 = \sum_i d_{1i}; \; d_6 = \frac{\sum_i d_{2i}y_i}{\sum_i y_i}; \; d_7 = \frac{\sum_i d_{3i}a_i}{\sum_i a_i}$$

$$C = \sum_i c_i; \; Y = \sum_i y_i; \; A = \sum_i a_i$$

Similarly we obtain

$$(19) \qquad B/p = e_4 + e_5 r + e_6 Y/p + e_7 A/p$$

$$(20) \qquad M/p = f_4 + f_5 r + f_6 Y/p + f_7 A/p$$

The variable A/p is equal to $M/p + B/p$. We can, obviously, eliminate B/p between (18), (19), and (20) to get

$$(18a) \qquad C/p = d_8 + d_9 r + d_{10} Y/p + d_{11} M/p$$

$$(20a) \qquad M/p = f_8 + f_9 r + f_{10} Y/p$$

These are the usual Keynesian consumption function and liquidity preference function respectively. In most cases, we assume, however, $d_{11} = 0$. Some empirical evidence supports this view.[3] Another method of transforming (18) and (20) directly into the Keynesian equations is to consider A/p as representative of the aggregate real wealth of the community. If this real wealth is capable of producing the income stream Y/p, we can write

$$(21) \qquad A/p = \frac{Y/p}{r}$$

which is the capitalization, at the going interest rate, of the income which the wealth of the community produces. By substituting (21) into (18) and (20), we can eliminate A/p as a separate variable of the system.

If income and consumption are variables of the system, we have the definition

$$(22) \quad S/p \equiv Y/p - C/p \equiv -d_4 - d_5 r + (1 - d_6)Y/p - d_7 A/p$$

in which S = savings.

[3] See L. R. Klein, "A Post-mortem on Transition Predictions of National Product," *Journal of Political Economy*, Vol. LIV, 1946, p. 289.

Equation (22) is the savings function. It is redundant to use both the savings function and the consumption function in the system.

It should be noted that in the above derivations the variable y was called non-interest income. However, in the constraining equation (2), interest income and non-interest income always enter additively; hence we can consider (10), (11), (12) as solved in terms of income including interest as well as in terms of non-interest income. Equations (18) and (20) are more convenient if the variable Y includes interest income. It should also be noted that d_6, d_7, e_6, e_7, f_6, and f_7 are weighted averages of individual parameters, the weights being the individual money incomes or liquid assets. If the distribution of income and that of wealth do not change radically over short periods, these weighted averages may be regarded as stable parameters of the system rather than as variables.

The Investment Function, General Case. The entrepreneur will be assumed to behave, with regard to the purchase of capital assets, according to the principles of profit maximization over the anticipated future life of the asset in question. The anticipated profits which are to be maximized can be written as

$$(23) \qquad \pi = \int_0^T (py - wN)e^{-\rho\theta}d\theta - q\left(\frac{I}{q}\right)$$

where p = price level of output, y = volume of output, w = wage rate, N = employment, ρ = discount rate, T = entrepreneurial horizon, q = price of new capital goods, I = money value of investment.†

The last term is not included under the integral sign because it represents an outlay on durable equipment, which will produce goods and services over the whole horizon. The input of labor and the output of goods will be flows coming forth during the entire period $(0, T)$, but the capital outlay will be made once and for all at the beginning of the planning period. Other terms, such as the market value of existing capital, could also appear in the profit function although they have no influence on the maximizing conditions.

The rational entrepreneur will now behave so as to maximize π subject to the production function

$$(24) \qquad y = y\left(N, \frac{I}{q}, K\right)^4$$

---

[4] We write the production function this way in order to show the technological distinction between new and old capital. The distinction can be carried much further to show the technological differences between capital goods of all age groups. The function (24) is a convenient compromise between the most general case and the case where no distinction is made.*

where $K = \int_{-\infty}^{0} \left(\frac{I}{q}\right) d\theta$, the accumulated volume of capital at the beginning of the period. The resulting maximization condition will be

(25) $$\frac{\partial \pi}{\partial \left(\frac{I}{q}\right)} = \int_0^T p\left(1 - \frac{1}{\eta}\right) \frac{\partial y}{\partial \left(\frac{I}{q}\right)} e^{-\rho\theta} d\theta - q = 0$$

when η = elasticity of demand. This equation establishes a relation between p, y, N, K, ρ, q, and $\frac{I}{q}$, which can be called the investment function or the schedule of the marginal efficiency of capital. The term under the integral is the discounted stream of future returns expected to be realized from the use of the newly purchased capital equipment, $\frac{I}{q}$. The discount rate, ρ, is that rate which discounts this stream to the current purchase price of new capital, q. This is precisely Keynes' formulation of the marginal efficiency of capital.

The demand for labor, as well as new capital, follows in a similar fashion from this model of profit maximization. We can maximize profits with respect to small variations in labor input. This leads to

(26) $$\frac{\partial \pi}{\partial N} = p\left(1 - \frac{1}{\eta}\right) \frac{\partial y}{\partial N} - w = 0$$

The marginal value productivity of labor is equated to the wage rate, giving us the demand schedule for labor.[5]

The Investment Function, Special Case. There are two unknown functions which enter into the make-up of the marginal efficiency of capital, the elasticity of demand and the marginal productivity of new capital. We know the elasticity of demand in the case of perfect competition, but if competition is assumed to be imperfect we can simplify the problem by assuming the elasticity coefficient to be constant. In view of much

[5] In this demonstration we have assumed a very simplified type of economy. To say that firms maximize the profit function (23) is not as realistic as it should be; some firms, as well as households, are concerned about the structure of their assets. A more complete theory should assume that firms maximize a utility function which depends on the time patterns of future profits, of the stock of fixed capital, of the stock of liquid assets, of the stock of inventories. The more general theory leads to many more equations in the micro-system — but can also be reduced to macro-systems like that of Keynes. We have merely attempted to demonstrate simple theories that lead to the Keynesian system. In the case of the theory of the household, we could not have been much less general, because we had to show the foundations of the theory of liquidity preference, which is not possible without introducing the asset structure specifically.

empirical evidence that constant elasticity demand functions fit the observed data well, the latter assumption is not bad. We also have much empirical evidence concerning the production function. A slight variation of the familiar Cobb-Douglas production function to the form

$$(27) \qquad y = BN^{\alpha}\left(\gamma_1 K + \gamma_2 \frac{I}{q}\right)^{\beta} e^{g(t)}$$

is consistent with the output-input data of many industries and also of the economy as a whole.

By making use of these two empirical facts and substituting in our profit-maximizing equation, we obtain

$$(28) \qquad \frac{\partial \pi}{\partial \left(\dfrac{I}{q}\right)} = \int_0^T p\left(1 - \frac{1}{\eta}\right) \frac{\beta \gamma_2 y}{\gamma_1 K + \gamma_2 \left(\dfrac{I}{q}\right)} e^{-\rho\theta} d\theta - q = 0$$

Let us assume that the entrepreneur who does not know the value of the integrand over each time period of the horizon anticipates the integrand to take on the same value (current value) for each time point of this horizon. We then have

$$(29) \qquad q = \beta\gamma_2\left(1 - \frac{1}{\eta}\right)\frac{py}{\gamma_1 K + \gamma_2\left(\dfrac{I}{q}\right)} \int_0^T e^{-\rho\theta} d\theta$$

$$\frac{I}{q} = \beta\left(1 - \frac{1}{\eta}\right)\frac{py}{q}\frac{1}{\rho}(1 - e^{-T\rho}) - \frac{\gamma_1}{\gamma_2} K$$

This is our Keynesian investment function. If $p = q$ or $p = \nu q$, then we get the customary version of the Keynesian function

$$(30) \qquad \frac{I}{p} = \beta\left(1 - \frac{1}{\eta}\right)y\frac{1}{\rho}(1 - e^{-T\rho}) - \frac{\gamma_1}{\gamma_2} K$$

or

$$\frac{I}{p} = f(y, \rho, K)$$

We can also write this result in terms of money values instead of real values to get

$$(31) \qquad I = f^*(py, \rho, q K)$$

In all the short-run theories, we assume that K or qK is given by the past history of the system and enters only as a parameter in the investment function. We also assume that we can write r, the interest rate, for ρ because the difference between the two can only be accounted for by subjective risk elements which are not to be explained by our theory and must be taken as given.

We can also see clearly why the investment function is likely to be interest-elastic as the horizon, T, is shortened, which we believe to be the case today.

(32)
$$\frac{\partial\left(\frac{I}{p}\right)}{\partial\rho} = -\beta\left(1 - \frac{1}{\eta}\right)\frac{y}{\rho^2}(1 - e^{-T\rho}) + \beta\left(1 - \frac{1}{\eta}\right)\frac{y}{\rho}Te^{-T\rho}$$
$$= \beta\left(1 - \frac{1}{\eta}\right)\frac{y}{\rho}\left[Te^{-T\rho} - \frac{1}{\rho}(1 - e^{-T\rho})\right]$$

(33)
$$\frac{\partial^2\left(\frac{I}{p}\right)}{\partial\rho\partial T} = \beta\left(1 - \frac{1}{\eta}\right)\frac{y}{\rho}(-T\rho e^{-T\rho}) < 0$$

Investment is less sensitive to the discount rate as the period $(0, T)$ is contracted, because the *absolute value* of $\dfrac{\partial\left(\frac{I}{p}\right)}{\partial\rho}$ falls with declining T.

The steps which were completed in order to derive the Keynesian investment function can be considered to apply either to the individual firm or to the community. The justification for their application to the community is based on the theory that the profit maximizing equations of micro-economics hold in analogy for the macro-system if the aggregates of the latter system are properly measured.[6]

MATHEMATICAL MODELS OF KEYNESIAN AND CLASSICAL ECONOMICS

In order to compare two different economic theories, it is very helpful to construct mathematical skeletons of the system supported by each theory. The differences in analytical structure between these two skeletons should show clearly the essential differences between the two theories.

The most general form of the Keynesian system consists of the savings-investment equation, the liquidity-preference equation, and the background relations from the real part of the system. It can be written as follows:

(34) $$S(r, Y) = I(r, Y)$$
(35) $$M = L(r, Y)$$
(36) $$Y = py$$
(37) $$y = y(N)$$
(38) $$w = p\left(1 - \frac{1}{\eta}\right)y'(N)$$
(39) $$N = F(w)$$

[6] See L. R. Klein, "Macroeconomics and the Theory of Rational Behavior," *Econometrica*, Vol. XIV, 1946, p. 93.

where S = money savings, I = money investment, M = the stock of cash balances, r = the interest rate, Y = money income, y = real income, p = the price level, N = employment, w = the wage rate, η = the elasticity of demand.[7] In this short-run model we assume that the stock of capital is given, *i.e.* $K = \overline{K}$. It is further assumed that these equations have particular shapes. Specifically,

$$\frac{\partial S}{\partial r} \geqq 0 \quad \text{and small in absolute value}$$

$$\frac{\partial S}{\partial Y} > 0$$

$$\frac{\partial I}{\partial r} \leqq 0 \quad \text{and small in absolute value}$$

$$\frac{\partial I}{\partial Y} > 0$$

$$\frac{\partial L}{\partial r} < 0 \quad \text{and large in absolute value}$$

$$\frac{\partial L}{\partial Y} > 0$$

$$\frac{dF}{dw} = \infty \quad \text{for } N \leqq No \text{ where } No \text{ is full employment}$$

$$0 \leqq \frac{dF}{dw} < \infty \quad \text{for } N > No$$

It is true, of course, that there are just enough equations to determine all the independent variables except M, which is assumed given by bank policy.

The classical model can also be written in terms of a few simple equations. It is

(40)		$S(r) = I(r)$
(41)		$M = kY$
(42)		$Y = py$
(43)		$y = y(N)$
(44)		$w = py'(N)$
(45)		$N = f\left(\dfrac{w}{p}\right)$

---

[7] We have suppressed the price level as an explicit variable in the savings function.

with the conditions

$$\frac{\partial S}{\partial r} > 0$$

$$\frac{\partial I}{\partial r} < 0$$

$$K = \overline{K}$$

Many economists have maintained that the principal difference in these two systems rests in the substitution of $N = F(w)$ for $N = f\!\left(\dfrac{w}{p}\right)$. This we do not believe to be true, for by inserting the latter supply equation into the Keynesian system in place of the former, we can still get a system which does not automatically obtain full employment. A more significant distinction between the systems occurs in the determination of the variable Y. In the classical system, we can always solve the last three equations uniquely for $\dfrac{w}{p}$, N, and y. Then the quantity equation serves merely to determine the absolute level of prices, p (or wages, w), while r is obtained from the savings-investment equation. There is no direct theory of the determination of Y, merely one of the determination of p for a given level of full employment. We can call the employment full in this case because the value calculated for N lies on the supply curve of labor — all who want to work at the going real wage rate are hired.

It has been argued that the classical economists really thought of the savings-investment equation as depending upon Y as well as r, and the money equation as depending upon r as well as Y. If this argument is correct, does it mean that the classical economists had a theory of effective demand? We shall now show that it does not. One method of showing this is to construct a very general system which includes, formally, both classical and Keynesian economics. Then we shall show that one result follows if we use classical reasoning, and another result follows if we become Keynesians.

This system will be one that is homogeneous of order zero in prices in all equations except that dealing with cash balances. If we change all prices and wages by the same proportions, we do not change any of the real magnitudes in the homogeneous equations. Furthermore, there will be perfect competition in all markets.

Our system can be written in terms of any *numéraire*. Following Keynes, we shall use the wage-rate as our *numéraire;* thus the following relations will hold.

(46) $Y = wY_w, S = wS_w, I = wI_w, M = wM_w, L = wL_w$

where the subscripts denote variables measured in wage units. The model is

$$(47) \qquad S_w(r, Y_w) = I_w(r, Y_w)$$
$$(48) \qquad M_w = L_w(r, Y_w)$$
$$(49) \qquad wY_w = py$$
$$(50) \qquad y = y(N)$$
$$(51) \qquad w = py'(N)$$
$$(52) \qquad N = f\left(\frac{w}{p}\right)$$

If every equation holds simultaneously, then we have a perfect equilibrium of perfect competition. The classical solution fits this case. From the solution of (49)–(52) we obtain

$$\left(\frac{w}{p}\right) = \left(\frac{w}{p}\right)_0$$
$$N = N_0$$
$$y = y_0$$
$$Y_w = (Y_w)_0$$

Substitute $(Y_w)_0$ into the savings-investment equation and solve the equation

$$S_w(r,(Y_w)_0) = I_w(r,(Y_w)_0)$$

for $r = r_0$. Substitute r_0 and $(Y_w)_0$ into the money equation and calculate the level of money wages from

$$M_w = \frac{\overline{M}}{w} = L_w(r_0,(Y_w)_0)$$

Since we know $\left(\frac{w}{p}\right) = \left(\frac{w}{p}\right)_0$ and w_0, we can get p_0. Every variable takes on a unique value, and we have full employment because all willing workers are hired at the real wage $\left(\frac{w}{p}\right)_0$.

Now, let us proceed as Keynesians. Solve again (49)–(52). Substitute the full-employment income, $(Y_w)_0$, into the savings-investment equation. Is there always a solution for $r > 0$ from the equation

$$S_w(r,(Y_w)_0) = I_w(r,(Y_w)_0)?$$

There is always such a solution within the framework of classical economics because the classicals assumed shapes for these functions so that they would always intersect in the positive quadrant of the $(S_w\text{-}I_w, r)$-plane. The classical theory of interest assumes that savings decisions and investment decisions both respond sensitively to changes in the rate of interest. But Keynesian economics assumes that both functions are interest-inelastic. Under these conditions there may be no solution ($r > 0$) to the above equation when Y_w is at a full-employment level. In order for the equation to hold something must give way, either r or Y_w. Obviously r cannot give way because it is bounded by the restriction $r > 0$. But (Y_w) can change. If Y_w falls from $(Y_w)_0$ to $(Y_w)_1$, we may be able to get savings equal to investment. In fact, Y_w will fall until the two surfaces $S_w(r, Y_w)$ and $I_w(r, Y_w)$ adjust to an equilibrium. If we have the plausible conditions

$$S_w(0,(Y_w)_0) > I_w(0,(Y_w)_0)$$

and

$$\frac{\partial S_w}{\partial Y_w} > \frac{\partial I_w}{\partial Y_w}$$

then falling income will finally bring savings and investment into equilibrium. But falling incomes bring about decreased employment. In the equation

(49) $$wY_w = py$$

substitute (51) to get

$$Y_w = \frac{p}{w} y = \frac{y(N)}{y'(N)}$$

This substitution implies that regardless of the shifting adjustments, the demand curve for labor will hold. If there is ever any conflict between the demand and supply of labor in the perfectly competitive case like the one we are considering (*e.g.* one of no trade-union influence), we can be certain that a short demand will dominate a long supply. Hence in the latter equation, with $y'(N)$ a decreasing function of N, a smaller value of Y_w can be balanced only by a smaller value of N. It is not meaningful to assume that employed workers move downward along their supply schedule of labor,[8] for they would be accepting a smaller real wage than employers would be willing to pay. But it is meaningful to assume that they move upward along the demand curve for labor [9] and get the highest possible real wage offered for the amount of labor corresponding to the reduced level of income. In this position, the demand for labor at the going real wage will be less than the supply, and the difference represents unemployment.

[8] See Fig. 5, Ch. III.
[9] See Fig. 5, Ch. III.

We conclude from this argument that a perfect equilibrium of perfect competition is always possible in classical economics and is incompatible with Keynesian economics. The only type of unemployment that can appear in a classical model is that due to friction and other imperfections or the unwillingness to work at going real wage rates. To explain unemployment in the Keynesian model, it is not necessary to introduce any frictions; it is only necessary to substitute a theory of effective demand for a theory of interest.

Will this unemployment which we have explained above be an equilibrium position? It is true within the classical system that money wage cuts always increase the level of employment and income. If wage cuts operate with the same force in the Keynesian system, the unemployment position will quickly be wiped out, since we have assumed perfect competition in every market, including the labor market. Classicists would argue that the excess supply of workers will be wiped out because they will compete with each other for jobs by cutting wages and thus restore full employment. But the two systems have different structures. An employment-creating process in one system may not have the same effects in the other system.

Since we have a completely determined system we can truncate it at any place we choose. Hence we can write

$$(47) \qquad S_w(r, Y_w) = I_w(r, Y_w)$$
$$(48) \qquad M_w = L_w(r, Y_w)$$
$$(53) \qquad w = \overline{w}$$

which is equivalent to the entire system above.[10] The first two equations can be solved for r, and Y_w in terms of M_w, which in turn equals $\dfrac{M}{w}$. Assume a bank policy favorable to the orthodox argument, namely, $M = \overline{M}$ is held constant. Then output, Y_w, is a function of $\overline{w}$, the wage rate. Suppose that the unemployed workers cut wages. What is the effect on Y_w? It is easy to calculate a multiplier of the form

$$(54) \qquad dY_w = \frac{dY_w}{dM_w} dM_w$$

which will tell us the increment to output as a result of a wage cut.

[10] The fact that all equations do not hold exactly in the Keynesian system does not prevent us from taking this system as completely determined. Every equation except one holds, but all the variables take on unique values because the demand for labor dominates the supply. From the imperfect relation we get $\left(\dfrac{w}{p}\right)_1 , N_1$.

Differentiating, totally, the first two equations of the truncated system, we get

$$(55) \qquad \frac{\partial S_w}{\partial r} \frac{dr}{dM_w} + \frac{\partial S_w}{\partial Y_w} \frac{dY_w}{dM_w} = \frac{\partial I_w}{\partial r} \frac{dr}{dM_w} + \frac{\partial I_w}{\partial Y_w} \frac{dY_w}{dM_w}$$

$$(56) \qquad 1 = \frac{\partial L_w}{\partial r} \frac{dr}{dM_w} + \frac{\partial L_w}{\partial Y_w} \frac{dY_w}{dM_w}$$

Treating this system as two equations in the two variables, $\dfrac{dY_w}{dM_w}$, $\dfrac{dr}{dM_w}$, we can solve to obtain

$$(57) \qquad \frac{dY_w}{dM_w} = \frac{\dfrac{\partial I_w}{\partial r} - \dfrac{\partial S_w}{\partial r}}{\dfrac{\partial L_w}{\partial Y_w}\left(\dfrac{\partial I_w}{\partial r} - \dfrac{\partial S_w}{\partial r}\right) - \dfrac{\partial L_w}{\partial r}\left(\dfrac{\partial I_w}{\partial Y_w} - \dfrac{\partial S_w}{\partial Y_w}\right)}$$

Professor Samuelson has shown that if a dynamic model, for which our static system is the stationary solution, is to be stable then the denominator must be negative.[11] It follows that

$$(58) \qquad \frac{dY_w}{dM_w} \geqq 0;$$

there are some positive effects from wage cuts. But the fact that these positive effects are seriously limited in magnitude may have some bearing on the result.

In the limiting case where the investment schedule is completely interest-inelastic and/or the liquidity-preference schedule is infinitely interest-elastic there is zero stimulus as a result of wage cuts.

$$(59) \qquad \begin{aligned} &\lim \qquad \frac{dY_w}{dM_w} = 0 \\ &\frac{\partial I_w}{\partial r} \to 0 \\ &\frac{\partial L_w}{\partial r} \to -\infty \end{aligned}$$

Wages can be cut endlessly, but no increased output and employment will result. After some short period of high-level unemployment in an environment of wage cuts, hyper-deflation will set in. Producers will continuously find it more profitable to wait for wage costs to fall further and will postpone economic activity. If there are no frictions in the system, this process will go on until social revolution explodes the economy.

[11] Behind this result, there is the very reasonable assumption that $0 < \dfrac{\partial I_w}{\partial Y_w} < 1$.

In the case where we do not go to the limit, the multiplier, $\dfrac{dY_w}{dM_w}$, will be a small positive quantity.[12] In this event, a sufficiently large multiplicand will make the product (of multiplier and multiplicand) a sizable quantity. However, the wage-cutting argument must rest upon a small multiplicand. Wage cuts will engender anticipations of further wage cuts unless they are kept small. A large multiplicand and small multiplier will lead to results identical with those of the limiting case — hyper-deflation. A small multiplicand and a small multiplier will do no good; their joint effect will not cure unemployment. We really need a small multiplicand and large multiplier to bring the standard arguments into their own, but this situation is not feasible in a Keynesian system.

The possibility exists (though small) that wage cuts may alter the schedules of decisions to invest and to save. If we write

$$(60) \qquad I_w(r, Y_w) - S_w(r, Y_w) = -\alpha$$
$$(48) \qquad M_w = L_w(r, Y_w)$$

where α represents a positive shift of the investment schedule relative to the savings schedule, we can also calculate

$$(61) \qquad \frac{dY_w}{d\alpha} = \frac{\dfrac{\partial L_w}{\partial r}}{\dfrac{\partial L_w}{\partial Y_w}\left(\dfrac{\partial I_w}{\partial r} - \dfrac{\partial S_w}{\partial r}\right) - \dfrac{\partial L_w}{\partial r}\left(\dfrac{\partial I_w}{\partial Y_w} - \dfrac{\partial S_w}{\partial Y_w}\right)}$$

In this multiplier equation, it is not the multiplier which is limited, rather the multiplicand. The multiplier is positive and will stimulate employment if coupled with a large enough multiplicand, $d\alpha$. There will be forces acting to increase savings and thus reduce $d\alpha$, while there will be other forces which will stimulate and also retard investment. Whatever positive forces exist to make $d\alpha$ large will be counteracted by the negative forces so that the final result is uncertain, though probably not large. The reasons for this final judgment are presented more fully in the text above.

THE LONG-RUN EQUILIBRIUM

At any point of time the economic system can be regarded as tending toward a long-run stationary state in which there is no net investment

---

[12] We are assuming $\dfrac{\partial I_w}{\partial r} = -\epsilon(r, Y_w)$ and $\dfrac{\partial L_w}{\partial r} = -\dfrac{1}{\delta(r, Y_w)}$ where ϵ and δ are small positive quantities.

and in which all existing capital equipment is exactly replaced. This idea does not mean to imply that the stationary state will necessarily be reached, but any dynamical system can be considered as approaching a stationary norm which changes at different periods of time but always exists as a useful concept. Outside factors will from time to time introduce shocks within the dynamical system which will make it tend toward a different stationary state. The question to be investigated now, in the light of Keynesian economics, is concerned with the level of employment in the long run. Will the stationary state be one of full employment? The classical economists who first talked about the stationary state certainly assumed full employment for their long-run theory. Recently, Professor Hansen [13] has disputed the classical position with the argument that the institutional and psychological makeup behind the determinants of effective demand may be such that the system will settle down to a long-run, under-employment equilibrium. Professor Pigou [14] was not long in coming to the rescue of the classical writers, and attempted to salvage their theory. It will be very useful to consider, in some detail, Professor Pigou's case and to trace its full implications.

Reckoning in terms of wage units we can easily write down a system to represent the long-run equilibrium, which is consistent with that of Pigou.

$$(48) \qquad M_w = L_w(r, Y_w)$$
$$(62) \qquad S_w(r, Y_w, K_w) = 0$$
$$(63) \qquad I_w(r, K_w) = 0$$
$$(49) \qquad wY_w = py$$
$$(64) \qquad wK_w = pK$$
$$(65) \qquad y = y(N, K)$$
$$(66) \qquad w = p\,\frac{\partial y}{\partial N}$$
$$(52) \qquad N = f\left(\frac{w}{p}\right)$$

The above model for the long-run equilibrium is essentially that of Pigou and not the result that would follow from a dynamical Keynesian model, where the variable representing time is allowed to increase without limit. In the Keynesian versions of this model, Y_w would appear in the investment equation and K_w would not appear in the savings equation.

[13] *Fiscal Policy and Business Cycles*, Norton, New York, 1941, p. 288.
[14] "The Classical Stationary State," *Economic Journal*, Vol. LIII, 1943, p. 343.

If an economically meaningful solution to these equations should exist, then full employment would follow, and the stationary state would represent perfect equilibrium of perfect competition. But Pigou has agreed that the added condition, $r > 0$ may make the system over-determined. That is to say, there may be no solution for r which has economic meaning when all other variables are at a full-employment level. There must be some least value of $r > 0$, and if this value will not bring savings and investment into equilibrium at their zero levels, then something must give way in the system. In reality employment is the thing that will give way,[15] such that a solution for r exists consistent with less-than-full employment values of the other variables. However, Pigou represented this system of equations as an impasse. He did not object to the conclusions of the classical economists, but he objected to the structure of their model because he refused to admit the existence of an imperfect equilibrium condition. For Keynesians this system represents a situation of unemployment due to the overthrow of the classical interest theory. The market phenomenon of sticky wages will explain why the unemployment position is one of equilibrium.

The ace in the hole for Pigou was a slight modification of the savings schedule to the form

$$(67) \qquad S_w(r, Y_w, K_w, M_w) = 0$$

The substitution of this function for the other savings function (62) in conjunction with the other equations of the system, Pigou thought, enabled him to save the classical doctrine. His argument was the following: Since it is reasonable to assume $\dfrac{\partial S_w}{\partial M_w} < 0$, a flexible-wage policy will always push savings to the required zero level, even after r has been lowered to its minimum value. It is obvious from the relation, $M_w = \dfrac{\overline{M}}{w}$, that wage cuts serve to increase the stock of money, M_w. If increases in M_w diminish the desire to save, then a flexible-wage policy can always insure the zero level of savings at full employment because unemployed workers will always bid w to such a low value that just the correct amount of savings is forthcoming. In this case the added condition on the interest rate does not make the system over-determined.

Pigou's argument, however, is not quite convincing, and the classical point of view has not yet been saved. The assumption of unlimited wage

<hr>

[15] It is employment and not something else which gives way for reasons similar to those given previously in connection with the short-run models.

cuts, as has been pointed out above, is a very dangerous tool when we take into account any realistic considerations of anticipations in the economic process. Professor Pigou *must* rest his argument on the fact that a very small wage cut will immediately restore high levels of employment, so that a deflationary spiral is to be avoided. In particular, he must show that in his system the relation

$$(68) \qquad dY_w = \frac{dY_w}{dM_w} \, dM_w$$

yields a large positive multiplier, $\frac{dY_w}{dM_w}$, so that a small multiplicand can induce a large increment in income, dY_w. We must consider, then, the conditions which make for large or small values of $\frac{dY_w}{dM_w}$.

The system

$$(48) \qquad\qquad M_w = L_w \, (r, \, Y_w)$$
$$(67) \qquad S(r, \, Y_w, \, K_w, \, M_w) = 0$$
$$(63) \qquad\qquad I(r, \, K_w) = 0$$
$$(53) \qquad\qquad w = \overline{w}$$

is equivalent to the larger system with the background equations because with $\overline{M}$, given by the banking system, the first three equations in conjunction with the background equations are sufficient in number to solve for all variables. Thus we can consider the first three equations as solved for r, Y_w, K_w in terms of w (or M_w) and w as determined along with p, N, K from the background equations. Whatever this value of w turns out to be, we shall call it $\overline{w}$. Pigou, in his paper, actually assumed $Y_w = \overline{Y}_w$ instead of $w = \overline{w}$, but the difference is not essential. As a matter of fact, in his *Employment and Equilibrium*, he pointed out that either $w = \overline{w}$ or $Y_w = \overline{Y}_w$ was implicitly assumed by the classical economists.

Suppose now that the solution to the abbreviated system is one of less than full employment with $w = \overline{w}$, in other words, forces are imposed upon the system so that the relations hold only imperfectly. Pigou's process is then to lower w in the equations as a result of the competition for jobs. The stimulus to employment from this lowering of w can be seen from

$$(69) \qquad \frac{dY_w}{dM_w} = \frac{\dfrac{\partial S_w}{\partial K_w} \dfrac{\partial I_w}{\partial r} - \dfrac{\partial I_w}{\partial K_w} \left(\dfrac{\partial S_w}{\partial r} + \dfrac{\partial S_w}{\partial M_w} \dfrac{\partial L_w}{\partial r} \right)}{\dfrac{\partial S_w}{\partial K_w} \dfrac{\partial I_w}{\partial r} \dfrac{\partial L_w}{\partial Y_w} - \dfrac{\partial I_w}{\partial K_w} \left(\dfrac{\partial S_w}{\partial r} \dfrac{\partial L_w}{\partial Y_w} - \dfrac{\partial L_w}{\partial r} \dfrac{\partial S_w}{\partial Y_w} \right)}$$

With Pigou's assumptions

$$(70) \quad \frac{\partial S_w}{\partial K_w} \lessgtr 0, \frac{\partial S_w}{\partial r} \gtrless 0, \frac{\partial S_w}{\partial Y_w} > 0, \frac{\partial S_w}{\partial M_w} < 0, \frac{\partial I_w}{\partial r} < 0, \frac{\partial I_w}{\partial K_w} < 0,$$

$$\frac{\partial L_w}{\partial r} < 0, \frac{\partial L_w}{\partial Y_w} > 0$$

it follows that

$$(71) \qquad\qquad\qquad \frac{dY_w}{dM_w} > 0$$

But' the size of the multiplier will depend, as in the short-run models, on the structure of the entire system.

In the long run, it is reasonable to expect that the rate of interest will be pushed toward its least possible value. If the stationary state is one of such foresight that there are no minimum risks connected with borrowing, the interest rate can fall to the minimum costs of making loans on the part of the banks. This will undoubtedly bring the rate near zero. In the case of the presence of borrowing risks, the bottom to the interest rate may be somewhat higher, but no matter which point of view is adopted, the rate should be in a range in which the liquidity-preference schedule has great interest-elasticity. While the condition of interest-elasticity seems to follow directly from the Keynesian assumptions about the bottom to the interest rate, it can easily be shown that this condition follows also from Pigou's system.

Instead of the liquidity function, as we have written it, he used the relation

$$(72) \qquad\qquad\qquad r = g\left(\frac{M_w}{Y_w}\right)$$

in which $\frac{M_w}{Y_w}$ represents the Marshall "k." He assumed

$$g\left(\frac{M_w}{Y_w}\right) > 0$$

and

$$\frac{dr}{d\left(\frac{M_w}{Y_w}\right)} < 0$$

for all

$$\frac{M_w}{Y_w} > 0$$

In addition he stated that the function g falls asymptotically towards zero for large values of $\dfrac{M_w}{Y_w}$. Thus when the interest rate is small and near zero, as it will be in the stationary state, we get

$$\frac{dr}{d\left(\dfrac{M_w}{Y_w}\right)} < 0$$

and small in absolute value. From the inverse relation

(73) $$\frac{M_w}{Y_w} = g^{-1}(r)$$

we can calculate

(74) $$\frac{\partial M_w}{\partial r} = Y_w \frac{d[g^{-1}(r)]}{dr} = Y_w \frac{d\left(\dfrac{M_w}{Y_w}\right)}{dr} < 0$$

Where r is small, Pigou's assumptions imply that $\dfrac{d\left(\dfrac{M_w}{Y_w}\right)}{dr}$ is large in absolute value, so that $\dfrac{\partial M_w}{\partial r}$ will also be numerically large, although negative.

The consequences of an elastic liquidity-preference schedule are that the stimulative effects of wage cuts will be very slight. In the multiplier expression, all terms not involving $\dfrac{\partial L_w}{\partial r}$ do involve either $\dfrac{\partial S_w}{\partial r}$ or $\dfrac{\partial S_w}{\partial K_w}$ as factors. Pigou admitted that the magnitude of both these slopes of the savings function would be extremely small, numerically. In the limiting case where these terms tend to zero and the liquidity preference function tends toward infinite interest-elasticity we get

(75) $$\begin{array}{c} \lim \\ \dfrac{\partial S_w}{\partial r} \to 0 \\[2mm] \dfrac{\partial S_w}{\partial K_w} \to 0 \\[2mm] \dfrac{\partial L_w}{\partial r} \to -\infty \end{array} \qquad \frac{dY_w}{dM_w} = -\frac{\dfrac{\partial S_w}{\partial M_w}}{\dfrac{\partial S_w}{\partial Y_w}}$$

The size of the multiplier depends upon the relative sizes of $\dfrac{\partial S_w}{\partial M_w}$ and $\dfrac{\partial S_w}{\partial Y_w}$. The only way to determine the multiplier is to obtain quantitative estimates of the parameters of the savings function. Econometric results show that $\dfrac{\partial S_w}{\partial Y_w}$ is in the neighborhood of 0.2 or 0.3, but the past data have never shown a significant correlation between S_w and M_w when all other variables are taken into account. It is likely that $\dfrac{\partial S_w}{\partial M_w}$ is numerically small. This is consistent with Pigou's admission of the possibility that $\dfrac{\partial S_w}{\partial K_w}$ is small. The respective influences of M_w and K_w on S_w would be expected, *a priori*, to be of the same order of magnitude.

The modification of the savings function has really done very little to enable Pigou to abstract from the deflationary aspects of expectations. In this case, even if we admit flexible wages, full employment will not be readily achieved. With the existence of unemployment, workers will continue to cut wages in their competitive struggle for jobs, but there will be little stimulus to increased employment, and expectations of further wage cuts must certainly develop. Producers will postpone action in anticipation of further wage cuts; prices will be depressed; and the economy will travel downward in a hopeless spiral. As before, we introduce the condition of rigid wages to show why the system will stay in the imperfect equilibrium condition and not collapse as a result of the deflationary spiral.

However, there is one case which may be labeled as an extremely classical situation in which Pigou's results can be obtained but which does not follow from his assumptions. One of the important aspects of this situation is contained within the following statement by Keynes:

> In a static society or in a society in which for any other reason no one feels any uncertainty about the future rates of interest, the Liquidity Function L_2, or the propensity to hoard (as we might term it) will always be zero in equilibrium. . . . Thus if it is practicable to measure the quantity, O, and the price, P, of current output, we have $Y = OP$, and, therefore, $MV = OP$; which is much the same as the Quantity Theory of Money in its traditional form.[16]

If we assume, as a characteristic of the stationary state, that there is no uncertainty as to the future rate of interest, then the liquidity-preference equation can be replaced by the quantity equation, and the effects of wage cuts should be favorable to employment. In fact for this case it follows that

$$(76) \qquad \frac{dY_w}{dM_w} = \frac{1}{\dfrac{\partial L_w}{\partial Y_w}}$$

[16] *General Theory*, pp. 208–209.

The multiplier is the income velocity of circulation of cash balances (or the reciprocal of the Marshall " k "). This value has been estimated at two or three for the United States; consequently we should expect, in this case, a favorable result from wage cuts which could quickly restore full employment and avoid the disastrous results of hyper-deflation. If this model is what the classical economists had in mind for their stationary state, then perhaps they were correctly following their assumptions.

NOTES TO THE ORIGINAL EDITION

† PAGE 262.   A superior accounting treatment of this same problem is given by D. Jorgenson in *The Brookings Quarterly Econometric Model of the U.S. Economy*, ed. J. Duesenberry, G. Fromm, L. R. Klein, and E. Kuh, Rand McNally, Chicago, 1965.   The beauty of his approach is that the relevant price concept becomes *user cost* of capital, thus placing Keynes' concept in its proper role.

* PAGE 262.   In recent work the idea of distinguishing between old and new capital has been more formally and completely treated in vintage models of production.

INDEX